THE SPIRIT OF SELF-HELP
A Life of Samuel Smiles

1 Samuel Smiles at 47, in the year *Self-Help* was published.
(The Mary Evans Picture Library)

THE SPIRIT OF
SELF-HELP

A Life of Samuel Smiles

*'The value of life lies not in the length of days
but in the use you make of them'*

Michel de Montaigne
Essais, 1580

John Hunter

SHEPHEARD-WALWYN (PUBLISHERS) LTD

First published in 2017 by
Shepheard-Walwyn (Publishers) Ltd
107 Parkway House, Sheen Lane,
London SW14 8LS
www.shepheard-walwyn.co.uk

British Library Cataloguing in Publication Data
A catalogue record of this book
is available from the British Library

ISBN: 978-0-85683-512-4

Jacket detail: From portrait of Samuel Smiles by Sir George Reid,
oil on canvas, 1877 (NPG 1377)
© National Portrait Gallery, London

Typeset by Alacrity, Chesterfield, Sandford, Somerset
Printed and bound in the United Kingdom
by Short Run Press, Exeter

CONTENTS

LIST OF ILLUSTRATIONS

INTRODUCTION

A NYONE walking along George IV Bridge in Edinburgh in 2014 might have examined with curiosity the line of decorated boards outside the National Library of Scotland. Put there to shield passers-by from building work going on inside, they'd been used to display images representing the library's great literary heritage. The choice was instructive. One of the most striking showed a trolley with a stack of books, and on their spines the names of selected giants of nineteenth-century writing: Sir Walter Scott, Lord Byron, Jane Austen, Washington Irving, Charles Darwin – and Samuel Smiles.[1] In this company Samuel Smiles is the name most twenty-first century readers might barely have heard of, yet he was, in his time, quite as famous as Sir Walter Scott, Lord Byron, or any of the others. In 1887 *Pall Mall Gazette* listed the capital's 'men of letters, savans (sic) and divines', including William Morris, Matthew Arnold, Christina Rossetti, Walter Pater, J A Symonds, Cardinal Newman, and Samuel Smiles. Indeed when Sir John Lubbock, polymath and long-term friend of Charles Darwin, published his *Hundred Best Books* in 1886, there, with the *Meditations of Marcus Aurelius* and Pascal's *Pensées*, with Thackeray, Dickens, and George Eliot, was Smiles's *Self-Help* (Smiles was delighted to note that 'I was the only living author whom Sir J Lubbock included on his list').[2]

Self-Help was, and remains, Samuel Smiles's best-known book, and when it appeared in 1859 it became a publishing sensation, not just in Britain, but across the world. The Khedive of Egypt[3] had panels on his palace walls inscribed with quotations from the Koran, and from Smiles's *Self-Help*. 'Indeed', the Khedive told an English visitor, 'they are principally from Smeelis.' 'Smeelis' was honoured in his lifetime by national leaders in foreign countries from Italy and Bohemia to Japan and Argentina (in Buenos Aires his works were collectively translated as *The Social Gospel*, and presented to the Argentinian President). *Self-Help* sold in Britain upwards of a quarter of a million copies in Smiles's lifetime, and worldwide, many times that number. It remains in print.

Self-Help was not Samuel Smiles's only successful book, nor his first. He wrote some thirty books, dozens of pamphlets, and many hundreds of newspaper and magazine articles. But *Self-Help's* title came to stand for more than a book. It represented an attitude to life, a response to the extraordinary conditions of its time, and, in the long term, a catch-all for a thousand theories on how each of us can become master of our own fate.

Samuel Smiles was born in the reign of George III, outlived George IV, William IV, and Queen Victoria, and survived into the Edwardian era. In his adult life he witnessed a century in which man changed the world faster and more dramatically then had ever before seemed possible. It was the time of the industrial revolution's second wave, the tidal wave of the manufacturing revolution. For the British people particularly, on whose doorstep most of this change had been generated, its speed was both exhilarating and alarming. 'Within the last half-century', a visitor to the 1851 Great Exhibition observed, 'there have been performed upon our island, unquestionably, the most prodigious feats of human industry and skill witnessed in any age of time or in any nation of the earth.' But Friedrich Engels[4] had noted a few years earlier during his time in Manchester, that early deaths and low wages were more prevalent in the manufacturing cities than in the countryside. To many intellectuals of the time, men like John Ruskin and Matthew Arnold, this surge toward the future caused great unease. Their instinct was to fear the machine, and to look to the past for a model of innocence and beauty. Matthew Arnold asked, in 1869:

> Which would excite most the love, interest, and admiration of mankind? ... The England of the last twenty years, or the England of Elizabeth, of a true, splendid, spiritual effort, but when our coal, and our industrial operations depending on coal, were very little developed? Well then, what an unsound habit of mind it must be which makes talk of things like coal, or iron as constituting the greatness of England.[5]

With his Hellenist hankerings, Arnold turned his fire on the emerging dream. 'The university of Mr Ezra Cornell ... seems to rest on a provincial misconception of what culture truly is, and to be calculated to produce miners, or engineers, or architects, not sweetness and light.' This was the Victorian dilemma – how to pursue economic progress without destroying sweetness and light.

Samuel Smiles's work grew from personal experience of this paradox in action. As a young working journalist in the manufacturing town of Leeds he saw the power of technology to create enormous wealth, and crucially, to democratise the wealth-producing process. Prosperity no longer needed ancestry. But at the same time he could see the lives of thousands of uneducated and unrepresented people reduced to squalor and deprived of meaning. Yet Smiles believed that these operative classes were, as he said in a speech in Leeds in 1839, 'the fabricators of our national greatness ... the working men and mechanics, the true creators of our national wealth'.[6]

His books were about working men and mechanics, about the miners, engineers, and architects who worried Matthew Arnold so much, but also about cobblers and bakers and poets, and their route, each in his own way, to what Smiles called 'happiness and well-being' – one of his favourite phrases. 'The grand object aimed at' he said, 'should be to make the great mass of the people virtuous, intelligent, well-informed, and well conducted; and open up to them new sources of pleasure and happiness.' This, Smiles believed, was a man's true mission, and his individual responsibility. But Smiles was no utopian. His vision was of happiness as an expression of work, of difficulty overcome, of self-discipline and moral courage, and an acceptance of the hardship that accompanies a life fully lived.

The voice that Samuel Smiles gave to this vision, in *Self-Help* and in his other books, touched a chord in millions of ordinary people, struggling to see, in a world of frightening change, a meaning for their own lives. 'There are few books in history', Asa Briggs wrote in 1958, 'which have reflected the spirit of their age more faithfully and successfully than *Self-Help*'.[7] Samuel Smiles, and *Self-Help*, remain a reference point for much of the discourse on ideas about 'the search for happiness' in the twenty-first century. What significance had Smiles's work in generating the self-help movement so pervasive today? A quick examination of titles on Amazon (and there are thousands) suggests the answer 'not much'. *Change Your Life in Seven Days*; *How to be a Property Millionaire*; or *59 Seconds: Think a Little, Change a Lot* – these and innumerable others run directly counter to the Smiles ethos. Their themes are quick, effort-free solutions, instant wealth, and life enhancement through mind games. Where is the patient, hard-slogging, pick-yourself-up-and-try-again Smiles hero?

The idea of self-help, as elaborated by Samuel Smiles in his writing, and in his life, has been charged with representing a particular set of 'Victorian values'. But at root it is an idea which is intensely personal, addressing questions about the nature of happiness, the meaning of success and failure, the relation between the two sets of ideas, and the moral dimension of both – in other words the questions which occupied Aristotle, Plato and the ancients, and every serious philosopher since. 'How should we live?' Aristotle asked, and answered: 'by seeking happiness'.

Samuel Smiles's contribution (without any pretensions to being a philosopher, or even a particularly original thinker), and the reason I suggest that his work has enduring significance, is that he was the first to find a voice, and a medium – biography – to make these ideas relevant to the everyday lives of everyday people. And not just Victorians.

PROLOGUE
An Evening Reimagined

T HE OLD MAN, silver-haired, with a smartly trimmed white beard, dresses with special care for this evening – starched shirt, white tie, black tail-coat – before inspection by his wife Sarah Anne,[1] and a steadying hand from his driver as he steps into his brougham for the drive to the City. Dr Samuel Smiles is on his way to dine at London's Mansion House.

It is high summer, Saturday 18 June 1887. As his carriage moves through Kensington High Street and on past Kensington Gardens he can see on every building and lamp post, and among the crowds strolling in the park, flags and emblems in a rash of loyal colour. God Save the Queen! Victoria Regina! Red, white and blue, purple and gold, laughter and waves in the late evening sun. Celebration of the Queen Empress's Golden Jubilee has already begun and Samuel Smiles has been invited by the Lord Mayor, Sir Reginald Hanson, to a 'Banquet to representatives of Literature, Science and Art'. But what does Samuel Smiles really think about the Queen's majesty? Almost fifty years earlier, as a young newspaper editor, he had introduced himself to the readers of the *Leeds Times* by advising them that 'From the puppetry of thrones they have nothing to hope, except new demands for money, for friends and for army, to support the pomp and parade of monarchy ...'[2] The Crown he had dismissed as 'the mere plaything of the aristocracy and its wearer, for the time being, but their pensioned creature and puppet'. His attitude to the monarchy was, at best, sceptical. 'If it be not productive of good, royalty is not worth a sow's bristle, nor is loyalty worth a sow's grunt.' But that had been in 1839. How hot now is the radical blood?

Under the Mansion House banqueting hall's chandeliers over three hundred gentlemen sit down to dinner (no ladies, of course) – eminent scientists, and a host of Royal Academicians, but Literature is in truth rather thinly represented. Thomas Hardy is here, Edmund Gosse, the wildly popular Henry Rider Haggard (*She* has just been published), and 33-year old Oscar Wilde, though none of the work that will make him famous has yet been seen. For English literature it is a time of changing generations.

Tonight Samuel Smiles has little competition. Most of the Victorian giants, Smiles's contemporaries, are dead. Thomas Carlyle and John Stuart Mill, Charles Dickens, Anthony Trollope, Thackeray and George Eliot ... all gone, as is the man who had achieved public fame in the same year as Smiles, Charles Darwin. Both Darwin's *On The Origin of Species* and Smiles's *Self-Help* had been published by Murray's back in the autumn of 1859. Now, thirty years later, John Murray III, head of the famous publishing house, sits with Samuel Smiles among the Lord Mayor's guests. As Smiles's publisher, and a friend and collaborator for over thirty years, he and the seventy-four-year-old author might be seen in this company as twin icons of their generation; and Smiles as a sort of Grand Old Man of English letters. But Smiles, in spite of the huge sales and the international fame, suspects that he is not regarded in that way, and he is probably right. His peers do not embrace him.

In the intellectual discourse of the age, dominated by the voices of men like Carlyle, John Stuart Mill, Ruskin, and Matthew Arnold, Samuel Smiles spoke to a wider audience, and in a different voice – a voice much more like their own. As Humphrey Carpenter, chronicler of the House of Murray[3] commented, Smiles's *Self-Help* had almost as much influence on the Victorian outlook as *The Origin of Species*; but among the intellectual establishment Smiles felt an outsider. 'I have received more recognition from the King and Queen [of Italy] down to their humblest subjects than in my own country', he wrote in his *Autobiography*. This sense of alienation, of exclusion from élite circles, was something he felt from his earliest days. On the Smiles shoulder a chip is never completely invisible. He acquired it as a child and perhaps unknowingly treasured it all his life, as the driver of his work and the inspiration for his relentless insistence on the loser as winner, on the inversion of privilege. 'What,' he asked about his school contemporaries 'became of the favourites at one school and the prize boys at the other? I do not think any of them made a mark in the world. Some became insufferable prigs, stuck up with self-conceit. The prize boys began as prodigies and ended up as failures.' Samuels Smiles's work, and his career, are full of contradiction and paradox – of intolerance matched with understanding, severity with compassion, certainty with doubt – all originating from a childhood of happiness haunted by rejection, both real and perceived.

I

The Smiling Country

A FEW YEARS after that Jubilee dinner Smiles sat down to write an autobiography, unpublished until 1905, a year after his death. He needed a good memory, for the eminent Victorian was born a Georgian, on 23 December 1812, in the small town of Haddington, in the Scottish lowlands twenty miles from Edinburgh. He had, as we all have, memories of times beyond memory. 'It seems to me like a dream,'[1] he wrote of the days after the Battle of Waterloo, 'to remember the rejoicings on that occasion – the bands of the militia, the drums and pipes that paraded the town, and the illuminations.' Writing his *Autobiography,* the eighty year-old Smiles could see a picture of his childhood, of himself, aged barely three, at the open window of the room above his father's shop, hanging out too far no doubt, and scaring his mother, battling with his older brother John for a better view of the kilted soldiers in the street below. His eye even then was alert to impressions, and to information: a very Smilesian trait. He remembered the 42nd Highlanders, the glorious Black Watch, marching through Haddington the next year. He remembered the fireside talks about the war, the price of bread, so expensive at sixteen pence for a loaf, the eventual pulling down of the soldiers' barracks, and his father's coup on army surplus stores – 'he bought a large quantity ... principally blankets and greatcoats'. Smiles senior was a conscientious shopkeeper.

Young Sam found a lot to love about Haddington and, only later, a lot to resent. But for all the resentment, for all the later urge to escape, he still looked back to distant enchantments, to the small-world familiarity so precious to children. 'I knew everybody,' he wrote, 'even the cocks and hens running about the streets.' The boy he remembered used to climb, on a fine day, to a high point on the Garleton hills that rose above the town, then look down and see a sort of Eden. To the south the grey buildings of the town gathered like friends, with the high tower of the cathedral church where the 'higher' people worshipped, and the lower slate roof of the dissenters' chapel, where God met the other sort, like Sam's family. He could see the little private school in St Ann's Street, fiefdom of the hated Mr Hardie, and nearby, the buildings of the Grammar School. The old narrow roof and long windows of the Town Library sat behind the High Street. Two other libraries snuggled between the houses and shops. No child in Haddington had to go without books or learning. And when he had taken in all this, he would have been able find the straight line of the High Street, and near the top the business place of S. Smiles, General Merchant. Then he would have felt an innocent pride, for just as Sam knew every cock and hen running about the streets, so every citizen of Haddington knew S. Smiles, General Merchant, who gave good value in ex-army blankets.

On Wednesday and Saturday afternoons Sam and his brothers and sisters had their free times; free that is from school, though their father made sure they did their stint helping in the narrow garden behind the house, among the tulips and red and yellow polyanthus. Then, if the work had not been too hard, he could run off, across the river and up the hills even higher, to look north, to the far-spread plain, rich with some of the finest agricultural land in East Lothian. Samuel Smiles has been patronised for his utilitarian style of writing. Even a kind critic called it 'serviceable prose' and his obituarist in the *London Standard* sneered that 'the standard at which the veteran author aimed was, perhaps, not the loftiest'.[2] But the descriptions of the place of his boyhood have a touching lyricism that he rarely showed. 'All around this smiling country,' he wrote, 'lies the Firth of Forth, and in the northern distance the blue hills of Fife. Beyond Musselburgh Bay, Arthur's seat lies like an elephant at rest ... and the smoke of Edinburgh in the distance.'

He would have come down the hill then, into the town, to the big Smiles family packed into their few rooms above the shop. Samuel Smiles senior and his wife Janet worked hard. Sam saw his mother tied all day to the shop, serving, stacking, keeping the books; he watched her help tend the cow in the byre at the end of the garden, feed her husband and children and then, in her so-called 'spare hours', at her spinning wheel, for 'she not only wished to keep up the house store of linen, but to spin for the plenishing of her daughters'. In the end there were three of those (and one who died in infancy), and eight sons, with Sam the second eldest born in 1812,[3] two years after his brother John.

He knew how fortunate he was. In spite of 'the smiling country' all about, life in the years after the Napoleonic wars was tough. The cost of war kept taxes and prices high. Men were pouring back from the army and navy looking for work on the land, or for any job they could find in towns like Haddington. Edinburgh, a day's walk to the west, was full of men without work. Mass employment in manufacturing, the great absorber of labour, was still unusual. But Sam's parents, as he put it, 'were neither "hunden doon" by poverty, nor oppressed by riches'. Almost every year another child arrived, every one fed wholesomely, clothed warmly, and most importantly, in Sam's eyes, 'sedulously started on the road to knowledge'.

Sedulously – it is a very Smilesian word, a Sunday-school word, packed with persistence, application and honest diligence, a word children may not have understood but whose meaning they would have sensed (Smiles, a sharp etymologist, no doubt appreciated its Latin root in *se dolo:* without guile). This straightness, the sort of diligence Sam saw at home, was stern but benevolent, and applied with assumed love. But as soon as his small white legs were old enough to carry him down the street and through the doors of St Ann's school, he found them exposed to the rod of its master, Patrick Hardie. 'I have seen,' Smiles wrote, 'Hardie flog a boy so hard and so long that he had to hold his sides and sit down exhausted.' Unfortunately for Sam, a year or so later Hardie was appointed to the mathematical school, the first level of the Burgh schools which constituted the famous Haddington Grammar School, a jewel in East Lothian education. So when Sam moved on there, Hardie was waiting. With his bilious pale complexion and yellowish-red hair he must have been a terrifying figure for the children whose parents, apparently without question, left them day after day, unprotected, in his power.

Sam learned several lessons from Mr Hardie. 'He was a good teacher. He taught reading, writing and arithmetic very well. He cultivated in his pupils the gift of memory. He made us learn by heart, and recite, poetry and speeches by memorable orators.' He also gave Sam his first lessons in class discrimination and its hypocrisies. Sam saw Hardie trying to wheedle his way into acceptance by 'the well to do men, who could give him dinners and drink'. Though he would thrash the poorer boys and yell at them, his favourites were spared. These favourites were not the clever or well-behaved but the sons of provosts, bailies, or town council-lors. The fierce light in Hardie's eyes – sure sign of a storm coming on – was kindled by the humble and unconnected, and especially by Dissenters. 'I will flog you sir, within an inch of your life; I will dash your brains against the wall; I will split your skull into a thousand pieces!' But to his favourites the master was always mild and sleek. 'The cut of the leather would never be used to raise wales on their backs.' Yet apparently not everyone shared Smiles's unhappy memories of Patrick Hardie. When the teacher died in 1837 some of his ex-pupils erected a tombstone to his memory 'In grateful recollection of his talents, acquirements and zealous perseverance as a successful teacher of youth.' Mr Hardie's favourites were apparently loyal.

The other lesson Sam took from the Hardie terror was that, though education was priceless, its worth could be poisoned by brutality. 'Learning is not advanced by harshness and tyranny on the part of the masters. These are enough to drive a boy into stupidity and make him reckless.' Smiles maintained a life-long interest in education and became a significant voice in the debate on Victorian educational policies, always inspired by a resolutely anti-Hardie approach.

People who met Smiles in later life almost universally used words like 'kindly,' 'genial' or 'gentle'. As a boy he clearly responded to qualities like these – to gentleness (if not to gentility), to being led not pushed, to what he called 'moral suasion'. When, at the age of about ten, he escaped Hardie's reign, his life opened and learning became a source of joy. The change came when he moved up to the classical division of the Grammar School, under Rector Graham.

William Graham, plump, jovial, with a smile for every child, ran the Classical School and was Hardie's opposite – 'as much a gentleman as the other was a tyrant,' Smiles wrote. Graham had the gift of enthusing children, and Sam discovered that Greek, Latin and French could be enjoyed. But even in this enlightened air, young Smiles, son of a small tradesman and Anti-burgher (a narrow sect that refused to vote for burghers or councillors) continued to twitch at the whiff of social exclusion and privilege. He was very aware of 'the better sort' who attended the Grammar School – the English, or the sons of Indian officers, or county men with large farms. Sam's father had to save hard to send him to the Grammar School; it was not the natural habitat of a boy from his background. Even the minister's sons had the advantage of cramming at home so that they could win prizes. Sam won nothing, and affected disdain for the school-boy winners.

In the Smiles household no one had time to help Sam with cramming. For his parents the hours not spent on trading, cleaning, feeding, caring for babies and infants, spinning, washing, milking and keeping the garden were devoted to religion – heads-down, eyes fixed, unquestioning religion of the most strict Calvinist sort. Sam's father's people had been Cameronians, followers of a flint-eyed Covenanter called Richard Cameron. In the seventeenth century Cameron had seen a new light when he decided that the Covenanters were altogether too liberal, too easy with the papists, and must be discarded. So he moved off to the sternest edge of the Protestant faith to preach, not in chapels, but in the fields of God. Field preaching became the Cameronians' favoured style of worship. When Sam visited his grandfather the old man was still an elder of the Cameronians, and an active preacher. Sam heard him, his voice carried on the wind to the congregation gathered in the field like birds of a single dark feather, from vast distances, for holy reasons. The boy sat among them on the grass, all day, through prayer upon prayer, psalm upon psalm, sermon upon sermon; for the preachers came in relays, so that the day darkened and not until the sun had set did the service end. Sam does not say what these relentless ministers told him. Perhaps the crowd, and the sunset, and his increasingly numb backside distracted his mind from their message.

On Sundays at home not even the sunset was visible to lift his spirit. The hard work of the sabbath started straight after breakfast, in the grey dawn. Then the Smiles children, a small congregation in their own right, squeezed round the table for prayers led by their father. After prayers they were set to learning their catechism and paraphrase – with no whispering and no fidgeting; they would be tested on these lessons later. But when they were at last released into the light of the High Street it was for a cold, silent walk to the kirk, and a morning of psalms, prayers, and a sermon of over an hour long. At one o'clock they went home again, to grace and quiet and a slice of meat, but not freedom. By two o'clock they were back in their pew in the kirk, for another sermon until four, then home to be tested on their paraphrases and catechism and, holy of holies, back to the kirk for a third sermon at six, taking the day's observances up to eight o'clock. And then, even then, the dreaded paraphrase and catechism had to be repeated, by a line of small voices by that time surely shredded by their devotions.

None of this inspired or stimulated Sam. 'Our preacher,' he remembered, 'preached the narrowest form of Calvinism and there was far more fear than love in his sermons.' Just as Hardie failed to beat in knowledge, this regime failed to hammer in doctrine. The preacher was 'wearisome and unsympathetic, and his doctrines, though intended to frighten us into goodness, had perhaps the reverse effect'. For the rest of his life Smiles showed little interest in the church, and contempt for any religious organisation that tried to stand above its people.

But it would be wrong to see Sam's boyhood as dominated by severe schooling and a scowling God at his shoulder. The smiling countryside was still there, friends and brothers and sisters, to go hunting for birds' nests, or sloes, or haws, to play shinty with, or football on the sands. And whatever he felt about his father's field-preaching family, Sam had an altogether softer affection for his mother's side, the Wilsons and Yellowlees.

The magic was with her cousin William Yellowlees, a young artist from the borders near Berwick, learning his trade in Edinburgh. Yellowlees came over to Haddington to paint the portraits of Sam's parents. He was an exquisite draughtsman – he later became cabinet portrait painter to King William's brother, the Duke of Sussex, and was dubbed 'the Little Romney'. His skill dazzled Sam. The boy watched as the small canvases came alive with the faces of his mother and father. He sat, wide-eyed, as Cousin William dashed off superb drawings of the Union and Mail coaches, waiting for the change of horses at the George Inn lower down the High Street for their last stage between London and Edinburgh.

Sam thought he might become an artist. He later illustrated some of his own lectures, and at least one of his books. Sketches in pen and wash of engineering works, made in his later career as a railway official, show sensitivity and talent. Their feeling for line and colour suggest the work of a man more romantic than the author of the no-nonsense books that were to make him famous. The contrast is deceptive. In his books Smiles may have chosen practical language for what he saw as a practical purpose, but a belief in the power of the human spirit drove that purpose. In that sense, at least, Samuel Smiles was a true romantic.

It was not only the bewitching Yellowlees who attracted Sam. He found his Wilson uncles equally fascinating. They were inventors, men of practical ingenuity and real, tangible usefulness. Neither of them made it into his 1884 book, *Men of Invention and Industry*, but young Sam was proud of the prize Uncle George won at the Dalkeith Farming Club for his invention of one of the first reaping machines, and of his Uncle Robert's success as a builder and carpenter. Uncle Robert Wilson gave his name to Sam's younger brother, Robert Wilson Smiles, and later the two Smiles brothers were to find much in common, particularly in trying to bring education, untainted by privilege or piety, to the people they believed needed it most.

The eldest boy in the Smiles family, John, was seven years old when he became very ill with lung inflammation. The drama at the time made a deep impression on Sam – the doctor's visit, John's thin arm stretched out on the table for bleeding, and the cups, first one, then another, then a third, filling with the child's dark blood. When Sam wrote about this sixty years later, bleeding had almost disappeared from accepted medical practice. He made no judgement, except to note that it had worked. 'Though the boy was only seven years old, the bleeding at once cured him. Doctors were not afraid to bleed in those days.'

His brother's healer Dr Welsh was, like Sam's favourite schoolmaster Rector Graham, 'a most agreeable and cheerful man. Everybody loved him. He had a comely face and expressive features.' Not, apparently, like his daughter Jane's – the Jane who, as Jane Welsh Carlyle, later became

Haddington's most famous daughter. She was eleven years older than Sam, a haughty sixteen-year-old at the time, with a number of admirers, in spite of being outshone, in Sam's opinion, by her tall, beautiful mother. 'Jeanie was less lovely,' he wrote. 'Her face was too angular,' as, apparently, was her disposition. She later wrote cruelly of Haddington, calling it 'the dimmest, deadliest spot in the Creator's universe ... the very air one breathes is impregnated with stupidity'.⁴ Jane Welsh enjoyed the keen edge of her own tongue. It amused her friends, intimidated her critics, and later helped to make her probably the most admired letter writer of the nineteenth century. Provincial Haddington and its small-town people made an easy target. Of an encounter with Samuel Smiles (not dignified with a name in an 1849 letter to her husband Thomas Carlyle), she wrote describing 'a gentleman who dined at Forster's⁵ yesterday and claimed acquaintance with me on the strength of his vivid recollection of my "white veil" at Haddington (having lived exactly at the bottom of our entry!) his father keeping a china shop ...'

In fact after Dr Welsh died in 1819 Mrs Welsh and Jane moved into what Smiles called 'the upper flat of Mr Roughhead's large mansion almost opposite the house in the High street which my father had bought'. She may have lived in a large mansion, but Jane Welsh Carlyle's dismissal of the china shop 'at the bottom of our entry' seems a little, well, Jane Welsh Carlyle. Later her view of her home town softened noticeably. In 1855 she wrote to Richard Tait during a visit to Haddington that it 'is like being pretty well up towards heaven, being here'.

'Up towards heaven' was probably never Smiles's view of his home town. Undoubtedly the idea of Haddington was attractive to him, the idea of a community on a comfortable scale where change happened at a measurable pace and you always knew who you were talking to. On the other hand, in a small town this same assumption of familiarity could breed small, corruptive poisons, of the sort he perceived in Mr Hardie's behaviour, and in his own characterisation of 'the better sort' at his school. In a small town a man might, he said later, 'be muzzled or shouted down on account of his opinions, or exposed to the petty persecutions he sometimes has to endure in the provinces'.

Though Haddington in the 1820s was a small town, it was no mere village. The Royal Burgh had a population of about 3,800 and a proud history as the ancient capital of East Lothian. The London to Edinburgh coaches had their last stage there, and busy markets flourished. Big farmers and aristocratic landowners like the Earl of Wemyss lived all about. Many of them sent their sons to the Grammar School and patronised the local merchants and professional people like Dr Welsh and his partners, lending status by their patronage. The churches were a key part of local life, giving prestige to ministers and nodding rights to the good when they met the great. Haddington had its society. The Veneerings in Dickens's *Our Mutual Friend*, published almost fifty years later, were alive and well and living in Haddington in 1820. Society there had its pecking order, and the Smiles family, with their eleven children packed into two floors over the shop, their uncertain 'general trade', but most of all with their adherence to the narrow, anti-establishment Cameronian sect, were on its lower rungs. Sam was aware of these distinctions, of the circles from which he was deemed to be excluded. His later work is marked by impatience with 'circles'. 'When work of importance needs to be done,' he wrote, 'nobody cares to ask where the man who can do it best comes from ... but what he is, and what he can do.' At an early age he seems to have acquired an inner life, not of fantasy or colourful imagination, but of serious reflection on the ways of the world. Did the boy who recoiled from the idea of an élite at school, who sat on the grass among hundreds of worshippers, unmoved, and who used to climb alone to view the world from the top of a mountain, use those times to ponder what he was and what he could do?

2

A Learning Game

IN HIS final years at the Grammar School, as his fourteenth birthday approached, Sam may not have bid for the glittering prizes, but he surely gained a greater reward. He learned how to learn. The cumulative effect of Mr Hardie's rote learning regime, Rector Graham's clarity and leadership, even the training of each Sunday's ordeal by catechism, all contributed to the mental muscle that allowed him to take a grip of any subject that might confront him.

As they moved, one by one, to the cut-off point marked by their fourteenth year, each of the Smiles children had to face the serious question of how they might lift their burden from the family and start to work for their own living. Sam's older brother went into the business; it was to be his inheritance. When Sam's turn came, his parents, surprisingly given their apparent sternness, asked his opinion. He suggested following his cousin Yellowlees as a painter, but the idea was quickly dismissed. His mother thought he might become a minister. Smiles recorded in his *Autobiography* a snatch of the dialogue between them:

'Would you no like to be a minister?'
'Oh no. I'll no be a minister.'

For a moment it is possible to hear his voice and to catch the simple Scottish accent. The language and the accent obviously changed, became 'educated', after he left home and when he had spent so many years living in England. A journalist who interviewed him[1] in 1883 described his 'big, soft tones, with just the echo of the Lothians in them'. But the fourteen-year-old Smiles talked like his own folk.

His future, at least the first part of it, was finally settled when he agreed that he would become a doctor. The opportunity came by accident, literally. One of the local practitioners, Dr Lewins, had stitched Sam's wound after a fall and Mrs Smiles seized the chance to ask the doctor if he could take the boy on as an apprentice. She was ambitious for her son, ready to make sacrifices for him. Janet Smiles was obviously an exceptional woman. Smiles wrote of her with real feeling: 'She had wonderful pluck, and abundant common sense. Her character seemed to develop with the calls made upon her ... I could not fail to be influenced by so good a mother. I was inspired by her and obeyed her.'

Interestingly he makes no mention of his father in these conversations. Mr Smiles must have been a good father. He, too, worked hard to give his children the best education he could. He took Sam on outings, to see King George IV's ship in the Firth of Forth, to see Walter Scott in Edinburgh, but in Smiles's *Autobiography* all his warmth is for his mother. Of course because she outlived her husband by thirty years, and became 'Granny Smiles', this is understandable, but a sense remains that Sam regarded his father with limited affection.

2 Samuel Smiles's mother: 'I was inspired by her and obeyed her...'
(Aileen Smiles, *The Life and Times of Samuel Smiles*, Robert Hale, 1956))

On 6 November 1826, a month before his fourteenth birthday, Sam was indentured for five years to Dr Lewins and his partner Dr Robert Lorimer. Their practice was not the smartest or most prosperous in Haddington. That eminence was occupied by the late Dr John Welsh's partnership, now flourishing under Dr Benjamin Welsh and Drs Howden and Fife. Dr Lewins probably did not like them. Their practice had a history of partners from an established church background and with private wealth and good connections. Dr Welsh had some years earlier beaten Dr Lewins[2] to the committee-appointed role of town's Dispensary doctor, with privileged access to the customers with paying power. The better people did not call Dr Lewins. In his apprenticeship Sam again found himself outside the circle, but he may have been fortunate. He got more practical experience more quickly with Dr Lewins than the competition would have given him.

Free now of the routine of school and of school's mass instruction and compulsion, Sam was able to experience a life separate from home and the irksome attention of parents. Even though this time is described in the *Autobiography* in Smiles's flattest style, there is a sense that the sap of enthusiasm is rising. For the first time he was discovering the satisfaction of directing his energy into the things that interested him. Proper society, as others perceived it, was of no consequence for him. Now he existed in the society of the mind, where his only competition was with himself.

In these years Sam absorbed knowledge and experience from every direction. At first things may have seemed a little dull. He spent his days in the shabby dispensing room learning about the strange substances in the jars and bottles that lined the walls. He was taught how to make pills and potions, ointments, liniments, tinctures and infusions. No patient would be happy until the doctor had bestowed upon them a bottle of coloured fluid or a box of important pills. Only then might the gods of sickness be propitiated. Sam's first task was to discover the characteristics, positive, negative or neutral, of every substance and every combination in the dispensary. The doctors showed great patience in teaching him, but he was a quick and conscientious pupil. They must also have given thanks for the exceptional apprentice they seemed to have acquired. Lewins, Lorimer and Smiles were what we might call a dream team.

But this was not enough for Sam. His mind fidgeted, pushed by curiosity and a determination not to be hampered by lack of knowledge. For his self-education he could set his own syllabus, and the great glory was that Haddington's array of libraries could serve every subject: history, literature, travel, theology, languages, science, mechanics, agriculture, and philosophy. The Town Library had a decent offering of books, but when he went there to consult Gibbon's *Decline and Fall*, his old perse-cutor Patrick Hardie materialised as one of the volunteer librarians, so Sam generally avoided it. His favourite was the East Lothian Itinerating Library,[3] a system by which sets of about fifty books each moved, a set at a time, from town to town at regular intervals, to be replaced by the ensuing set. By the mid-1830s, forty-seven sets were in circulation in the County. This wonderful institution had been conceived by one of Haddington's most admirable sons, Samuel Brown, and of course the Haddington branch of the Itinerating Library was its fountainhead and starting point. Everything itinerated from Haddington and there Sam had first access to all the latest books. The little Begbie library, a modest collection started by local worthy Mr Begbie, often had interesting titles, and for a few years the local bookseller and printer, George Tait, operated a lending service. Tait was an interesting character,[4] obviously a man smitten by literature. He not only sold books but, for a few years between 1822 and 1828, published a periodical, the *East Lothian Magazine*. 'It was supported by a number of young literati of the locality who,' according to contemporary local historian John Martine, 'contributed articles of great ability on history, agriculture and general literature. Mr Tait himself wrote well.' Sam was moving towards an awareness of his own need to write, but the *East Lothian Magazine* was just a few years too soon for him – even if he had been acceptable to the young literati of the locality.

Dr Lorimer, obviously aware of the boy's appetite for knowledge, encouraged him to get involved with the Haddington School of Arts. This institution was another boon bestowed on the town with the help of Samuel Brown. It provided an adult education centre, where those with higher education or specialist knowledge provided lectures for the benefit of working people. Dr Lorimer was one of the first lecturers, on mechanics and chemistry. Sam not only attended the School of Arts but went on to assist Dr Lorimer with his lectures. Both doctors treated Sam as a protégé. Dr Lewins gave him the run of his own library, enticing him with the fine stock of medical and scientific books and the novels of the old masters: Samuel Richardson, Henry Fielding and Tobias Smollett.

But the clearest sign of Sam's dedication in those years was his arrangement with Mr Johnstone, teacher at Haddington's Parish school.

Smiles showed disdain when he wrote about prizes. Now there was no competition, no other boys in the class to overcome. He wanted to learn because he found it rewarding. And so he went in the evenings to Mr Johnstone, whom he describes fondly as 'a most accomplished man, full of accumulated knowledge; he was a good linguist, a good mathematician, and stored with information, which ebbed out in every word of his discourses'. Writing about his days at the Grammar School, Smiles may have been dismissive of cramming, but he had thought of that as competitive cramming, to beat others to the prizes. Much later Smiles discovered that Johnstone had been a close friend of Thomas Carlyle's and had in fact been appointed to the Parish school with the help of Jane Welsh, on Carlyle's recommendation. Now this modest, learned man sat in the evenings with young Sam, instructed him in mathematics, Latin and French, and in his conversation surely taught him a great deal more.

In the meantime, of course, Sam was not allowed to forget the reality of wounds and burns and sick people in poor homes. He went round their cottages and small houses, often working in bad light and cramped conditions, usually assisting one of the doctors. But in the dispensary he might have to deal with a patient on his own. In his education the complexities of anatomy and physiology were for later, and although he may have administered not much more than first aid, he had to learn to understand symptoms, to prescribe and compound with common sense, and to bleed and bind with sensitivity. The apprentice probably attended only the poorer patients, but for them he represented the practice; for them he was the doctor. For a teenage boy this was a pressing responsibility. During those years he obviously met his master's expectations, because in 1829, when Dr Lewins decided to move to a practice in the Edinburgh suburb of Leith, he took Sam with him. The sixteen-year-old still had two years to run on his apprenticeship, but now his medical training was to start in earnest, and he was about to take a significant step away from his roots.

3

Doctor in Waiting

IT WAS a time for everyone to be challenged – Sam, his parents, and
Dr Lewins. By the autumn of 1829, a few months before Sam's seventeenth birthday, he had been apprenticed to Dr Lewins for three years.
By then he would have had a pretty good grounding in the basic skills of
medical care. At the same time he had, by his own account, used his
leisure seriously – reading and learning widely, living wisely – a perfect
model, it seems, for the earnest, self-improving, non-conformist Scot of
popular tradition. If this also casts him as a bit of an over-earnest swot it
may be kinder and more realistic to understand the responsibility he felt
towards his parents, who had sacrificed a great deal to help his education,
and to Dr Lewins, who had been a thoughtful master.

But now he could go no further in Haddington. If he was really to
become a doctor he would have to move away, go to Edinburgh, and put
in the necessary years of study at one of the medical schools there. In
those days it was theoretically possible to treat patients and charge fees
without a formal qualification. But realistically no serious practitioner
would consider that option. For Sam the stamp of academic approval
was essential. In the event, a change in Dr Lewins's circumstances came
to the rescue.

Whether this was just Sam's good luck or part of some pre-arranged
plan, the timing for him was perfect. Dr Lewins, whose wife had died a
few months earlier,[1] announced that he would be leaving Haddington to
take over the practice of his own former master Dr Kellie, in Leith (the
port district of Edinburgh). He would be glad to have Samuel Smiles

complete his apprenticeship there and at the same time attend lectures at the University. Equally generously, Sam's parents were prepared to let him go, and to continue supporting him until he qualified, despite their small-town suspicions of the city's fleshpots. Their son may have proved himself to be thoroughly conscientious, but his freedom would not be without conditions.

A remarkable letter,[2] dated 17 October 1829, began: 'Dear son. You are now about to leave us, permit us to give you an advice...' It went on to warn him that he would be going to a place 'where much depravity and wickedness is prevelent (*sic*) now when you are away from our parental eye'. Interspersed with much invocation of an all-seeing God, and their own affection for their son, the Smiles parents make the bargain with young Sam abundantly clear:

> you will be provided with the means of making you respectable in the world, you will also have our prayers, and affectionately esteemed by us, but if you act contrary, to your disgrace and our shame your now fair prospects will be forever blasted, we will withhold our support and give it to another if more deserving, but we cherish the hope that your conduct will be as becometh a Christian and be deserving of our approbation.

The long letter, meticulously transcribed on ruled paper by one hand, bears at its foot, in the same hand, the names of

Your loving and affectionate
> *Father and Mother*
> *Sam Smiles*
> *Janet Smiles*

Then, squeezed as a last plaintive appeal along the bottom of the page: '*Samuel Smiles Jnr read this letter often & peruse the Sacred Book.*'

The letter survived (the earliest of all Smiles's correspondence to do so) and with it Smiles's regard and affection for his mother. Forty-five years later he wrote of her: 'Though her income was less than that of many highly paid working men, she educated her children well and brought them up religiously and virtuously.'

In going to Edinburgh, Smiles was travelling more than the twenty miles between Haddington and the city. He was travelling from small-town culture into one of the great intellectual hubs of Europe, the seat of the Scottish Enlightenment, to a city glowing with pride in its architectural and scenic beauty, and to an educational opportunity envied across the world.[3]

Edinburgh offered Smiles two paths to the recognition he would need to practice as a doctor. One was through Edinburgh University's medical faculty, leading to a university degree: MD Edinburgh. The other was through the Royal College of Surgeons, leading to the College's diploma, and designation as Licentiate of the Royal College. In fact, in almost everything the two paths merged. Each establishment had its own curriculum and examinations. At institutional and governance level the relationship between the two bodies was complex and often fiercely competitive. But self-interest led them to co-operate in most practical matters. George Bell told a Royal Commission in 1826 that 'there ought to be no rivalry ... Every additional number of students attracted to Edinburgh by the Surgical School may be regarded at the same time as so many added to the University and vice versa.'

In a social sense many may have preferred a university degree, for the university tradition was one of scholarship for its own sake, free from the taint of trade or of a gentleman's need to earn a living. 'Society' regarded with suspicion a doctor who depended on his practice for his livelihood, for he might then be more interested in their cash than in their cough. At Edinburgh University a classical-humanities strand was assumed to be part of every degree, including medicine. So in Edinburgh the sons of gentlemen, destined to become the doctors of gentlemen, tended to apply to the university.

But many others started their medical education as apprentices. For most of these the more practical regime of the College of Surgeons, with its lower costs, was the more attractive choice. The College encouraged apprenticeship,[4] commenting in its 1832 regulations that

> the College are also desirous to point out to the public, that the profession of Surgery is a practical art, which cannot be acquired without actual experience, and familiarity with the phenomena of disease; and they believe these objects to be best attained by serving an apprenticeship to a regular practitioner.

Samuel Smiles himself wrote in his *Autobiography* of his move to Leith that 'I then began to attend the medical classes at the University of Edinburgh ...', leading down the years to his being wrongly credited with an Edinburgh MD.[5]

For Samuel Smiles the College of Surgeons was the automatic option. It is even tempting to detect both the shadow of his parents and the seeds of his later ideas in the splendidly earnest language of the College, who declared themselves to be

> aware that their best efforts to improve the course of study will be incapable of effecting this desirable end, unless they are seconded by the influence of parents and guardians, and by the strenuous exertions of those who are devoting themselves to the study of the arduous and responsible profession of Surgery.[6]

So in November 1829, with his few clothes, his parents' letter and no doubt a copy of the Sacred Book stored in his room at Dr Lewin's house in Leith, the boy, not yet seventeen, walked up the hill, over two miles, to the admissions office in the Old Surgeons' Hall in High School Yard,[7] and enrolled.

He was one of over a thousand men, from all social classes and nationalities, studying medicine in Edinburgh at the time. Apprentices often lived with their masters, as Sam did with Dr Lewins in his stone-grey house in Leith's Quality Street (now called Maritime Street). Most others found rooms or lodging houses in the warren of mediaeval streets inside Edinburgh's city wall, near the University. They flooded into to the town in October to be ready for the start of medical lectures in the first week in November. 'The student of medicine is placed under no restraints',[8] a contemporary writer remarked, 'even in the slippery period of early youth he is exposed to every temptation, and often sinks to the lowest debauchery.' Sam's parental warning in The Letter followed him as he walked these streets: *'be particularly careful as to your companions ... let your companies be few and select'*. He seems to have avoided debauchery. For Sam it wasn't difficult. He had neither the time nor the money, for his schedule was relentless and his allowance tiny.

Down on Leith's harbour-front in winter the icy east wind is prone to blow in from the sea, and the Forth mist makes the dark mornings seem even darker. Sam was out of bed each morning well before eight o'clock, taking his breakfast porridge, and starting up the hill for the walk to the old town while it was still barely daylight. Up in Edinburgh lectures started at nine o'clock, first materia medica with Dr Duncan, then Dr Hope for chemistry, and Mr Lizars for anatomy. Some of this was dull stuff. Four years earlier another seventeen-year-old medical student in Edinburgh, Charles Darwin, found the whole thing both tedious and distressing. He too had Dr Duncan for early morning materia medica and Dr Hope for chemistry. He called the anatomy lectures 'as dull as [the lecturer] was himself,' and although he was fascinated by Lizars' operation on 'a beautiful dead body of a female, quite fresh,'[9] he found the stench in the dissecting room suffocating. Smiles, devoted to the arduous, didn't complain. He absorbed it all and each day by midday was back in Leith 'to give such assistance as I could to Dr Lewins'.

Sam enjoyed that first academic year living in Leith. The port had none of the Georgian elegance of Edinburgh's New Town, where 'persons of title and rank abound' and where he appreciated what he called 'the picturesque beauty of Edinburgh, which never tires'. But the vast new harbour works at Leith offered him a different and more lasting excitement – the prospect, dominating the water-front, of modern engineering creating a new world through the vision of men like John Rennie, whose massive docks were making Leith the greatest port on the east coast. He later described Rennie as among the 'strong-minded, resolute, and ingenious men; impelled to their special pursuits by the force of their constructive instincts'. For Smiles there was a sort of beauty in all this, and beauty in the idea that man's imagination need put no limit on his ambition. Edinburgh may have had style; Leith had energy.

'My life then', he said, 'was very pleasant. There was the bustle of the seaport, the scenery by the seaside, the daily walks to and from the College ...' – and, so different from his narrow life in Haddington, the chance to make friends – 'all of these made life very agreeable and enjoyable'. One of Sam's closest friends from those days, Adam Hope, eventually emigrated to Canada where, after triumphing over repeated business difficulties, he became a Director of the Canadian Bank of Commerce and a member of the Senate. With a career like that and a name like Hope, he seems now an almost uncannily Smilesian character.

'Having come to Canada alone and without capital,' says the *Dictionary of Canadian Biography*, 'Adam Hope had made his own way by hard work, ability, and integrity.' The entry could have been compiled by Samuel Smiles himself.

In his second year of college the knives, literally, came out. Practical anatomy and surgery joined the curriculum.[10] Now every day there would be long hours in the dissecting room and, even more demanding, in the cruel world of surgery without anaesthetic. Young Charles Darwin had found the experience so disturbing he had been forced to leave the room before the operation was over.[11] Knowing the pressure his apprentice would be under, Dr Lewins agreed that Sam should move out and for the rest of his time take lodgings nearer the college. The serious boy from Haddington was now a truly serious medical student.

If Darwin was sickened by the ordeal of patients subjected to surgery without anaesthetic, Samuel Smiles was able to admire how his teacher Robert Liston, whom he described as 'perhaps the most dexterous surgeon of his time', minimised their pain by his legendary speed. 'Time me gentlemen, time me!'[12] Liston would urge his students as he started to cut. Richard Gordon described how, to free both hands for the saw, Liston would 'clasp the bloody knife between his teeth'. Apart from the benefit to the patient of such alarming behaviour, Smiles had other reasons to admire the flamboyant surgeon, for, more quietly, Liston gave a great deal of his time to working with the poor, operating in their homes and, with Dr Lizars, helping with the Public Dispensary for poor citizens.[13]

A more scholarly model was Dr Fletcher, who lectured in what was then called 'the institutions of medicine' – in today's language, physiology. Smiles later called Dr Fletcher 'a most profound lecturer on his branch of science. He was an extensive reader, and brought the science of all Europe to bear upon his subject.' In fact a closer affinity existed between John Fletcher and Samuel Smiles than simply between teacher and student. Fletcher, like Smiles, had been a protégé of Dr Lewins almost twenty years earlier, having arrived in Haddington from London with a letter of introduction to the local doctor. 'Although rather my senior in years,' Lewins noted, 'he did me the honour to consider himself my pupil',[14] and for some time he lived in the Lewins household in

Haddington. Then, like Smiles, Fletcher moved on to Edinburgh where, in 1816, he took his MD at the University.

Later, by introducing an Oxford-style tutorial teaching system to Edinburgh, Fletcher transformed the learning experience of his students. By the time Sam Smiles encountered him John Fletcher had not only made the so-called Argyle Square Medical School a magnet for ambitious students, he regularly attracted audiences of hundreds to his public lectures, where he railed against the 'prudery and bigotry' which tried to restrict the open discussion of animal and human physiology. 'When the works of Darwin afterwards came out,' Smiles wrote in his *Autobiography*, 'I felt Fletcher had long before expounded very much the same views; or at all events, had heralded his approach.'

Perhaps for Smiles, too, John Fletcher heralded something. He 'required correct thoughts in correct words, and whilst taste was improved, the memory and understanding were vigorously exercised'. One reads of his insistence that 'whatever was said, written, or done might be said, written, or done in a certain assigned space ... intending to devote three hours a day to that particular occupation [writing a treatise] with well-concocted plans and a command of time he finished his task in thirty-two days'. With the language of medical science Dr Fletcher was apparently dispensing the language of self-help.

But outside the lecture room and the hospital Smiles learned other lessons in his Edinburgh years. He learned about politics, about the mob, and about the exploitation of people by politicians with slogans. Though victory over Napoleon had given Britain a sense of itself as a European superpower, memories of the blood-lust of the French revolution still sent shivers down the well-clothed backs of Westminster's aristocratic politicians, and of the propertied classes whose votes kept them in power. When the so-called July Revolution flared in Paris in 1830, and a rash of rick-burning and street protest broke out across Britain, the political response at Westminster was nervy and ambiguous – on the one hand a hardening of reaction by authority against any sign of unrest, on the other a liberal impulse to address inequality. Quickly the debate, in Parliament and on the streets, focused on reforming the electoral system.

The campaign for the first Reform Bill reached Edinburgh in the spring of 1831, while the lecture term was finishing for Smiles. As he wandered through the city he was both fascinated and horrified by what he saw. Though his own instincts favoured reform, he was shocked by how easily the debate was reduced to a battle-cry. When the Bill's first draft was passed by a single vote at Westminster – 'the glorious majority of one!' – he saw how the bullying crowd demanded celebration. Light up your house to show you're on our side, they demanded, or stay dark and take the consequences: a fusillade of bricks and iron bars through your windows. The malign power of the mob, 'always the biggest despots of all', made an indelible impression on Sam.[15] That sense of distancing himself, so apparent in his Haddington school days, reappeared.

When he went home to Haddington for the summer break he found the same fever of excitement about the Reform Bill. Haddington was one of a group of burghs jointly returning a member to parliament, and favoured the Reform candidate. Though Smiles would not have had a vote, he was welcomed by the leading reformers and their candidate Robert Stewart to their election-day headquarters in Lauder, where polling was due to take place. But Sam's enthusiasm was more clearly for the quiet, wide spaces of the mountains he travelled through when he walked from Haddington to Lauder to see the election, across 'a perfect sea of hills – lying silent and sublime, as far as the eye could reach. Not a sound was heard, except the whirr of a moorfowl on its way to cover, or the occasional cry of a startled sheep.' The shepherd he saw, the first man he had encountered for many miles, seemed to affect him more profoundly than all the next day's political commotion. He pictures the man standing above a deep glen, signalling to his dog on the further slope, working with the sheep on a distant hill. No battle-cries, no mob, just the shepherd, signalling with his arms and 'in the course of time he brought the flock all together, home to the sheep-farm'.

That walk, by Gifford and the woods of Yester, up to the summit of Lammerlaw and down through the Lammermuir Hills to the small town of Lauder, was a journey of over twenty miles. But it was a fine day in May, the mountain air was crisp and fresh, and Sam was eighteen years old. What young man would not thrive on such a life? And now he could look forward to several months of this freedom, interspersed with hours of study and helping in the family home – months in the smiling country before the last, long haul in Edinburgh and his diploma examination, waiting, just a year away.

He came up to Edinburgh again in November, to the narrow lanes of the Old Town, to the sulphurous reek of the dissecting rooms and the blood-soaked floors of the operating theatres. John Lizars had become professor of Surgery at the Royal College. Robert Liston's flashing blade still amazed his watching students; no surgical challenge seemed to faze him. Between them Liston and Lizars tackled all the most important operations at the Royal Infirmary. Sam was now a senior student with both these great men. At the same time he had to keep up his anatomy and general medical classes – according to the syllabus at least five lectures a week for at least five months[16] – as well as walking the wards at the Infirmary several times a week, often at night. It was a heavy load, but after his time away Sam was fresh and fit. Licentiate of the Royal College of Surgeons was in sight.

A talking point in the medical world at this time (and in the world beyond) was the appearance of Asiatic Cholera in southern Europe. Deaths were being reported in a swathe from Spain and Italy and up through France. By the time Sam returned to Edinburgh, the disease had reached Hamburg, where ships moved every day between the city harbour and Britain's North Sea ports. The first cases of cholera were reported in Gateshead and the direction of travel was north.

One January morning before daylight Sam heard a frantic knocking on his door and shouting from the street below his window. With some dread he recognised the voice of Forsyth from the livery stable in Haddington. Smiles's father was ill, Forsyth shouted, and Sam must come at once to Haddington. The morning was cold and dry, and though Forsyth drove his gig as fast as possible through silent streets and out over Birslae Brae, they arrived at Haddington too late. Sam climbed the narrow stairs above the shop knowing that his father was already dead. As he stood looking down at the bed he saw reflected in the pale mask on the pillow, his own face – in death a likeness he had never seen in life.

Haddington had 125 confirmed cases of cholera in that outbreak, and 57 deaths.[17] The unclean water and foul drains that eventually proved to be the carriers of the disease were a subject of later Smiles campaigns. His present problem was a widowed mother with a family of eleven to

support, the youngest only three months old. Sam stayed on in Haddington, comforting his mother, realising that in the changed circumstances
he might have to sacrifice his medical education. Though the shop's business had been growing and his elder brother John contributed a lot, their
father had been the driver. Could Sam really return to Edinburgh and
expect his family to go on paying his costs?

With the question still in the air, another blow hit the grieving family.
Their dead father had guaranteed a loan for his brother John, who ran a
paper-making business near Edinburgh. The business had failed over a
tax problem and now the Smiles guarantee, over £300, was being called
in. Somehow the huge amount was raised. Sam was dispatched to the
lawyers' office in Edinburgh to hand over the money, and when he
returned he believed he had no alternative but to drop out from college
to relieve his family of the burden. His mother's answer was firm:
'You must go back to Edinburgh, and do as your father desired: God
will provide.' Between God and his mother the subsequent debt was
discharged, the business of S. Smiles General Merchant survived, and
Sam's education stayed on track.

In the final year it would be non-stop. Rather than going home in April
as in other years, he stayed in Edinburgh for a long summer of clinical
experience and unbroken study. Liston's rival James Syme ran an
advanced course in clinical surgery, Dr Mackintosh in midwifery. There
was no pause in the pursuit of encyclopaedic knowledge of anatomy or,
after a quick supper at his lodgings, in evenings of grim reality in ward
rounds at the Royal Infirmary. Between all of this, almost universally
at the time students prepared for the final medical examination by
employing a coach, or 'grinder' as they called him, for one-to-one
tutorials. It was an expense Sam wouldn't contemplate. Instead he and
a fellow student, Henry Smith, met every day to help each other with
revision. They knew how demanding the examination could be.

Since gaining its Royal Charter just over fifty years earlier (in 1778) the
Royal College of Surgeons had placed a high value on its rank as a
learned society and on instilling in its students a corresponding sense
of their own value. No one must take the Diploma for granted. That
splendid scroll, engraved in copperplate, made out in Latin: *In praesentia
Collegii Regii Chirurgorem Edinensium*, and bearing the armorial seal of

the College, was to be highly prized. In a fine frame on a surgeon's wall it would testify both to his parents, who had paid for it, and to his patients who might benefit from it, the august nature of his education. To let all that slip after three years' work, to be rejected by the examiners, was hardly bearable. At least one failed student committed suicide, putting 'a period to his existence on Arthur's seat'.[18] [the rocky hill dominating the centre of Edinburgh]. Another used an engraver to forge his certificate, so crudely that it was written in English and carried the seal of a local trader. Some felt compelled to dress especially for the occasion. 'I must have a new waistcoat before my examination,' wrote one to his parents. 'Black silk is generally worn on that day by those who can afford it.'[19]

When his day came Samuel Smiles probably didn't wear black silk, though no doubt he felt a proper sense of awe as he passed between the classical columns and through the massive doors of William Playfair's new Surgeons' Hall in Nicolson Street, almost opposite the university. Inside, he and Henry Smith, in a cluster of hushed students, waited to be called one-by-one into the presence of the examiners. The whole thing was conducted viva voce, so that, instead of written papers, students were inspected face-to-face by their examiners. Sam watched others come and go. Years later he described the ordeal: 'first one then another candidate came out – rejected! One was much older than myself. I thought if he had not been able to pass, there was little chance for me. Then Henry Smith was called in. After what I thought was a very long time of 'heckling' he made his appearance with a beaming face.' "I have passed," he said. "Is it difficult?" "No, not at all. I know what you can do. You will find it easy!" Accordingly, when I was next called in, I went with good heart.' Apparently the Smiles-Smith self-help programme paid off. Sam got through, he records, 'without difficulty'. On 6 November 1832 he was back, in lighter mood, to the Surgeons' Hall to receive his Diploma – the magnificent document that he hoped might ensure a flow of Haddington's ailing to the rooms of their newest doctor.

4

Doctor in Doubt

AS HE PACKED up his books and clothes in his Edinburgh lodgings for the last time, Samuel no doubt contemplated his future with mixed feelings. The assumption all those years earlier, when he was indentured to Dr Lewins in Haddington, would have been that when qualified he would return to his home town, settle down as a country surgeon, and help to support his family. His love for his mother was genuine and his admiration for her deep-rooted. But he was twenty. At that age three years is a big part of anyone's life and Sam had spent it in one of the most exciting cities in Europe, consistently stimulated by new knowledge, new ideas and new possibilities. A lifetime back in the town of his birth was in comparison a grey prospect.

Besides, the market was overcrowded. After years of peace the army, as Smiles recorded in his *Autobiography*, 'instead of absorbing surgeons, discharged them; and in Haddington, as elsewhere, there were experienced army surgeons on half pay, competing with the local practitioners'. Seven of those now jostled for the patronage of a population of about 3,500 people. That average of 500 per doctor (most of whom couldn't afford to pay) compares with over 2,000 registered patients for a typical general practitioner in today's National Health Service.

Smiles thought of going abroad, considered India, but without contacts or influence, dropped the idea. A break-out nearer home, to Galashiels, tempted him. His cousins the Yellowlees, whose artist father he had so much admired, lived nearby. A College friend had set up practice in the attractive town. Perhaps there was room for another new doctor – more room, at any rate, than in Haddington? His friend's response was brief:

'If you come I will go.' Samuel knew, anyway, where duty called: 'I was the son whom my mother most relied on for assistance, and as she wished me to remain at home for some years, I finally consented.'

During those years, between 1833 and 1837, he stayed at home, now the eighth doctor in the town and clearly not the most successful. He was left, he wearily records, with 'some remnants of practice, mostly among the poor'. They consulted him infrequently and paid him even less frequently. But he admired the dignity of the country poor, their hardiness, their thrift, their industry. Above all he noted their devotion to the education of their children, somehow managing, out of incomes of no more than ten shillings a week, to send them to school. Wryly he adds, 'how little remained for the doctor who attended them in their trials and troubles?'

Smiles knew before he started that Haddington had too many doctors. He knew he would have to live on scraps. Much of his work was done, as he said, 'gratuitously', so he could give precious little financial support to his mother. Years later his granddaughter Aileen suggested that his presence itself was his main contribution to the family. 'He was needed at home,' she said.[1] The younger children 'looked on him as their own father'. Aileen Smiles gives an impression of her grandfather at this time as unfailingly upbeat:

> one of those rarities, a man delighted with life and with his fellow human beings ... To more ordinary people those five years in Haddington would have seemed years of frustration, that fashionable word of the present day [she was writing in 1956]. It was a word which Grandpa never used for, whatever his faults, he was not lily-livered.

Indeed not, but in spite of his granddaughter's dismissal of frustration, that seems to have been exactly what he felt about his medical career in Haddington. He found the life of a country doctor monotonous. He quoted the explorer Mungo Park, who had tried practising in the nearby town of Peebles: 'I would rather go back to Africa than practise again in Peebles.' One can hear the Smiles 'Amen', and the weary sigh as he dismisses the subject: 'It is unnecessary for me to go into all the details of my life while practising as a country surgeon. My employment was very fitful.'

The picture is not hard to imagine, of a young man in an empty room, his desk before him and his framed Diploma gathering dust on the wall behind, waiting through the long, grey Scottish days for someone to knock on his door. Those unproductive hours were anathema to a man imbued with the sense of time as capital, who later wrote in praise of those 'who turned all things to gold – even time itself'. Smiles found his own sort of gold, first in the kind of activities that might be expected of any intelligent, energetic individual with time on his hands. He engaged in what he described as 'amusements', offering a glimpse perhaps of some sort of social metamorphosis, from humble shopkeeper's boy to Edinburgh-educated young doctor playing a leading role in community culture. He took up drawing and painting again, confident enough to let his work be seen in public. Inspired no doubt by the success of John Fletcher's public lectures to the great and good of Edinburgh, he put together his own set of fifteen talks on 'Physiology and the Conditions of Health', which he delivered to audiences of Haddingtonians packed into the oak-panelled solemnity of the Sheriff's Court-room. Like Fletcher, he embellished his lectures with his own watercolour illustrations. He studied music and learned the violin, again happy to share his enthusiasm with the community. Samuel Smiles, who had muttered resentfully against Mr Hardie's favourites, 'the sons of provosts, bailies and town-councillors', found himself joining Provost Lea to form what he called 'a quartette party' to give charity concerts in the town.

These were Smiles's amusements, little more than social pathways, but by their nature – based on application and knowledge rather than wealth and manners – they suggest an earnestness of purpose that sign-posted the direction he would take. Amusement would not be enough. At every spare moment he read and studied with hunger, for ideas, for a view of life and how it should be lived. He read French philosophers and polemicists, Australian feminists (before that word was known), and English radical journalists. It was a rich diet for a young country surgeon who had never travelled more than twenty miles from home, but it all fed in to a career which, in spite of apparent patchiness, was in fact remarkably coherent. Whatever else he did, from this time forward Smiles was always a writer.

When, in his own words 'I set to work at my French,' one of the authors he set to work on was Louis Aimé-Martin, whose *Éducation des Mères de famille* promoted ideas about the role of women, which in the twenty-first century seem at best delightfully quaint, at worst chauvinistic and patronising.[2] But in the 1830s Aimé-Martin would have been seen as cautiously progressive. He aimed to advance the role of women, especially as mothers. When the Emperor Napoleon, as reported by Aimé-Martin, asked Madame Campion, 'What is wanting, in order that the youth of France be well educated?' 'Mothers!' she replied. 'Here' said he 'is a system of education in one word. Be it your care to train up mothers who know how to educate their children.'

Smiles said that Aimé-Martin gave him 'views about the power of women which I later turned to good account'. In *Character* (1871) he was to write that 'the enlightenment or ignorance, the civilization or barbarism of the world, depends to a very high degree upon the exercise of women's power within her special kingdom of home'. The writing itch had started. *Éducation des Mères* may have prompted Smiles's first book, but while that was in gestation other, weightier ideas, other voices, were flooding his mind. He read London's most admired radical newspaper, *The Examiner*, whose brilliant editor Albany Fonblanque offered an exciting, elegantly articulated vision of liberal political thought. In the *Monthly Repository* Smiles discovered a free-thinking Unitarian intelligentsia – W J Fox, Southwood Smith, and Mary Leman Grimstone. Later he came particularly to admire and befriend Mrs Grimstone (by then Mrs Gillies). But of all the writers the young doctor studied at this time, one offers the most enticing link to Smiles's much later, career-defining book, if only because of its title: *Du Perfectionnement moral; ou l'Éducation de soi-même* by the Huguenot philosopher Baron de Gérando[3] – in English, *Self-Education; or the Means and Art of Moral Progress*. Smiles's *Self-Help* would not be published for another twenty-five years, but from this early exposure, de Gérando's ideas became firmly embedded.

The Frenchman's proposition, often tortuously expressed, is based on his concept of 'the Love of Excellence', in which he binds the excellence of a life to the moral excellence of the man – an achievable excellence because it is inherent. 'The perfection of all beings,' de Gérando declared 'consists in the faithfulness in which they conform themselves to their nature.' (To thine own self be true). The high spiritual-moral assumption behind *Self-Education,* and its emphasis on personal responsibility, fed into the thinking of the New England Transcendentalists like Henry David Thoreau, Margaret Fuller and Ralph Waldo Emerson. 'Self-Culture' was the title of the Franklin lecture delivered in Boston by the leading Unitarian preacher of the time, William Ellery Channing, when he essentially recycled de Gérando's text. This Unitarian transcendentalist vision was of the innate goodness of nature, and by corollary of people – original virtue rather than original sin, but vulnerable to the effects of society and its institutions, particularly organised religion and political parties. Thus, to be true to themselves people had to be independent of such forces. 'We will walk on our own feet', Emerson said, 'we will work with our own hands; we will speak with our own minds.'[4] From de Gérando, through Channing and Emerson and their cheerleaders among the London Unitarians, Samuels Smiles was working his way towards a view of life. Their argument for individual responsibility based on moral integrity informed everything he subsequently wrote.

It would be wrong to imagine Smiles, among his musical soirées and public talks on personal health, as a visionary in the Emerson mould. His impulse to communicate, and the nature of his message, were robustly practical, but in what was to be his first modest venture into publication, the core Smiles message would already be apparent: the integrity of the individual is the prerequisite for happiness and well-being, and we must, above all, 'seek elevation[5] of character, without which capacity is worthless and worldly success is naught'.

So to defeat the *longueurs* of medical life in the provinces Smiles set himself to write a book. He didn't find it easy, but in characteristic Smilesian mode 'I made up my mind, read and studied diligently, and prepared the sheets for the printer.' When he had finished, the twenty-four-year-old bachelor had written a book advising mothers how to rear their children.

Immediately the manuscript was ready, he took the coach from outside the George Hotel in Haddington to Edinburgh, walked through the familiar streets to the offices of his first choice publisher, W & R Chambers, and presented the manuscript to Mr William Chambers. Unfortunately Chambers was already in discussion for such a book with a much more distinguished Edinburgh physician, the fashionable Dr Andrew

Combe. Smiles, somewhat in awe of Combe, whose work he had studied, moved on to visit Oliver & Boyd in Tweedale Court. He knew George Boyd and quickly agreed a deal for the printing of 750 copies. *Physical Education, or The Nurture and management of Children, founded on the study of their Nature and Constitution*, by Samuel Smiles, Surgeon, was published in Edinburgh in 1836, and in London by Simkin, Marshall & Co in 1838.

Not all 750 copies sold, but for Samuel Smiles's career as a writer the book was important. At one level it is a manual of practical advice to mothers on the care of small children, with early chapter headings like 'Food', 'Teething' and 'Regular meals'. But as Smiles develops his argument, a more innovative and radical approach becomes apparent. He doesn't miss the value of an arresting opening line: 'It is a melancholy but undoubted fact, that of the whole number of children born in this country, considerably more than one-third die under five years of age!' From that platform he launches a series of attacks on what he perceives as conventional practice in child-rearing. His targets include social disadvantage, urban overcrowding, the poor education of women and the attitude to girls, 'middling' class stupidity, but most of all, behaviour which goes against nature. He points to 'the perfection of structure observed in the human frame – its admirable adaptation to external nature – and the efficiency of the laws provided for its healthy existence...' and goes on to blame the high rate of child sickness and mortality on 'a want of knowledge, a lamentable ignorance of the nature of the human frame and the means of preserving its adaptation to external nature'.

The Smiles cure, delivered through detailed advice on healthy diet, fresh air, sensible clothing, and vigorous exercise (for girls as well as boys) might be summed up in Juvenal's dictum: *mens sana in corpore sano*, a healthy mind in a healthy body, with heavy emphasis on the *corpore*. A parent's first concern for the infant, Smiles insisted, must be for its physical well-being. Look to the natural health of its body and the healthy development of its mind will naturally follow: 'physical health, which requires as its essential condition physical exercise, is the soundest basis of intellectual enjoyment'. For a man so dedicated to his own development through books and study, there is some surprise in his emphasis on the avoidance of 'book learning' in early years. Again, the reliance must be on what, in Smiles's view, is natural. 'Forced studies, like the forced labour of factory children, are alike bad. But place some object in view – give an interest in the pursuit, whatever it be ... and he will enter into it with interest, and reap the benefit of the pursuit.' Here is an early hint of the later Smiles doctrine – the importance of 'interest'. His heroes rise by single-minded pursuit of an inner aim, undeflected by the judgements or distractions of the world.

Of course the urgings of Aimé-Martin, of de Gérando, of Leman Grimstone, are everywhere apparent in *Physical Education* – above all in the high moral tone. Smiles quotes with enthusiasm words from Leman Grimstone's *Character*: 'If the earth heaved, and cried 'there is gold', should we fail to dig it forth? And how much more precious is the moral ore of the human breast?' His own final lines do not shirk the rhetorical flourish of a man with a message, not just for the mothers of Scotland, but for the world: 'Thus carried to its legitimate results, Physical Education will greatly improve the condition of mankind, promote human happiness and enjoyment, and by enabling him to cultivate his higher faculties and affections, raise man, on earth, to the very summit of nature.'

One can imagine the light in the eyes, the flush on the cheek of the young doctor, as he finished these words and hurried off to Edinburgh to find a publisher. There is a certain pathos in his later account of the book's fate, of its being superseded by a similar book 'much better done' by the ubiquitous Dr Coombe in his *Treatise on the Physiological and Moral Management of Infancy*, and of the final, hundred unbound copies which Smiles carried about with him and gave, after a few years, to a fugitive London bookseller on his way to Australia. 'The book sold fairly well,' Smiles later shrugged, 'but if it paid its expenses, that was all.'

But that was not all. Samuel Smiles was an author now. He had a book that his mother could see, with her son's name on the cover. Now, at last, he might be deserving of her approbation, as urged in that parental letter of 1832. Others, even beyond Edinburgh, might see the book. Doors might open. *Chambers's Journal*, even the great *Athenaeum* in London, noticed *Physical Education* favourably. Mrs Leman Gillies, to whom he had dared to send a copy, wrote in effusive praise. Perhaps now he could swap his under-used role as a country surgeon for life as a writer. He had come to the notice of Thomas Murray, a political philosopher, popular public lecturer and editor of the *Edinburgh Weekly Chronicle*. Murray invited the young author to submit a short article to his paper. Starting with what Smiles called 'pieces of intelligence', he gained the editor's confidence and soon became a regular contributor. Over the next year his opinionated columns were promoted to leader status, carrying, as he proudly recorded, the magic '"we" as if I were the editor.'

His pieces appeared between 1836 and 1838. What did he write about? What views did 'we' offer the Edinburgh public? Sadly the fruits of Samuel Smiles's first adventure in journalism have disappeared, for no copies of the *Edinburgh Weekly Chronicle* for those years have survived. What we do know is the editorial stance of the paper's stablemate, *Tait's Edinburgh Magazine*, whose proprietors John and Isobel Johnstone were among Edinburgh's leading liberals.[6] An address to subscribers in *Tait's* in October 1833 set out the *Chronicle's* manifesto: 'The Edinburgh Chronicle steadily adheres[7] to the CAUSE of the PEOPLE; supporting Ministers only when their measures deserve the approbation of Independent Journalists.' And the cause of the people? The writer is in no doubt: 'the abolition of the Corn Laws, Tithes, Church Rates, Pensions, Sinecures; for a total separation between Church and State, the Repeal of Taxes on Knowledge; and for those grand securities for responsible government, the Ballot, short Parliaments, and an extension of the Electoral Franchise.'

If such views were indeed echoed by Samuel Smiles in his leader columns in the *Edinburgh Weekly Chronicle* it would hardly be surprising, for they represent a fair catalogue of the policies he would later advocate when he became a newspaper editor in his own right, though not in Edinburgh and not until a year later. The links may be tenuous, but they are richly tempting – the resentment of the aristocracy, the enthusiasm for 'that important section of our countrymen, now fast emerging from ignorance and apathy', the admiration for 'industrious operatives' and their need for 'political, moral and literary instruction', and, most explicitly, the proudly-struck Benthamite utilitarian stance: 'in the words of our great master in political and moral science, 'the greatest happiness of the greatest number' is our leading object'.[8]

While he worked in his Haddington room on articles for the *Edinburgh Chronicle*, followed the fortunes of *Physical Education*, and answered infrequent calls from the local sick, he made *Tait's Edinburgh Magazine* part of his reading. There, probably early in 1838, he saw an advertisement for the vacant post of editor of the *Leeds Times* (a newspaper commended in the pages of *Tait's* for its radical stance).[9] The job opportunity had been caused by the death in December 1837 of the then *Leeds Times* editor, the Scottish poet Robert Nicoll. Isobel Johnstone, as a considerable literary figure in Edinburgh, had been able to foster Nicoll's early poetic talent and, when he became ill, had cared for him in her Edinburgh home in his last days. The thread joining the vacancy at the *Leeds Times*, Isobel Johnstone (mentor to its late editor), and Samuel Smiles, is thin but visible. What we know is that he answered the advertisement, was asked to submit a sample piece (on Suffrage) and that, though it was approved, he wasn't offered the job.

In November 1837 a newcomer had arrived on Leeds's lively media scene – the *Northern Star*, strident voice of Feargus O'Connor and of militant Chartism. The People's Charter, that great hope for a fairer society in Britain, had emerged through the work of the London Working Men's Association in 1838. Its headline aim was a vote for every adult man. This, and its five other aims,[10] had won the support of a broad range of liberal opinion, including a number of Members of Parliament. But a militant Chartist wing, led by Feargus O'Connor, an ultra-radical member of the LWMA, had started to advocate violence as the best way to achieve the Charter's objectives. This so-called 'physical force' appeal had grown alarmingly, particularly in the north, and the circulation of the *Northern Star* was swelling fast.

The *Leeds Times* owner, an independent-minded Yorkshireman called Frederick Hobson, believed his paper needed to counter this threat with a more experienced journalist than young Smiles. He appointed Charles Hooton, who had been a sub-editor at the London radical paper the *True Sun*. In view of subsequent events it is hard not to detect some irony in Smiles's comment on the appointment: 'He was a most accomplished man, an able writer, the author of the Adventures of Bilberry Thurland, Colin Clink, and other clever works of fiction.' So much for the struggle with violent Chartism.

In Haddington, life for Samuel Smiles had at last palled. At twenty-five, well educated, widely read, full of vigorous curiosity, with friends across a whole spectrum of society, he had still seen nothing beyond the

Lothians of his birth. The editor's job in Leeds might have provided the break, but it wasn't his. It was time to move on, perhaps eventually to England, perhaps even to Australia. For the present he set himself a short-term goal – to travel to the continent, take an MD at Heidelberg or Leyden, and at the same time learn German and improve his French. By the spring of 1838 he had tidied his affairs in Haddington, sold what he could, gathered the letters of introduction essential for any traveller in those days, and made his way to Leith where he took ship for Hull, the departure point for Rotterdam.

Smiles was exhilarated by his freedom, by the open sea, 'the gulls and solan geese ... wheeling in loud convulsions round the cliffs,' even by the challenge of sea-sickness on the 24-hour journey from Hull to Rotterdam – 'the first and only time I have ever been discomfited at sea'. He was enchanted by the strange, flat land of Holland, the windmills and canals reaching into the distance, but mainly by the people. The urge to travel and learn never left Smiles, nor his interest in the life and history of the people in the places he visited. Pausing briefly at Rotterdam to take advice from the local Scottish minister, he decided on Leyden for his degree. A few days later he joined the passengers on a horse-drawn canal barge for the gentle day's journey to the old university city. Its distant roofs and towers, seen that evening against the setting sun, made a lasting impression on him and gave him a sense of a different world.

Smiles was an affable man who made acquaintances easily. A fellow passenger on the barge not only recommended a private hotel in a quiet part of Leyden, but took the Scotsman there and introduced him to the family. An almost Vermeer-like sense of calm, of solemn Dutch smiles and restrained enjoyment, is suggested by Smiles's account of the time he spent with them. Through those early summer weeks he was the only boarder in the small hotel, set in what he describes as 'a retired part of the town'. During the days he prepared for the coming examination at the University. In the evenings the whole family – mother, father, three daughters and two sons – enjoyed the company of their English-speaking guest. Father and daughters, 'very musical', played for him (shades of Haddington's 'quartette parties'), and conversation was lively. Soon, Smiles says, he 'felt quite at home and got to know a great deal about Dutch manners and customs'. This interest in other societies became a habit for life. One imagines Samuel Smiles always travelling with a notebook. Though sadly no notebook has survived, most of his travels resulted in published works. Of this first adventure he recorded that he 'took copious notes during my residence abroad. I afterwards worked them up into a series of articles which were published in a London journal.' When the day for the examination arrived at what was Holland's oldest university, Smiles found himself before a group of eminent Dutch medical men headed by Professor van Hoeven, Dean of a school venerated throughout the medical world. Young Smiles was not impressed. Loyal to Edinburgh and the polished grammar of Dr Fletcher, he sniffed at the Dutchmen's 'dog Latin' and found the whole process 'by no means so thorough as the one at Edinburgh some years before'. But, in awarding him its degree, the university fulfilled his objective. Dr Smiles could now wear the title MD.

Perhaps the real attraction of this continental enterprise now began. Free of medical books and dog Latin, he left his luggage with his kind hosts, shouldered his knapsack, and on a sunny morning set off by Leyden's east gate for a walking tour of Holland and the Rhine. He spent that whole long summer 'staff in hand and kit on back ... this is the true way to see and enjoy a country. To appreciate nature, you must walk'. He did, for almost three months, learning all the way, 'something of modern languages; and a good deal of human nature'. He also thought a lot about his own future, including the possibility of emigrating to America or Australia. London seemed to be the place to find out more, so at the beginning of September, his walking tour over, he collected his luggage in Leyden, said goodbye to the musical Dutch family, and sailed for England and 'the great city which is the centre of so many aspirations'. Certainly this visit was to shape the aspirations of Samuel Smiles.

As Edinburgh had been a different world from Haddington, London in 1838 revealed itself as a vastly, strangely different world from Edinburgh, or anywhere else Samuel Smiles could have imagined. Drawn in through dark fog that lay across the Thames estuary, his cross-channel steamer edged its way up river in a thickening traffic of tall ships, yawls, lighters, wherries and smacks, a vision of river banks lined with workshops, sheds, manufactories and the lines of cannon and cannon balls along the Royal Dockyard wharf, a rising wave of sound, of crewmen's shouts and ringing bells, and the deep, dark smell of water passing through a great city. Ashore, this sense of infinite activity, of infinite strangeness grew, the sense that leaves a person in a crowd at once intimidated and exhilarated, at once part of everything, and isolated from it. But, as he noted, 'youth is vigorous, hopeful, and naturally cheerful', so once settled in the lodging house in Soho's Poland Street recommended by his brother Robert, Samuel Smiles set melancholy thoughts aside and rediscovered his gift for focussing on the positive. He treasured his anonymity in the big city, enjoying what he called the extreme mental liberty, and freedom from the petty persecutions of the provinces. In London, he declared, 'private opinion is active, free, and independent – one of the greatest privileges which free-minded men can desire'. More than anything, he valued the people he did meet, the very exemplars of active, free and independent opinion.

Such a one was the fugitive Italian patriot Giuseppe Mazzini. Robert Smiles, an educationist in Manchester, probably knew him through this work, for Samuel, directed by his brother, found himself sharing the Poland Street lodgings with Mazzini, who was involved, among much else, in education for the poor in London. Mazzini, passionate in the cause of Italian republicanism and unification, fired Smiles with his ideas for the brotherhood of men and 'the amelioration of all through the work of all'. In what is almost a parody of later Smiles attitudes,[11] Mazzini is described as lecturing to Italian working men 'on the outlines of natural philosophy, and the lives of great men, so as to elevate them above subjection and poverty, and fortify their minds in serious thought and earnest purpose'.

Serious thought and earnest purpose; true, active and independent opinion – stranded in Haddington Smiles had read of them in the books and periodicals he had so eagerly studied. Now, in London, he could engage with not just the writings but some of the writers. If he did not become exactly an intellectual saloniste, the drawing rooms that opened to him certainly influenced the course of his career, and gave him valuable confidence for the work ahead.

From his mentor, Provost Lea of Haddington, Smiles had learned about Lea's nephew Rowland Hill (now best-known for having introduced the penny post) and about the original work Hill was doing in education. Both at Hazelwood[12] School and in his writings, Hill promoted the principle of learning based on encouragement rather than prescription. In his treatise on public education he advocated kindness and moral influence rather than discipline and punishment. He believed that through self-education pupils would become most useful to society and most happy to themselves.

How thrilling for Smiles when he was not only welcomed by the great man, but was also offered generous praise, encouragement, and advice. Hill had a special interest in the Australian colonies (where Smiles thought of emigrating as a doctor). Hill thought there was little opportunity at the time for 'professional men' in Australia. 'Stay at home,' he advised his young guest. 'With an active mind like yours, there is plenty of room for you here. I find that, like myself, you have written about Education. I have read your book – it is very good; my uncle sent it to me. Go on in the same direction; there is plenty of room.'

At dinner in the Hill's Burton Terrace home Smiles had other opportunities to hear the great questions of the day discussed. He met Rowland Hill's family, and the language scholar John Bowring.[13] Both Hill and Bowring were some twenty years older that Samuel Smiles – political and intellectual heavyweights. Bowring had been MP for Kilmarnock, a close friend of Jeremy Bentham's, and an editor of the *Westminster Review*. One can imagine the effect on the twenty-five-year-old newcomer to London of sitting round the dinner table with these men. Popular education, reform of Parliament, free trade, religious liberalism – these were their causes. Smiles was able to feel, by admission to the company of such men, a rising belief in his own ideas, an authentication, and permission to build. He was the modern man, given a torch to take forward.

This growing excitement followed him to 43 Allsop Terrace in Regent's Park, the London home of Mary Leman Gillies. There, and at her sister's house in Highgate, he experienced the same sense of admission to a select community, as he talked with the woman whose articles in the *Monthly Repository* he had studied, and who had so warmly praised his own work. The same strand of radical thought, the treasured 'free and independent opinion', flourished there among her friends, the great Unitarians and advocates of modern ideas on everything from women's rights to public health – men like Thomas Southwood Smith and Edwin

Chadwick. In his *Autobiography* Smiles wrote that at these gatherings he also met the young Octavia Hill, who would spend a lifetime campaigning for progressive causes. 'I thought that she was precocious, but she was merely quick and cultivated by mixing in the best society.' But any such encounter must have come years later, for Octavia Hill,[14] Southwood Smith's granddaughter, had, in 1838, just been born.

But however stimulated he may have been by radical ideas, when Smiles had the opportunity in London to experience radical politics on the street, he did not like what he saw. At a Chartist rally in New Palace Yard Westminster he heard the emerging Chartist leader Feargus O'Connor hurling his words across the crowd, no doubt to reach the ears of Members hurrying to their business in the nearby House. Smiles was repelled by the mood of verbal and physical threat, by the same bully-boy mood he had noticed as a student during the reform campaign in Scotland. A Smiles hero, Ebenezer Elliot 'the Corn law Rhymer', was on the platform that night and told Smiles, when they met later: 'that fellow O'Connor will ruin that cause. The threat of physical force will never do: we want the power of public opinion.' One of the founders[15] of Chartism, William Lovett, secretary of the Working Men's Association, believed O'Connor's 'violent ravings about physical force' that evening helped to drive liberal middle-class support away from the Chartist cause.

When Samuel Smiles left London a few days later, and just weeks before his twenty-sixth birthday, he had matured in more than years. Yet fired as he was by the zeal of Mazzini, and by the enthusiasm of Hill, Bowring, Gillies and the others, for political and social improvement, he felt committed to the responsible path of rebuilding his career as a doctor. So when he visited his friend Dr Carstairs, practising in Sheffield, and Carstairs pointed him to an opportunity in nearby Doncaster, Smiles felt obliged to give it a chance. He hurried back to Haddington to collect his books and instruments. A few weeks later he returned to Doncaster with the intention of taking rooms and presenting Samuel Smiles MD to the local population. But first he called on a friend living locally and to whose lodgings he had arranged for his mail to be directed. Only one letter is recorded. It was from the *Leeds Times*.

5

Beautiful Undulations

THE LETTER was from a Mr Bingley, senior *Leeds Times* reporter, writing on behalf of his proprietor, Frederick Hobson. Mr Hobson was unhappy. His first editor, the late Robert Nichol, an energetic young Scot, had built a loyal readership for the paper in Leeds, and had worked hard for the non-violent radical cause in the area. His successor Charles Hooton, whatever his literary merits, had failed to keep up the good work. Under fire from Feargus O'Connor's new *Northern Star,* the circulation of the *Leeds Times* had started to slip. Hobson had now decided he needed another energetic young Scot to replace the departing Hooton. Bingley's letter offered Samuel Smiles the job. In Carstairs's home Smiles had met John Bridgeford, proprietor of the *Sheffield Iris*, a paper with a strongly liberal background. When Bridgeford heard of the *Leeds Times* offer he strongly urged Smiles to accept.

> I went over to Leeds by coach ... and duly arrived at the great manufacturing town, overhung by clouds of smoke. There I was to remain for nearly twenty years; there I married, there all my children were born; and there I spent about the happiest and most fruitful period of my life.

Smiles wrote those words as an old man, looking back over a sixty-year career. Yet the time of his greatest success, when he wrote his best-selling books and was courted by his publisher, achieved world fame, lived in fine houses, travelled widely, and was honoured by foreign royalty – came only after he had left Leeds. So what was there about those northern years that made him, on reflection, favour them above such apparent triumph? The unknown perhaps – idealism untainted by experience, the prospect rather than the arrival – and the thrill of meeting the modern world.

Smiles was joining a community in transformation. With a population across the borough of about 150,000 (London's population was over ten times larger), Leeds was not yet a city, much less a large one. But it was a borough growing and changing fast. Smiles described Leeds as a great manufacturing town. It had always been proud of its place as a 'cloth' town, described in a directory of the time as 'the most populous town of the West Riding of Yorkshire, and the principal seat and emporium of the great woollen manufacture of England'.[1] But the role of 'emporium', of a trading centre where makers brought their wares for sale, had been overtaken by the machine age. No longer was cloth spun and woven in cottages, and packaged in small parcels for sale in the local market. It was produced in factories, on a huge scale, for sale to national and international traders. Spinners and weavers had become 'operatives', paid a wage to tend a machine which could do the work of hundreds of human hands. And recently the even more modern industry of machine-making had arrived in Leeds. With the vast Yorkshire coalfields on its doorstep, Leeds was well placed to exploit the power of steam, both to drive the thousands of spindles in its flax and woollen mills, and to fire the furnaces for the iron fabricating monsters in the new engineering works. The smoke stacks clustered, seen from afar by Smiles as he approached the town, besmirching the sky, towering above the older buildings.

But Leeds still had its open spaces, a river, gracious Georgian buildings, and pride. The river Aire, flowing through the town, was lined on either side by workshops, small factories, and dyeworks, staining the water with bright colour. Self-employed artisans, craftspeople and small tradesmen still made up a significant part of the workforce. Leeds cherished its identity as a place where people valued their tradition of skill and hard work, their independence of mind, and their sense of a community confident to face the world. After visiting Leeds, the social reformer Anthony Ashley-Cooper wrote, 'What a sin it is to be ignorant of the sterling value and merit of these poor men.' The new generation of business titans, men like John Garth Marshall and James Kitson, came from modest, nonconformist backgrounds, with a liberal, tolerant tradition. After the Reform Bill of 1832 Leeds had been given two seats in Parliament. Its voters had elected two liberal Whigs, John G Marshall and Anthony Babington Macaulay. In 1838 the spirit of its former self survived in Leeds, and its people were determined not to let it go.

All over Britain these were years of depression and over-capacity in the textile business. Economic shifts and greedy building speculators were changing and darkening the character of Leeds. Foreign competition and new technology were affecting exports and driving down demand, which meant, for workers, lower wages or unemployment.

At the time of Smiles's arrival in Leeds, the 'hungry forties' were approaching everywhere in England. The town was feeling the national pain and joining the national debate. Pressure for reform had been on the agenda for a decade, but the new conditions had created a new, more confrontational atmosphere. Spokesmen across the political and social spectrum agreed that there was a problem. They disagreed vigorously both about its cause, and about its solution. Two ideas, two words, suffused public statements – 'radicalism' and the 'People'. Everyone who demanded change claimed to be radical, and every 'radical' claimed to be speaking for the People.

The people themselves, the great mass of working-class, unpropertied people, had no say, because they had no vote. Now many of them had no bread either, its price having been driven up by the Corn Laws, which protected wealthy farmers and land-owning aristocrats from cheap imported grain. That, at least, was the radical argument. One shade of radicalism advocated abolition of the Corn Laws, for the sake of the people. Another argued for abolition of voting restrictions – universal suffrage – and let the people then sort out their own answer to the price of bread. And there were many shades of radicalism in between. Politicians shouted at each other at Westminster, on behalf of the people, of course. Newspaper editors shouted at each other in print, on behalf of the people, of course – including the newspaper editors in Leeds.

But this was not simply a debate carefully choreographed by the newspapers and conducted in print. In towns like Leeds, people got involved in real political activity, in holding meetings, forming campaign groups, taking the arguments to local level in local elections. Newspaper owners, journalists and business leaders, came out from their offices and joined the live debate, in large meetings and small groups, in drawing rooms, in hotel rooms and in workrooms, and everyone with an axe to grind or an injustice to expose joined in. The air was thick with ideas and debate, and Samuel Smiles loved it.

By this time Smiles was no naïve, starry-eyed stripling. His experience with the *Edinburgh Chronicle*, the publication of his book, his travels in Holland and Germany, and his reception by writers and intellectuals in London, gave him, during those first winter weeks in Leeds, the clarity and the confidence to do his research effectively, and to start forming his own opinions. He had arrived a month before he was due to take over the editor's chair in the new year – plenty of time to look round and get a feel for the people and the politics he would be dealing with. He could walk through the whole town, barely two miles in any direction, in a morning, talk to the people in the streets, read the banners announcing a Chartist torch-light rally. He could witness at first hand the pain and poverty that gave the Charter such impetus. Off Kirkgate, only yards from his own newspaper office, he might peer into the grim Boot-and-Shoe Yard, where 'a fetid water course commencing in Vicar Lane receives much of the soil [sewage] from George's Street'[2] and where the two-room cottages housed on average six people per room. He could wonder at the vast and under-used Cloth Hall market, catch the smell of cattle, pigs and vegetables in the Free Market in Vicar Lane, and mingle with the crowd looking in the shops and moving between the offices on the six-hundred-yard long Briggate, Leeds's principal street. This great thoroughfare, described as one of the broadest, handsomest, and busiest in the north of England, sloped gently upwards from the bridge at its southern end to the distant St John's Parish Church, 'whence the suburbs rise in beautiful undulations northward to Woodhouse and Buslingthorp ... through a prosperous part of the town'.[3] A pleasant district, he might have thought, for a newspaper editor to live, some day.

Back down in Briggate he could pass, at number 149, the office of the hundred-year-old *Leeds Mercury*. Somewhere behind those doors the paper's Whig editor Edward Baines might at that very moment be working on one of his 'Radical-Whig' articles, arguing for abolition of the Corn Laws but saying nothing on one of Smiles's favourite subjects, universal suffrage. If he had diverted a few yards into Market Street, Smiles might, as he passed number 14, almost have felt the hot breath of

Feargus O'Connor's *Northern Star*, stirring the banner of the People's Charter, demanding universal male suffrage by force of argument if possible, by physical force if necessary. And were he curious to see the home of Leeds Toryism, he could have crossed Briggate again, into Commercial Street, where at number 19 the *Leeds Intelligencer*, deriding all its rivals, could be 'found at its post[4] ready to exert itself in the maintenance of Order, the Church, and the Monarchy'.

The *Mercury* might write of 'the audacious[5] insolence of the Tory organ'; the *Intelligencer* might accuse the *Mercury* of 'unparalleled impudence'.[6] The editors of Leeds's newspapers liked to exchange insults in print, though their offices were so close that they could as easily have exchanged them by shouting from their windows. Just along the road, at number 50 Briggate, in the office of the *Leeds Times*, Smiles's predecessor Charles Hooton was about to write his last editorial. On 29 December 1838 the paper carried Hooton's final message: 'The present number[7] of the *Leeds Times* is the last that will appear under my editorship.'

Smiles, in his *Autobiography*, ascribed Hooton's departure to a loss of circulation in the face of the *Northern Star*'s arrival. But Hooton hinted at darker forces: 'amidst all those, and there are many, with whom my situation has brought me into contact, one man, one moral assassin, and one alone (even now unknown to me, as his motives for striking at me in the dark are unknown) has raised his voice or pen against me'. In his two-column farewell editorial Mr Hooton does not slip away quietly: 'no man whose heart is in the cause ... can, while life is his, regard his task as finished ... I shall be found on the watch tower.' (A sadder story may lie behind Hooton's departure. Aileen Smiles recorded, in a footnote to her book on Smiles, that in 1847 Charles Hooton died of an overdose of morphia.)

His employer was rather less carried away. In announcing the editorial change he simply stated that

> The present number of this journal, being the last for which Mr Hooton is held responsible, we beg to inform our readers and the public that from this time the *Leeds Times* will be conducted by a gentleman who will, we trust and believe, be found fully capable of sustaining that character for fearlessness and uncompromising political honesty, by which the *Times* has ever sought to be distinguished.

How different this was from the flourish with which Smiles's predecessor had been heralded twelve months earlier: 'Charles Hooton, Esq.[8] of London has already arrived in Leeds. Next week he will state in detail the principles he will advocate ... his political writings have acquired for him a very high reputation.' Now he was gone, and Samuel Smiles had arrived from Scotland without name or reputation.

On 5 January 1839, a few weeks after his twenty-sixth birthday, Smiles quietly announced his presence to the readers of the *Leeds Times*: 'The readers of this journal have already been made aware of the change in its editorial management commencing this week. The editor considers it unnecessary to introduce himself to their notice by any formal address,' and closed his one-paragraph leader by reassuring them of 'the editor's resolution to conduct himself in the diffusion of sound political knowledge, and the strenuous advocacy of every means calculated to ameliorate and improve the condition of the People.'

The People again (capitalised in print, if not in property). Every editor[9] loved the People. That same day, Smiles's rival at the *Leeds Mercury* was telling readers that 'we take *the real and permanent welfare of the* PEOPLE for our governing principle', while across the road the *Northern Star* garnished its leader with four mentions of 'the people', warning of the cynical attempts of other parties to exploit them, and ending its leader by 'relying on the good sense and prudence of the people', in whose struggle the paper found 'much room for serious congratulation'. Even the patrician *Leeds Intelligencer*, having fingered its opponents as irresponsible agitators, reassured its readers that 'the great body of the People cannot now be persuaded to lend themselves any longer to the dirty purposes of their heterogeneous and self-seeking incitors'.

Of course newspapers want to court the people. People mean circulation and circulation means advertising revenue. But there was an obvious passion in these appeals that goes beyond mere circulation-building stunts. These newspapers reflected the real world of political and public concern, even fear – both *for* the people and *of* the people.

As he went about Leeds Samuel Smiles had seen their barely human housing conditions, their near starvation and hopelessness, the soulless and unsanitary state of the half-finished developments on the edges of the old town, and the slums just yards from his office. These conditions were common in many of England's towns and cities. As the industrial revolution entered a new phase – a manufacturing revolution – the shadow of an urban peasant revolt hovered. Just a few weeks earlier a letter signed by the Officers of a new Female Radical Association had been published in the *Northern Star*, talking of following husbands, sons and brothers to the battle-field, 'and if we perish in the attempt, we shall account our death a thousand times more desirable than ... that of perishing in a Whig bastile'.[10] The reference was hardly subtle. The authorities saw Feargus O'Connor's torch-light rallies as a real incitement to revolution by the masses. A Royal Proclamation referred to 'great numbers of evil-disposed and disorderly persons ... by torch-light, in large bodies, and in tumultuous manner, with banners, flags and other ensigns ... by loud shouts and noises, and by the discharge of firearms, and by the display of weapons of offence ...'[11]

This was the mood Smiles had sensed in the crowd in New Palace Yard in London, and, when he was a student, in the reform demonstrations in Edinburgh. Then, as now, he recognised and sympathised with the need for radical reform, but regardless of any legal constraint, he recoiled instinctively from violence. Fear of violence by the people, as much as compassion for their condition, was the defining factor in politics at the time he arrived in Leeds.

The three other newspapers there had already staked out the ground: the *Northern Star* on the hard-radical left, the *Leeds Intelligencer* on the Tory right, the *Leeds Mercury* in the Whig-radical centre. Where then was there a position for the *Leeds Times*, at one time the voice of the left?[12] Now, in his first job as a professional journalist, faced by older and vastly more experienced editorial rivals, Samuel Smiles had to rescue the *Leeds Times* from the risk of journalistic irrelevance, and the people, in his view, from party and factional hijack.

It may seem strange now, when local newspapers tend to be more concerned with car-parking and litter than with affairs of state, to see their 1830s precursors so exercised about national and international politics. Those were, in a sense, golden years for the provincial press. Earlier in the century, in the words of Edward Baines of the *Leeds Mercury*, 'the English newspaper press ... was such as to be barely adequate to satisfy the intelligence and curiosity of the rustics in a small village'.[13] But by

Baines's time far more people were learning to read, and a great many more (particularly during the 1832 Reform Bill debate) were becoming involved in the political argument. Provincial newspapers raised their sights; editors turned from being cut-and-paste recyclers of London copy to generators of their own stories. Most significantly they became spokesmen for proprietors with their own political agenda. Baines again: 'It happened that at a small party of friends, the defenceless position of reformers in Leeds was the subject of the conversation ... It was suggested that a new journal might be established, which would do justice to their opinions.' Opinion-forming became a principal role of local as well as of metropolitan newspapers. Without quick, cheap access to London newspapers, without radio or television, Leeds people formed their opinions, not just about Leeds but about the world, by reading Leeds newspapers. Smiles was about to take his place as an opinion-former, but that was not all. In his *Autobiography* he gently boasts that 'I had perhaps some of the qualities necessary for an editor. I had plenty of energy, and ability for work.'

He would have needed those qualities. Each Saturday, when all four Leeds papers came out, buyers parting with their fourpence-halfpenny would have expected a great deal more than the lucubrations of the editor. Eight pages had to be filled with local news, reports on council and parish meetings, charity events and public lectures, cattle and textile market prices, marriages and deaths, as well as the traditional recycled reports from other publications covering news from London and abroad. They were also given book reviews, poems and literary tit-bits. On page six the *Leeds Times* carried a weekly 'Varieties' column, with pithy quotations, aphorisms and excruciating jokes – a sort of nineteenth-century blog. Every page had to be filled with six tightly packed columns of type, unrelieved by illustrations. Size mattered. In its New Year address to readers in 1839 Smiles's rival, the *Leeds Mercury*, announced a size increase to the same as 'the largest newspaper in the Kingdom, namely the "Double" Times.'[14] Since 1801, when Edward Baines took over the *Mercury*, its content had grown from just over 20,000 words to well over 100,000 a week. In their competition with each other, words were the editors' weapons – the more the mightier.

Smiles, abundant with words, was undaunted. He 'read no end of newspapers, periodicals and reviews ... clipped and cut, and made piles of extracts ... used the paste pot with effect, and made up my slips for the paper ... much of my reading was skimming, but I was soon able to get the gist of a thing.' He was also required to produce occasional topical paragraphs and commentaries, write a column or two of book reviews, and deal with correspondence, before sitting down to the serious work of the week, the writing of the editorials, usually at least four columns, which were at the heart of the paper's opinion-forming mission. For over six years since leaving Edinburgh he had been on the margins, apparently un-needed as a doctor, tantalised by the possibilities as a writer, a young man seething with energy and ideas, but unstretched. Now every task, from the paste pot and the speed-reading to the drafting of leading articles, gave Smiles a sense of purpose, inspired no doubt by Milton's words carried at his newspaper's masthead: 'Give me the liberty to know, to utter, and to argue freely, according to conscience, above all liberties.'

In his first number, 5 January 1839, Smiles eschewed grand posturing in his self-introduction; but a position needed to be taken. The people had been invoked. Where, vis-à-vis the other papers and the parties they represented, did the *Leeds Times* stand on the great questions of the day? Sad, dead Robert Nicoll had written to his mother two years earlier, 'You will see I am speaking out boldly, and the people here like it ... we are beating both Whigs and Tories in Yorkshire'.[15]

Smiles sharpened that theme. His main leader in that first issue was headed 'Prospects of the People' and in the exposition that followed he sought to define an independent space, untainted by any party – a plague-on-both-your-houses position. He argued for the power of the minority in Parliament as the lever of the majority in the country, a stronger voice to speak for the unenfranchised. He had in mind a small number of radically-minded MPs, who had from the start been sympathetic to the People's Charter, including Joseph Hume, a supporter of William Lovett and the Working Men's Association, his acquaintance from London, Dr Bowring, Thomas Perronet Thompson, and the Irish MP, William Sharman Crawford. This was the group who came to represent the 'rational' as opposed to the physical force wing of the Chartist argument, where for a long time Smiles's true heart lay. In parliament they, 'the people's friends, though in a minority, are nevertheless formidable'.

Smiles dismissed 'the peddling work of the united Whigs and Tories'. The uncommitted minority, conversely, 'representing as they do the great mass of the people, they possess a moral as well as an intellectual power in which the other parties are found wanting'. No improvement, no amelioration of grievances, could be expected from the ruling cliques in the House of Commons, even less from the 'Lazar House of Incurables – that rotten and most corrupt of all corporations – the House of Peers.' There was a naivety about much of the rhetoric in this piece. What was the unemployed operative, trying to keep his family fed in one filthy room in Boot-and-Shoe Lane, to make of the promise that 'a light has dawned forth from the darkness of ages which has displayed to man his true position in society as a moral and intellectual being'?

Perhaps Smiles knew that the man in Boot-and-Shoe Lane (hardly a newspaper buyer) was not his real audience, that he was talking not *to* him but *for* him, and that the *Leeds Times* was issuing not a rallying call to the distressed, but a warning to their rulers. His closing lines declare that

> it were as vain for Mrs Partington[16] to attempt stemming the Atlantic tide with her mop, as for the Aristocrats of these days to resist the progress of the people in political improvement. Those who set up their puny barriers against popular improvement run the risk of being swept away in the onward rushing tide of human progression.

Strong stuff from a twenty-six-year-old in his first job, and in its broad policy no doubt influenced by at least an awareness of his proprietor's attitudes (though Frederick Hobson never saw the paper before it was printed).[17] Nevertheless, even at this embryonic stage of his career the Smilesian signposts are becoming apparent: the one that says, don't depend on governments for your salvation; look to yourselves. 'Where lie then our prospects for improvement? In the People themselves we answer; in the intelligence which pervades the masses.' And the one that says, let's have a working class-middle class coalition. 'In this [middle-class] body is to be found much of the intelligence and real *stamina* of the country – no movement will effect its object which does not carry the influence and weight of this class along with it.' He was not talking about the prosperous, prejudiced, bourgeois middle class of later stereotype. He had an almost romantic view of a class defined not in economic but in intellectual and moral terms. 'They too are as yet unrepresented – the honestest and best part of them, who will neither stoop to nor be influenced by, corrupt means, have as little exercise of the franchise as the Chartists of the working class themselves.' Even the enfranchised middle classes should be sure to think for themselves: 'Let them be wary ... in whom they repose their confidence, else this may only terminate in a continuance of that deception in which leaders have generally practised on them.' People should beware of leaders. 'To themselves alone must they look for means of progression.'[18]

The Smiles doctrine of individual responsibility may have been no more than a flickering presence in this early journalism, but it remained present. It became the consistent impulse in what was to be, at some levels, his remarkably inconsistent career.

In the meantime he needed, literally, to stand up and be counted.

6

The Fabricators of
Our Greatness

THREE DAYS after his editorial debut Samuel Smiles attended an Anti-Corn Law meeting in the Court House adjacent to Leeds Cloth Yard. The meeting had been organised by Edward Baines, Whig MP and owner of the *Leeds Mercury*, to demonstrate how strongly the people of Leeds supported Corn Law abolition as their top political priority. Baines, his son Edward Baines junior, Editor of the *Mercury*, and their cohort, probably expected an easy ride, straightforward endorsement, and an opportunity to put pressure on their party leaders at Westminster. From Leeds's working-class population a small group would turn up, according to the Baines script, behave well and agree with their MP (even though most of them probably hadn't had the opportunity to vote for him). Leeds was not known as an extreme radical town. Its working people could be depended upon to recognise where their self-interest lay.

That, at least, was the theory. The only spoiler might be the appearance of Feargus O'Connor and the militants. But O'Connor was booked to dine in Bradford the evening before, and at the Halfway House Inn in the village of Queenshead, beyond Bradford, on the evening of the meeting. So 'the mob' would be unlikely to turn up. The dignity of the Court House would be maintained and the Baines motion would be carried with acclaim.

But O'Connor did turn up, and a great many more besides (including the as yet unknown young editor of the *Leeds Times*). The meeting was scheduled to start at 12 noon. By then the Court House was packed and several thousand filled the Cloth Hall Yard outside. As the unfortunate Mayor, conscripted by Baines to chair proceedings, stumbled through his opening remarks, the noise increased. Baines junior suggested that the meeting be adjourned and reconvened in the Yard, where a crowd of at least three thousand had already gathered. By twelve-thirty the programme had restarted in the open, with the platform party trying to regain control and Alderman Goodman proposing a petition to Parliament calling, on behalf of the people of Leeds, for the repeal of the Corn Laws.

At once O'Connor was on his feet (loud cheers, 'Now for the bloody Whigs! Well done Feargus!')[1] to move an amendment effectively blocking the proposal in favour of one demanding universal suffrage as a pre-condition for any discussion of the Corn Laws.[2]

But before a vote could be taken, a stranger rose to speak, a young man of no more than medium height, with a pale, northern complexion and sandy hair above a high, clear brow. 'Who is he?' 'What is he?' they asked in the crowd. 'It's the new editor of the *Leeds Times*!'[3] Smiles, nervous no doubt, started clumsily, then gathered momentum. Open trade was important for everyone, he declared, especially for wage earners. 'Abolish the Corn Laws, and let us shake hands with the whole world ... I assert that the condition of the working man is thereby improved.' ('Aye if it gives us good wages, thou're reet lad!')[4] He went on to declare support for the O'Connor line on the extension of the franchise: 'But this is not the time to urge the question ... I move an amendment to the effect that Mr O'Connor's amendment shall lie over till we decide the other business of the day.'

The Mayor called for a vote on the O'Connor amendment, answered by a strong show of hands. Then, in spite of roars of apparent triumph from the O'Connor wing, the chairman asked for a show of those in favour of the Baines petition. When even more hands were raised (many, allegedly, misled about what they were voting for), his worship declared the Corn Law repeal proposal carried, to the dismay and rage of O'Connor and his supporters.

Who won? Which proposal truly had a majority? The answer depends on which of the next week's papers you believe. And how did these events affect Smiles's position in the town, and the development of his ideas? Again the answer depends on which of the papers you read.

The *Northern Star* declared the day a triumph for O'Connor and a humiliation for Baines and the Whigs. It was the

> Last struggle of the faction, the first appearance of the Mayor, and the last appearance of the Bainses. Complete annihilation of the Whigs as a party, and irretrievable defeat as a faction ... Mr O'Connor did attend, and did actually carry an amendment to the first resolution in a meeting of from 3000 to 4000, by a majority of nine to one.

(Misrepresentation, in this version, had been caused by the crowd thinking that on the last vote they were reaffirming their support for the amendment.)

Of the contribution of 'Mr Smiles, editor of the *Leeds Times*', The *Star*'s report offered a somewhat patronising account, suggesting ironic cheers ... groans ... laughter throughout his speech. His amendment to the amendment is barely taken seriously, finally greeted, in the *Star*'s account, with 'roars of laughter mingled with groans'. But at least they got his name and position right.

Baines's *Leeds Mercury* on the same day reported 'the perfectly unprincipled conduct of Mr Feargus O'Connor ... which received its appropriate reward in entire defeat, and in the loudly expressed disgust and contempt of the audience.' O'Connor's supporters (the 'Torch men') were 'a mere handful of the lowest and dirtiest fellows in the meeting, and well drilled to make a noise.' The paper ignored Smiles's intervention.

The Tory *Leeds Intelligencer* tried to hold itself above the fray: 'it is the province of parliament to decide between them, and to hold the balance as fairly as may be. We feel confirmed that Ministers are too wily to stake their office upon this question.' Referring to Smile's part, they called him 'Mr Miles', without designation.

As for Smiles himself, the conclusion was clear. On 19 January the *Leeds Times* declared that

> The working men of Leeds have achieved a great moral triumph ... they have eschewed the snare laid for them, and turned a deaf ear to the clap-traps of Mr O'Connor ... when the Mayor put the motion and Mr O'Connor's amendment to the audience, at the very lowest computation, two-to-one held up in favour of the former.

If Smiles felt bruised by his first engagement with local politics he certainly didn't show it. In the weeks and months ahead the *Leeds Times* stuck to its consistent line in favour of Corn Law abolition, and through his leaders Smiles continued to suggest that in the innate 'intelligence' of the working man lay the real hope for his salvation, and the salvation of society. O'Connor had lost the Cloth Hall debate because his argument found 'little favour with the more intelligent workmen of Leeds' – more intelligent than their deluded brothers in Manchester – 'he [O'Connor] had an amount of intelligence in its working classes to contend with, which is an effectual safeguard against imposture and delusion'.[5]

The poverty and suffering of the working classes drove almost everything that Smiles wrote in those years. His paper, in alliance with others, continued to campaign for Corn Law repeal. 'The work goes on gloriously. Our columns would be insufficient to record in detail the meetings which have been held during the last week ... anything short of total abolition is short of justice and what the people have a right to expect and demand.'[6] But he was shocked at least as much by the cruelty of the Poor Law Amendment Act. This 1834 legislation cut parish payments to destitute families, forcing them to choose between starvation and life in the workhouse, where they lived in conditions of near-slavery. Smiles linked the Corn Laws and Poor Laws as the twin wheels that ground the poor, the one driving them into the teeth devised by the other. He accused landowners, concerned only to keep up the price of both grain and rent, of squeezing the working man from both sides. They were insensitive to his plight and by their 'continued aspiration of a high price of food absorbing his wages ... make him increase his hours of toil till human endurance can go no farther; and broken in spirit, in health, and in frame, he is at length killed off, or forced into a workhouse'.[7] At a time of high unemployment, the Poor Law often treated its victims as malingerers, subjecting them in the workhouse to harsh and meaningless labour. Henry Wallis's 'The Stonebreaker', exhibited at the Royal Academy in 1858, offered the public a horrific example.

The *Leeds Times* had a campaigning role, and as its editor Samuel Smiles had an obligation to promote specific changes in legislation. But real anger and personal conviction blaze through much of his early editorial writing – a sense of a young man raging against privilege –

unearned privilege indulging itself by starving the poor. He saw the state of society as the rotten fruit of a violent past, characterising the landowning aristocrats who dominated parliament as the heirs of robber barons:

> Their origin was in those barbarous times when might took the place of right, and strength of power to seize and to preserve plunder were the sole title to nobility and right. Like all men in situations of uncontrolled power, they made laws for their self-aggrandisement without respect for the happiness of the people.[8]

During the four years when he was editor of the *Leeds Times* Samuel Smiles wrote upwards of half a million words of editorial comment, opinion and exposition, and the paper reported extensively on his contributions to local meetings and institutions. Collectively these newspaper years suggest, at one level, a working out of political position, and at another a growing disillusion with 'movements' and a preoccupation with personal conviction. The boy on the hilltop at Haddington is still there, but so is the ambitious young editor trying to make a place for himself in the world, and thrilled to find a world so congenial to his ideological instincts.

The *Leeds Times* was essentially a middle-class Radical publication (remember its endorsement from *Tait's Magazine*), broadly supportive of a group of manufacturing and commercial interests in Leeds and the West Riding. These men of business were the new class, representing the force behind the 1832 Reform Bill (but now impatient with its limitations). Their vision was of a new order based on technological progress bringing economic good for everyone, and an end at last to the consignment of the masses to misery and destitution. They not only believed in Benthamite utilitarianism – the greatest happiness of the greatest number – but were convinced that they knew how to achieve it. They were self-made men, happy to be role models for the less fortunate, believing in the potential in everyone for self-improvement. They were religious dissenters and non-conformists, convinced not only of the *right* of every man to self-improvement, but of his moral obligation to strive for it – so long as he didn't threaten economic stability in the process.

These were the new revolutionaries, the respectable revolutionaries, well dressed, well behaved, and well heeled. Every week the *Leeds Times* carried reports of the meetings organised by such men – to protest against the Corn Laws or the Poor Laws, to campaign for the extension of the franchise or the education of the poor, or simply to spread the message of 'progress'. The respectability of the gathering and the refinement of the proceedings were always apparent. 'A well-dressed, respectable and intelligent audience' were attracted to a meeting of New Wortley and Holbeck Youth Guardian Society.[9] A debate at Leeds Literary Institution – '*Is rational amusement the source of intellectual improvement?*' – 'was quite filled by a most respectable company'.[10]

The same names crop up time after time – Plint, Goodman, Stansfield, Middleton, Baines ... the almost great and the determinedly good. When they held a dinner to celebrate the return of John Bower, their Radical candidate in the municipal election of 1839, the walls may have been decorated with radical slogans – 'No Bread tax!' 'Vote by Ballot', 'Civil and Religious Liberty'.[11] When the mandatory toast, 'the Queen' was proposed, it may have been joined with 'the People, the true source of all legitimate power'. And when Mr Joseph Middleton responded by asking 'Who are the people?' he may have answered his own question: 'Not the well-fed and pampered aristocracy. No, the honest labourers, the manufacturers and merchants, the masses who work, and toil and produce all the wealth. What would become of the monarchy, of the aristocracy, but for the people?' But radical banners and radical words apart, the radical dinner bore all the marks of an impeccably bourgeois affair,

> in a large room provided by Laird, Kitson & Co, engineers and iron founders ... the company were admitted soon after six o'clock, a brilliant jet gas-light, describing the letters 'VR', pointing out the festive room to guests as they approached. Upwards of 370 sat down to a very excellent dinner provided by Mr and Mrs Thackrah, of the Swan-with-Two-Necks Inn at Highgate, Hunslet.

And Mr Middleton's careful embedding of manufacturers and merchants among the honest labourers is a strong clue to the diners' revolutionary strategy.

It was unequivocal and undisguised – an alliance of middle and working classes to effect radical change.

The taxes on the common necessities of life are as injurious to the interests of the manufacturers, merchants and others, as they are unjust and inequitable to the labouring classes ... the remedy? The people must be united, come forward, hand and heart for the good cause, we must be united for the great struggle for religious liberty. And how? By universal suffrage and the ballot. [Loud cheers.]

Samuel Smiles was among the guests, and responded to the Middleton toast. He spoke for the press, he said, which was 'a creature of the people, had its origin in the people, belonged to the people ... it was the great object of the press to make all men think, examine and decide for themselves as rational beings'. He cast the press in the role of educators, for 'so long as the education of the people is unaccomplished, so long had the press an important duty to perform.' His toast was 'to progress – the equality of man, equal at birth, equal at death – he might be made unequal by the laws of man but was equal in the sight of God.'

That dinner was on 5 December 1839, by which time Smiles had been in Leeds for a full year. At the start of the year, at the big Anti-Corn Law meeting in the Cloth Hall Yard, people had asked Who is he? What is he? Since then he had beaten his editorial drum for all the liberal-radical causes – repeal of the Corn Laws and of the 1834 Poor Law, free education (free of charge and free from Church control), freedom of dissenters from Church tax, protest at 'aristocratic' grip on political power, extension of suffrage, and even scepticism about the role of the monarchy. He had been a welcome guest at many dinners, spoken at dozens of meetings and rallies, given lectures, made donations to good causes, and become an accepted member of the Leeds radical set. No one now misspelt his name.

These accounts of dining and speechifying could give an impression of a certain amount of mutual back-slapping and self-congratulation in a liberal enclave. But the rising sound was one more of fear than of complacency. Britain, in the diners' view, was at a tipping point, between a descent into the sort of poverty, ignorance and ruined lives that lay all around them in the slums of Leeds, or a leap forward into prosperity for everyone, based on the wonders of machinery and technology. Their fear was that a landed political class with a vested interest in the past would block their road to a wealth-creating future. England's green and pleasant land fed the greed and extravagance of the few, who owned most of it. But her mills could feed and clothe and house the many. While land-owners and bishops controlled parliament, the people who depended on the mills had no voice, their dissenting religion no rights. Which then was more dark and satanic? This was the argument of the new collar-and-tie revolutionaries, and they were glad to have the energetic pen and voice of Samuel Smiles to help them to express it.

He was happy to fulminate, at length, in print, and on his feet, the Corn Laws being the focus, the 'starvation laws' as he came to call them. Every week the *Leeds Times* carried an editorial on the subject, or a report on a protest meeting, or both. The landowning aristocracy were always the villains, but their running dogs in the Church did not escape:

> The Established Church, as might be supposed, has stept forth to the aid of the Corn Law robbers, called on no doubt by the community of interest between the Church and the landlords ... this is not a 'labour of love', but a labour for landlords, on the part of the reverend gentleman, in order that his own corn, and wine, and oil may abound ...

Smiles clearly enjoyed these opportunities to develop his polemical muscles and to release some of his frustration. For someone whose core belief was in man's ability and God-given duty to improve his lot, the sight of unused machinery, unfinished buildings and, worst of all, unused, starving people, was a moral and intellectual affront – doubly so because he believed it to be unnecessary. What he could see was a modern world bursting with technical ingenuity and the energy of ordinary men, frustrated by a political establishment interested only in its own preservation.

The possibilities were there for all to see in the Leeds Mechanics Exhibition staged at the Music Hall in the summer of 1839. This was an exercise in debrutalising mechanical progress and promoting its soul. On 29 of July a special early morning train brought three hundred members of the York Institute for Popular Science and Literature over to Leeds for a vision of the future (a hundred more followed in the scheduled train arriving at eleven o'clock). After a five-hour tour of the exhibits they joined local worthies (ladies and gentlemen) at a packed reception in the adjoining Commercial Building where 'A plain and simple, but substantial repast, was provided for the occasion, there being besides tea, a plentiful supply of ham sandwiches.'[12] There was also provided a plentiful supply of speeches. The Mayor welcomed the guests, referring to the artistic exhibits on display, 'the results of the labours of Spagnaletto, Canaletti [sic], Rubens and others', but the Mayor's pride was in Leeds's contribution to mechanical invention, the gleaming modern spinning machines and carding machines on display, the achievements of 'Leeds's Marshall' in the application of engineering to his productions, and the Mayor's own contribution in transforming apparently worthless silk into something beautiful and valuable by the use of machinery. He then called on Mr Samuel Smiles to address the company. Smiles's message that day was of the human as well as the economic value of mechanical development. The exhibition

> afforded all classes the opportunity of seeing what study, science and art
> had accomplished for our country, and must promote to no small degree
> intellectual improvement and refinement ... Artisans had souls to relish
> works of art, equally with others, and were equally endowed with mind
> and faculties to look and admire and enjoy them ... Did not Opie and
> Bonnington and Romney rise up from the ranks of mechanics? Did not
> Bloomfield and Chatterton and Burns come from the huts of lowly men?

The political agenda was of course there. Though there was no reference, on this strictly non-political occasion, to the crimes of the aristocracy, neither was there any doubt about where the country must look for its salvation. The engineers and inventors, Smiles said, had been 'the true fabricators of our national greatness ... Who had been chiefly instrumental in bringing all this about? Had it not been working men and mechanics – James Watt, Crompton, Smeaton, Arkwright – the true creators of our national wealth.'

Smiles was showing already where his enthusiasms lay, who were his heroes, and how his future writing might be shaped. He was excited by the practical possibilities of science and engineering to improve man's happiness and well-being, but his more profound interest was in the men behind the machines. In studying their lives much later he became a biographical alchemist, demonstrating how gold could be spun from the base metal of ordinary men. His fame as a writer would be built on his difference from the main stream of biographers – men educated in the classical tradition, writing about statesmen, soldiers and bishops – about exceptional men. Smiles wrote about ordinary men who achieved extraordinary things, and offered them as examples not to be admired, but to be imitated. All his biographies were essentially self-help books, and all his self-help books were biographies.

But all that was decades ahead. For now he had a political mission to fulfil, and political dragons to slay. At the start of the year the message of the *Leeds Times* and its new editor had seemed relatively clear – abolish the Corn Laws, and then give every man the vote. The enemy had also seemed obvious: on one flank the O'Connorite Chartists opposing the Anti-Corn Law movement in favour of their Charter demands, and on the other the Tories and conservative Whigs opposing *any* change. For six months Smiles and the *Leeds Times* had campaigned on this platform, but by mid-summer little progress had been made. The Anti-Corn Law voice was in danger of being drowned out by more strident calls, and extremist elements on both sides were winning new recruits.

Unemployment and high food prices added every week to the great population of the starving and the hopeless. If they had ever had any faith in governments and constitutions, that faith seemed to have been killed. The ground was fertile for extremism on both sides. Extreme Chartists had moved further and further towards organised violence; even moderates saw little hope in anything short of physical protest – a bloodless revolution they hoped, but a revolution nevertheless. Among the governing classes the priority of property outweighed all other considerations. Tories demanded ruthless military response. Even moderates, 'middle-class' Whigs, supported law-and-order before reform. For everyone the examples of France and America were recent and graphic, and as the word 'revolution' spread its dangerous fire, the voices of conciliation became almost inaudible.

In that same week in 1839, while Samuel Smiles extolled for his York guests 'the fabicators of our national greatness ... the working men and mechanics, the true creators of our national wealth', the Chartists had called for a 'Sacred Month' of strikes, ritual self-sacrifice, and mass demonstrations, starting on 12 August. Concurrently the government had called for the recruitment of thousands of extra soldiers and police to guard property and put down any threat of violence among the people. In this they had won the support of middle-class members who might have voted against them on other issues. Smiles railed against both and seemed to be speaking from an increasingly isolated position.

In his leader of 3 August he was attacking the Chartists for intolerance:

> The Chartist coercion preached by the O'Briens and O'Connors of this day, is but a revival of old Tory coercion in its most odious form ... they declare their determination to bring about a total revolution of the present state of things. Now we shall not deny that such a thing may be greatly needed, nor shall we argue less intrepidly for the total removal of every political institution which is bad ... There is, however, as much difference between repairing and destroying as there is between the moral-force Chartists ... and the physical force pikemen and torchists of O'Connor and O'Brien. That reasonable men follow such leaders is unaccountable to us.

A week later the government was again in his sights, but with a difference. Now Smiles turned on his own middle-class allies. The Prime Minister, Lord Melbourne, proposed to raise more troops and constabulary,

> with the approbation of the middle classes. This is all: the sum of the efforts used to pacify the labouring classes, and remedy their grievances, is implied in the single word – COERCION ... Do the middle classes consider what may be the consequences of their apathy ... do they seriously consider for what purpose they are calling out for an addition to an army of fighting men? It is *to put down the working classes* because they complain of their sufferings – because they can endure their sufferings no longer ... *It is against a class which forms a great proportion of our population* ... it becomes the middle classes seriously to consider whether, in sanctioning the increase of the armies of the aristocracy, and in turning away the ear from their suffering fellow-creatures, they are not strengthening the hands of tyranny...[13]

Smiles had sat side-by-side every week or so, at dinner tables and public meetings, with Edward Baines junior, editor of the *Leeds Mercury* and declared fellow-advocate of middle-class working-class solidarity. They were business competitors but seemingly of a mind ideologically. Not any longer. In the *Mercury* Baines applauded

the response made by the middle classes of all political parties to their call
in behalf of law and order ... the comparative advantage of employing
moral and physical means for effecting political objects is impressed on
many a broken head at Leigh and Bolton, by the staves of the policemen.[14]

This support for the staves of the policemen signified a sharper difference between the two men, which soon grew. Baines was almost forty
years old. His father, Edward Baines senior, was a Whig MP. Edward
Baines junior would himself later enter Parliament as a Whig. He was
essentially a member of an establishment, even though it may have been
a liberal establishment. Samuel Smiles, in his mid-twenties at the time,
was suspicious of all establishments – state, church or monarchy. He
looked beyond them for his inspiration, to Bentham, to James Mill
(Smiles's persistent argument for the people's right to 'happiness' was an
overtly utilitarian argument), but perhaps most of all to Milton, quoted
with approval in one of his earliest pieces: 'Who knows not that the truth
is strong next to the almighty; she needs no policies, nor stratagems, nor
licensings to make her victorious', and whose words led the *Leeds Times*
into battle every week.

In London that year, 1839, the press was exercising itself with rumours
of the young Queen Victoria's engagement to Prince Albert. Smiles let
his readers know his opinion: 'Should Prince Albert form the "Happy
Object" of the Queen's choice, the only difference to the people of the
country will be that they will have another German family pensioned on
them.'[15] His own interest was in an extraordinary crossfire which broke
out between Baines's *Mercury* and the *Leeds Times,* suggesting a much
more radical shift in Smiles's position. The trigger was an open letter in
the *Mercury* on 3 August addressed by the Editor to 'Jas Ibbetson, bookseller of Bradford', a real or invented Chartist. Ibbetson was lectured
sternly on the follies of the proposed Sacred Month and warned against
any resort to physical force for political ends: 'Think again, James Ibbetson – think often – before you enter yourself, or advise others to enter,
on the desperate hazards of an appeal to the sword.' A week later the
Leeds Times published a three-column response in the form of an open
letter addressed to the Editor of the *Leeds Mercury*, purportedly from
'James Ibbetson', rebutting the Baines arguments point by point. Next

week the *Mercury* replied, first making clear that it was not for a moment fooled by the disguise.

> The writer who figures in the *Leeds Times* under the name 'James Ibbetson' is so exceedingly unlike the James Ibbetson whom we have sometimes met in Bradford that we should never have suspected he was the same person ... The writer in the *Times* is altogether another man from the Bradford bookseller.[16]

The exchange went on into September, wordy, sometimes angry, often facetious in the manner of a college debate. But it revealed clearly the younger man's striving for a much more independent stance. Distancing himself from the party manoeuvres of the other so-called Leeds radicals, 'Ibbetson' accused the Baines camp of ganging up against the working classes, of supporting suppression by military force, of robbing them of representation, of turning their backs on the peoples' real plight.

> You justify it [physical force coercion of the people]. All the Whigs and Tories justify it ... You assert that the English government springs from the people ... instead of this it is sprung from William, the Norman robber – it depends on the Monarch, the Lords, the Aristocracy ... The labouring classes, embodying so large a proportion of the intelligence, skill and industry of the nation, are wholly unrepresented. For what purpose are you, Editors of the *Leeds Mercury* and others of the Whig brethren now crying out for the protection of the Suffrage? Is it not because the aristocracy have bought up ... those least informed 'middle class' persons whom you foolishly mistake for 'the people of England?

The *Leeds Mercury* had taken the line that, all-in-all, the people had little cause for complaint: 'There is no country where labourers, manufacturing and agricultural, are so well fed, so well clothed, and so well housed as in England.' Smiles (and presumably Edward Baines) could see, from their office windows, the real condition of England's labourers. This brought out 'Ibbetson's' final sally:

> Do you know, Mr Baines, that one of your own Whig ministers asserted and proved that eleven and three quarters per cent of the population of Manchester, and fifteen per cent of that of Liverpool, lived in CELLARS? Think on these things then, Editors of the *Leeds Mercury*. We do not believe

that you are so utterly lost to all sense of truth or justice that they may not yet be without some good effect on you.[17]

In expressing this arithmetic of misery, the piece gave a sharp foretaste of Friederich Engels's devastating analysis a few years later in *The Condition of the Working Class in England.*

In spite of the depth of the people's grievances, and the eloquence of their champions, the Chartists' Sacred Month produced only patchy outbreaks of civil disobedience. The schism between the physical-force and moral-force Chartists had sucked much of the energy from it. The government had used it as a pretext for arresting even anti-O'Connor leaders, like the Working Men's Association's William Lovett, on the grounds of sedition. Lovett was jailed, his health broken, and his career ruined. Smiles, aware of his plight, offered Lovett a job on the *Leeds Times,* but Lovett did not want to move to Yorkshire.[18] In Leeds, as Smiles recorded in his *Autobiography*, 'the working people suffered much ... though they complained [they] did not riot.' By autumn the local media had reverted to less divisive issues. Smiles again was headlining the Corn Laws as the current root of social evil: CORN LAWS PREVENT THE DISTRIBUTION OF WEALTH; AND BY INCREASING COMPETITION FOR FOOD, LOWER THE REAL WAGES OF THE WORKING CLASSES. A week later the *Mercury* was reporting on the failure of a free trade mission to Germany, and blaming it on the Corn Laws. On this question, at least, Smiles and Baines could agree.

Since his arrival in Leeds, Smiles had been on something of a treadmill of editorial duty and loyal commitment to a political agenda – a dull grind for a young, single man in a vibrant city. Smiles's workload on the paper and his involvement in meetings would have left precious little time for self-indulgence. The 'depravity and wickedness' his parents had warned him against when he first left Haddington seem, in Leeds, to have been limited to bread-throwing at some of the all-male dinners that passed for social life. A glimpse appears in an account of a dinner in January 'in honour of four Whigs' (with E Baines MP and Charles Hooton present; 'S. Smiles Esq' was also of the company). Baines's toast to the Queen seems to have been met by jeers from some 'notorious Jacobites and Republicans'. Others started singing the national anthem. One jumped on the table: 'Shout lads! Shout!' – during which guests went on 'guzzling, jesting, or cramming themselves with raisins, ginger-bread and other suchlike trash.' And it got worse: 'Previous to the disper-sion we observed several gentlemen taking a nap with their heads on the tables.' The *Leeds Times* representative obviously managed to avoid a hangover. Next day he was able to tut-tut: 'These are the pretty Whigs who talk about the morality of the working classes!'[19]

In these years the private life of Samuel Smiles has left no trail. He may have continued his violin playing, as in his Haddington days, and his painting. He certainly spoke at the Leeds Literary Institution – on topics like THE STATION AND INFLUENCE ON SOCIETY OF WOMEN, the subject of the June soirée. But if he had a hobby, and a hobby horse, it was the 'happiness' question, with education (in the Smiles sense) a major part of the answer. He explained his meaning for readers of the *Leeds Times*. His approach was what might now be called 'holistic':

> By the term Education we denote ... the development of man's whole constitution, physical, moral, and intellectual – by which his own happi-ness and enjoyment are to be promoted, and he is to be the best enabled to raise himself on earth, to the very summit of his nature ... So how is the community best to be educated? First by ameliorating the Physical condition of the people ... a provision for the daily and abundant food of the labouring population – until then it is as insulting and cruel as it is unwise to denounce the working population for ignorance ... It is physical improvement alone which can bring them within the sphere of morality and intelligence.

This appeared in the *Leeds Times* on 5 October 1839. The echo is faint but clear: the unifying of the physical, the moral and the intellectual as enunciated in his book published almost two years earlier.

Smiles must have had parcels of unsold copies of the book sent to his lodgings in Leeds, for an advertisement in the *Leeds Times* four weeks later announced, 'Lately published, 3s-6d, *PHYSICAL EDUCATION, OR THE NURTURE AND MANAGEMENT OF CHILDREN*, by Samuel Smiles MD. On sale at F. Hobson, the Times Office and other booksellers.' The people of Leeds now knew, if they had not known before, that their local news-paper editor was a published author, a Doctor of Medicine, and a man of very modern ideas. They knew, if they had not known before, his views on the urban poor, specifically their own urban poor. 'In Leeds,' the book reminded them, 'a manufacturing town, out of every 10,000 children born in it, 5286 on average die under five years of age.' And they knew that in his heart education was his abiding passion.

The paper's year-end review on 28 December asked: 'First and foremost – what has "Thirty-nine" done for the Education of the People? What number has it admitted to the enjoyment of enlightened reason, cultivated tastes, ennobling desires and humanising spirits?' Not much and not many, was Smiles's answer, with the Church as the main villain. But

> the present times are not without solid grounds for hope. Sound opinions are rapidly spreading. Knowledge is increasing the number of thinking minds almost without limit. The very discomfort of the present time is a matter of hope, for it indicates an aiming after better things – the realisation of a more healthy frame for society. Farewell then, to the old and worn-out year: and now for EIGHTEEN HUNDRED AND FORTY!

7

Sidestep

THE YEAR 1840 was not one to be welcomed. Any chirpiness Samuel Smiles may have displayed at the prospect of a brave new dawn was unjustified, and probably he knew it. Britain had entered a bleak decade, the infamous 'hungry forties'. Falling trade had combined with low wages and high food prices, artificially elevated by the Corn Laws, to create a perfect storm of deprivation for millions. Politicians raged at each other about the causes and solutions. The majority in Parliament, both Whig and Tory, argued that the ill fortune of weather and natural dips in the trade cycle were to blame. Things will inevitably get better they claimed. Their message in the meantime was: work harder when work is offered, pray harder all the time, and above all, don't even think of challenging the law. Conversely, the more radical Whig minority – the anti-Corn Law lobby – and their manufacturing supporters, blamed all on an incompetent and bloody-minded landowning aristocracy, on whose behalf legislators ignored both the cries of the poor and the solutions proposed by the new middle class in manufacturing towns like Leeds.

Ever since his arrival in Leeds Smiles had seen the suffering at first hand. He knew the radical heritage of the *Leeds Times*. His predecessor as editor, Robert Nicoll had been an unequivocal radical who had backed the formation in 1837 of the Leeds Working Men's Association, serving on committees with such men as William Ryder, who became a hardline Chartist, and George White who was later employed by Feargus O'Connor as a reporter on the *Northern Star*. Smiles's sympathies were

entirely with the People, the exploited working-class People, and
intuitively with the objectives of the People's Charter: male suffrage,
equal electoral districts, voting by secret ballot, annual parliaments,
abolition of property qualifications for MPs, and payment for MPs.
But hard radicalism was not the mood in Leeds. Its working people,
with their artisan background and (by nineteenth-century standards)
enlightened employers like the Marshalls and James Kitson, had little of
the militancy of their fellow workers in Bradford and Manchester.
Samuel Smiles, his radical idealism balanced by his recoil from violence,
found Leeds, and the *Leeds Times*, a natural home for his ideas.

Nevertheless over the next few years he had cause at times to become
both confused and bemused by the groups, institutes, and associations
swirling about him, pleading for relief, proposing solutions, and often
arguing with each other. Indeed, a few weeks earlier than his 'Welcome
to 1840' editorial, his paper carried an almost ironical account of a
mass meeting of unemployed workmen on Hunslet Moor. They had
assembled not to threaten, or even to demand, but merely to request
respectfully 'the wealthy and influential gentlemen of Leeds ... [for] a
meeting to ascertain the cause of the present alarming and unparalleled
distress and to propose some measure for removing and alleviating the
same'.[1] With this modest proposal the two thousand men then formed
themselves six abreast and, headed by 'a band of music', marched from
the moor, through the town streets, and up Briggate to meet the Mayor
and his colleagues. There a deputation put their request. His Worship's
response, as recorded, was a masterpiece of vacillation – '... steps to see
what might be required ... today or tomorrow expect to have further
communication with some leading gentlemen in the town ... some
measures will no doubt be agreed upon...' and so on. Having accepted
this waffle the men's deputation made just one more request: that they
might sing a hymn they had sung on the moor, composed by one of them
for the occasion. The following astonishing exchange then took place:

> Mayor – 'You have asked my permission to sing a hymn. I would rather
>   you did not.'
> Spokesman for the men – 'It is fully expected by the people, and it will be
>   merely sung, and then the people will retire peaceably to their homes.'
> Mayor – 'I would rather you did not.'

The crowd made no further protest. 'The mass of the persons in front of the building then separated, and in a few minutes the street was again clear.'

However high Smiles might have raised an eyebrow at this forelock-touching behaviour, he felt a good deal more comfortable with it than with the torch-light rallies of the physical force Chartists. Men he had sat beside in committees and dinners, whose words he had seconded at public meetings – J G Marshall, Edward Baines, and prosperous textile merchant Hamer Stansfield – were beside the Mayor that afternoon when the hymn-singers from Hunslet Moor were so shamefully sent packing. Yet Marshall, and particularly Stansfield, were the men whose causes Smiles supported in the years that followed. In looking for a place between the despot and the mob he found this the most reassuring environment.

But the Smiles sidestep was more than mere ideological compromise. Something apolitical and more subtle lay behind it – an Emersonian view of the moral autonomy of the individual and a belief in the possibility of happiness for everyone. In the self-determined independence of the creators of technical progress, he saw the best exemplars. A man with a big factory full of gleaming machinery was a man to be supported. Smiles despised equally the land-owning aristocrat who would inhibit such a man's trade and starve his operatives, and the rabble-rouser who would threaten the factory owner and alienate his workers. So Smiles's journey through affiliation and personal theorising – in search of not even the greatest happiness, but just for some hope of happiness for the greatest number – moved on through a landscape of growing misery and fading hope.

For the *Leeds Times*, in his first leader of the new year, Smiles tried to reassert a third-way policy 'between the timid inclining to Conservative Whiggism and Toryism on the one hand, and the over-ardent, who fly to revolutionary changes, on the other'. The paper's increase in circulation was, he said, due 'chiefly to the good opinion of our friends, as well as to the present diffusion of a taste for dispassionate, and at the same time bold and searching enquiry'.[2]

But in the same issue Samuel Smiles's real preoccupation showed through, in an article displaying an extraordinary world economic view, and his solution to society's problems. Forget about the Corn Laws or the Tories. The problem, and its solution, were to be found in the hands of a true Smiles hero, James Watt. In a pre-Watt era, he argued, wages were high compared to food prices and 'England exported but a small portion of her labour ... the labouring classes were generally contented, well fed and well clothed.' Then Watt's discovery of 'the infinitely productive powers of steam ... produced an influx of wealth upon England unparalleled in the history of the world'. It had been calculated, Smiles claimed, that James Watt's discovery had enabled Britain 'to exercise a productive power equal to that of 400,000,000 men – that the steam power which keeps in operation the beautiful manufactures of the British manufacturer is more than equal to the power that lies in the naked hands of half the population of the world'.

So Britannia ruled the economic waves? Not exactly. Apart from ransacking the earth for raw materials 'to feed the devouring maw of the British factory', world markets had been glutted, demand exhausted, and successive panics, crises and bankruptcies provoked. 'But this is not all', for the dastardly foreigners had imitated us

> to fabricate their own apparel ... the time is rapidly approaching when Europe and America, by employing a large part of their population in all of the branches of industry, will deluge the world with their manufactured productions ... once England prided herself as the workshop of the world ... but at length production got ahead of consumption ... wages fell, children's labour was employed, gluts and depressions of trade recurred, abandoning to destitution and want tens of thousands of our industrious people ... in less than twenty years we shall be producing more than six times the quantity of manufactured articles that the civilised world can consume.

Smiles was no Luddite. The fault was not with Watt's discovery. Mankind had simply not applied it to its proper purposes. Remarkably, for the man later represented as the high priest of the Victorian work ethic, these proper purposes were 'to abridge the hours of toil, and afford all that opportunity for mental and moral cultivation which the happiness and security and welfare of society absolutely requires'.[3] Smiles admits that the ultimate effect of mechanical inventions is 'impossible to divine', but assuredly 'the true application of them is to increase the sum of total human happiness, and thus extend the blessings of knowledge and civilisation among the members of the entire human family'. This perception of virtuous technology became an essential strand in everything Smiles later wrote.

One has to imagine Smiles at this time, still in his twenties, still a relative newcomer to the town and its youngest and most junior newspaper editor, still trying to work out his own ideas and priorities. He found contradictions everywhere. Middle-class people who had campaigned for the 1832 Reform Bill and who claimed to be on the side of the working classes, were now supporting the use of military force to subdue the appeals for relief from their plight of those same workers. He could see that 'The rich have become richer, the great more powerful, and new aristocracies have risen up among the middle classes ... while grasping selfishness has amassed property in heaps, it has proportionately impoverished and depressed millions.'[4] Yet Smiles found himself working, mixing and worshipping (at Mill Hill Unitarian Chapel, the 'enlightenment church') with the cream of Leeds's middle class, many of whom, like James Garth Marshall, living in Headingley House, the most splendid in the richest part of the district, had certainly 'amassed property in heaps'.

Smiles enjoyed being editor of the *Leeds Times*, and acknowledged that because of his job he had a place in local society. On the one hand he was pulled towards this life, and a public role in support of great causes like the abolition of the Corn Laws. On the other he was drawn to inward reflection and an urge to write, not as a public spokesman for the 'wealthy and influential gentlemen' petitioned by the workers from Hunslet Moor, but as a young man exploring new ideas.

His difficulty was that, though he could analyse the problems, always with sympathy for the underprivileged, when it came to solutions he was often forced into bland equivocation, or worse. In the James Watt article his best answer had been to let matters work themselves out. In August he talked himself into an even tougher dilemma. Quoting with approval an Address from the Woolcombers of Bradford to their masters, he was unafraid to let them describe their appalling condition, their once comfortable homes 'dwelling places of misery, receptacles of wretchedness', their wives clothed in rags, their children's frames emaciated. Working fourteen to sixteen hours a day, these workers 'have no time to be wise, no leisure to be good; we are sunken, debilitated, depressed, emasculated'.

Yet confronted by these horrors, brought about partly by his beloved machinery, Smiles is able to resort only to a kind of grim fatalism: 'though it may be through a course of much suffering and misery, mechanism and nature will finally accommodate themselves to each other, and enable the working classes to obtain the physical comforts of life with much less exertion than at present'.[5] Until then, he seems to suggest in a chilling analogy, the worker is, sadly, expendable. 'The mill owner is brought to look upon the sufferings of his operatives just as a general may look upon the carnage and mutilation of his soldiers.'

Smiles could never bring himself to demonise the mill owners, because he liked the ones he knew, sympathised with their problems, and believed they held the ultimate solution. He could never subdue his pity and respect for workers like the men from Hunslet Moor and the Woolcombers of Bradford (whose plea was for conciliation, not confrontation, with their masters). As for mechanisation, however harsh its short-term effects, in Smiles's view it represented a golden future, and must be encouraged. Where then was the enemy?

At Westminster of course, where in the Smiles narrative, a conspiracy between inherited wealth and the established church was the source of all society's harms. There, idle aristocrats and smug prelates made laws in their own interests, like the Corn Laws and the new Poor Law, and levied cruel taxes, stifling trade and impoverishing the working classes. So 'the Lazar House of Incurables', described in his first ever editorial, remained the target for Smiles's vituperation, and Corn Law abolition, for the time being, the focus of his energies.

Through the early months of 1840, as the plight of the country grew worse, the *Leeds Times* continued to argue the anti-Corn Law case. By turns, the paper pleaded on behalf of starving operatives and broken businesses. At meeting after meeting resolutions were passed petitioning the government to rescue the country by relaxing trade restrictions. Week after week Smiles wrote with a mix of anger and common sense: end the bread tax and save the nation. But while in the previous year he had attended dozens of anti-Corn law meetings, as lead speaker at many, now he was on the stump much less often. He appeared at a meeting of the people of the Kirkgate ward in Leeds on 28 February, proposing adoption of a motion for a petition to Parliament for 'the total and immediate repeal of the Corn laws'. At Westminster every week, almost every day, petitions from all parts of the country flooded in, praying for repeal, always on behalf of constituencies like Kirkgate, where manufacturing and business bled, and workers starved. Often these were matched, in the same sitting, by counter petitions demanding no change. This cry for the status quo came from 'country'constituencies. On 29 March *The Times* reported Lord Redesdale presenting such a pro-Corn Law petition from 'farmers, owners, occupiers of land, meeting in Hertford Corn Market; and from places in Dorset, Devon and Hertford'. The same paper on 26 March suggested a preponderance of abolitionists: 'a great number of petitions for the repeal of the Corn Laws, and several against any change'.

London was certainly for change. In February 1840 a large group of bankers, merchants, traders and inhabitants of the City met in the council chamber of the Guildhall to agree to petition Parliament for repeal, or at least modification. Perhaps it was the solemn weight of City voices that finally moved Parliament to serious consideration. On 26 May the Sheriffs of London came to the Bar of the House to present a petition from the Lord Mayor and Common Council of the City against the present Corn Laws. On that day a motion for a debate on abolition was finally heard. But too many Members were either landowners themselves or were dependent on the votes of farmers, and therefore unwilling to risk losing protection, or even to discuss change. They agreed with the Marquess of Salisbury, who had described the rash of Corn Law petitions as 'extremely inconvenient and only likely to agitate the public mind'.[6] In spite of the millions of petitioners for abolition, the poverty that blighted the country, and the warnings of the City, the motion failed. On division, 177 voted for the motion, but 300 voted against.

This curt rejection was an affront to the respectable businessmen of Leeds: 'our Marshalls and Stansfields, and Goodmans and Bowers ... men of substance who gave employment to thousands' – men who were used to having their opinions taken seriously.

Smiles, while still on the side of abolition, had for some time suspected that anti-Corn Law agitation in its present form was a lost cause. Another solution would have to be found. In February he had raged against 'the Corn Law ruffians, who enrich themselves at the expense of the blood and sinews of the poor and destitute'. These titled tyrants were not to be persuaded but must, through unanimity between middle and working classes, be driven 'like owls and bats, back into the caves and dens of corruption from which they first issued. Only by means of co-operation between the franchised and unenfranchised can aristocratic monopolies be beaten down, the Bread tax abolished and the burden of taxation repealed.'[7]

Many of the great and the good, the business barons in Leeds and other manufacturing towns, were reaching, in less colourful terms, similar conclusions. Until their constituents had more parliamentary representation nothing would change. And if the anti-Corn Law league had met a brick wall, the Chartist campaign for universal male suffrage had met an even higher one. Its leaders' emphasis on physical confrontation had driven away much of its moderate support. Now a coalition of moderates from both Chartists and Anti-Corn Law leaguers had started to seem attractive. So in the summer of 1840 the Leeds Parliamentary Reform Association came into being, led by James Garth Marshall and Hamer Stansfield, with Samuel Smiles as honorary secretary. Its first general meeting took place in the saloon of the Music Hall on 31 August 1840. Even by the standards of the day it was a long meeting, lasting until eleven o'clock at night. The *Leeds Times*, in over 12,000 words, reported speech after speech in which the infuriated burghers of Leeds expressed their hurt and frustration at the way their petitions had been treated, their fear at the outcome, and their determination to achieve change. Marshall, introducing the new organisation, referred to 'the ominous refusal ... sullen, unreasoning, without the decency of inquiry, and almost without the formality of a debate,' and warned that this attitude threatened to 'snap asunder the ties that bind society together'. Stansfield, revealing the fundamental utilitarian principles that underlay so much of this group's approach, declared that 'heaven designed man to be happy ... the true measure of the suffrage, in my humble opinion, should be its utility and its capability of conferring happiness on the greatest number'.

As almost the final act of the night Samuel Smiles was called on to propose the resolution for the formation of the new Society. Corn Law repeal would never be achieved, Smiles argued, until the root of the evil was dug out, and that evil, he said, 'lies in the conformation of the legislature, and will not be removed until that legislature has been reformed and remodelled'. Chartism's failure lay in its rejection of class solidarity. On the other hand 'It will be observed that the present association has as its principal feature the cooperation of the middle and operative classes. The movement will thus at the same time have heads to direct it, and masses to enable it to act with power and effect.'

This division between officers and other ranks was blatant and unashamed – hardly as brutal as the 'generals and soldiers' analogy Smiles had used when arguing the case for mechanisation, but an admission nevertheless of different roles for different classes. The acceptance of a divide becomes even clearer when in the last act of the meeting the names of the Committee of the Leeds Parliamentary Reform Association were recorded under two headings: 'Middle Class' and 'Operatives'.

Attitudes to class and perceptions of egalitarianism in 1840 were, of course, quite different from those of the twenty-first century. When Mr Atkinson of Mill Hill had proposed that 'one half of the officers of the new Association should be chosen from the operative class' he genuinely believed he was asking for inclusion, not division, and in the spirit of the time he was right. This was nineteenth-century positive discrimination.

For a while, disillusioned about the chances of Corn Law repeal and somewhat in awe of Hamer Stansfield ('Mr Stansfield was a man for whom I had the greatest esteem ... I felt it an honour to be consulted by such a man').[8] Smiles threw himself into the work of the new Association. At first the signs looked good. All the liberal gang – Goodman, Bower, Middleton, as well as Marshall and Stansfield – seemed to be on board. The *Leeds Times* was giving the movement a voice. National commentators were taking notice.

But one significant name was missing and one voice not heard – yet. Very soon, however, Smiles and his friends realised that the bitterest opposition to their new Association came not from predicable Toryism but from their old anti-Corn law ally Edward Baines, and the *Leeds Mercury*. Edward Baines senior had been elected to Parliament under the existing franchise. The 1832 Reform Act was reform enough for him and his editor son; further tinkering with representation was a threat to national stability. So when, in the autumn of 1840, Hamer Stansfield publicly declined the office of Chief Magistrate of Leeds in order to direct his energies to the cause of Household Suffrage, Edward Baines used the move as a pretext to attack the whole concept. A series of open letters addressed to 'Hamer Stansfield Esq', and signed by 'the Editors' appeared in the *Leeds Mercury* through November and December. Each week, tedious in their weight of statistical and psephological argument, these letters sought to make the case that household suffrage would enfranchise more 'country' than 'town' voters, advancing Tory strength in the House of Commons and further damaging the chances of Corn Law abolition. But through the mass of constituency numbers and voting figures there ran, like a polluted stream, the 'fitness to vote' concept. 'We think it dangerous to give power to the uneducated classes' Baines pronounced.[9]

> We require some evidence before the bestowal of so important a trust, that the parties are *fitted* to exercise it. Household Suffrage would not, we think, succeed because the people are not prepared for it ... we say that for a safe, intelligent, independent constituency, the substance and staple must be found in the middle classes.

By the third week in December Smiles and the *Leeds Times* had girded themselves for a counter-blast: 'the statements of the *Mercury* are not true. The thirteen columns which "the Editors" have devoted ... to the subject of Household Suffrage have been stuffed throughout with fallacies.' Rather than attacking the Baines statistical case (Stansfield himself did that in the *Mercury*'s letter pages), the *Leeds Times* chose a Smilesian riff of outrage:

> Their three letters to Mr Stansfield form the most extraordinary jumble of contradictory theories and facts, of arguments and opinions, of fallacies and truisms, of assertions and assumptions, of figures and tropes, of fancies and fictions, which it has ever been our lot to peruse.

Smiles's underlying concern was with what he saw as the danger of a total breakdown between government and governed:

The working classes are in fact at war with the governing classes. The people are broken up into sections and classes and parties – the Chartists, Socialists, Repealers, Voluntaries, and Household Suffrage Association – and the separation between the governing classes and the great mass of the people is all but complete.[10]

But in his emphasis on proliferation of protest Smiles had, maybe without knowing it, identified the flaw in the organisation he was striving to support.

Baines's full frontal attack on the Leeds Parliamentary Reform Association was not its sponsors' only cause for concern. The anticipated great wave of endorsement seemed slow in coming. Claims for support had a tentative note; evidence was unspecific: 'Societies spring up in various parts of the West Riding ... we are also glad to learn that application for lectures have been made from several quarters.' More worryingly, the authoritative voice of Richard Cobden, in a speech in Manchester, warned of the new movement's potential to dilute the anti-Corn Law effort. A letter in the *Spectator* seemed at first to back the Association, by reckoning that Baines had lost the argument with Stansfield, but then went on to point out that 'when Mr Stansfield comes to argue with the Chartists, we do not see how he can escape being worsted in his turn, for the arguments in his letter to Mr Baines clearly go to make up the Chartist case.' In this the *Spectator* turned out to be remarkably prescient.

In the meantime Smiles and his friends continued to be upbeat about the new Association's prospects. A meeting in Hunslet in early December suggested widespread local support for the Association, with new members signing up from across the political spectrum. Joshua Bower enthused the gathering of over three hundred 'not with a mere Whig speech, but with one of the soundest Radical speeches we have ever heard that man deliver'. Dr Smiles then 'entered at some length into the causes of the distressed state of the country, showing that bad, unjust, and partial legislation was at the root of the whole ... the only cure, a Radical Reform in the representation of the people'.[11] Attention from the national press was noted, in the *Sun*, the *Morning Chronicle*, and the *Morning Advertiser*, with the *Weekly Dispatch* and the *Statesman* being described as 'supportive, and friendly'. Even the spoiler campaign of

Smiles's rival paper, with its unpleasant strand of class stereotyping, was represented as a positive – the 'oxygen of publicity' argument: 'The three fallacy-stuffed articles of the *Leeds Mercury* have done more good to the cause of extended suffrage and redistribution than all the previous efforts of the Leeds Association.'[12] The vision of the Association's committee was, however, much wider – nothing less than a great coalition of all liberal and radical parties, from Chartists and Corn Law repealers to Socialists and Voluntaries. To this end they planned a Grand Festival of Suffrage in January, to be held at Marshall's magnificent new mill in Holbeck, built on a vast scale in the style of an Egyptian temple. MPs and leaders representing all reforming interests and organisations would be invited to attend, and to speak – a conclave of the faithful in the cathedral of the future. By understanding the sacredness of their common goal, these groups were to be united into a single, irresistible voice.

In the midst of all this excitement (perhaps prompted by it), Smiles's personal career in the newspaper business was taking a significant step forward. In implicit recognition of his contribution to 'The great and sustained increase in the circulation of the *Leeds Times* ... the commanding position which it has attained as an organ of enlightened and liberal opinions', the paper announced to its readers on 19 December 1840 that 'from and after the first of January next, the *Leeds Times* will be conducted under the joint proprietorship of FREDERICK HOBSON, printer and Publisher, and SAMUEL SMILES, for some time Editor of this Journal.'

Though improved circulation was, of course, important to the paper, it seems that Smiles's leading role in the Leeds Parliamentary Reform Association was a key factor in his elevation. In its first edition of 1841, the paper felt moved to explain further the change in proprietorship. By taking the lead in campaigning for the extension of suffrage and helping the reformers of Leeds to 'assume a position far in advance of any other population in the empire ... the Conductor of this paper [Smiles] has been induced permanently to attach himself to it'. The *Leeds Times* was now in partnership with the Leeds Parliamentary Reform Association, and Samuel Smiles was now in formal partnership with Frederick Hobson. As to how permanent 'permanently' would be, only events would show.

For now the Grand Festival of Suffrage was everyone's concern, and the *Leeds Times* was at its heart. In announcing the event it described in breathless detail the new mill which, 'as many of our readers will know has not its equal in England, if in the world'.[13] Smiles in his *Autobiography*, judged it as *the* largest, five times the size of Westminster Hall – a place, declared the *Leeds Times*, 'the inspection of which is worth all the money charged for admission to the festival proceedings'. Space would be provided for eight thousand. Thrilled by the size and splendour of this venue, Smiles and his friends looked forward to an outcome to match: a spectacular triumph for their movement.

Advertisements for the event noted the planned participation of a galaxy of MPs and leaders from every shade of reforming opinion and that 'the attendance of every honest and sincere Liberal is respectfully requested'. In the fading winter light of 20 January 1841 the anticipated 8,000 liberals duly turned up, and a dozen distinguished speakers.

Perhaps James Garth Marshall and Hamer Stansfield were too fair-minded, too anxious to offer an open agenda, to control the direction of the meeting. Fifty years later Smiles remembered it as very confused, 'on account of the heterogeneous audience, and the frequent howlings of the Chartists'.[14] At the time of the meeting, he wrote of a gathering of 'all grades and classes of reformers ... to hear and consider each other's opinions',[15] and described it as 'a great step forward to have got such a mass of individuals together for such a purpose'. But in the event the Chartists, by flooding the meeting with a single, unequivocal demand – universal male suffrage – had rendered the Association's spokesmen pale and directionless.

On the same day, describing the same meeting, the *Leeds Mercury* was less restrained in its comments.

> Our friends Mr James G Marshall and Mr Hamer Stansfield must now concede to us that we were right ...We ask where was the manliness in allowing themselves to be invaded, turned round, and the meeting absolutely appropriated by the Chartists without one act of defence or of protest?

Distasteful as he must have found the *Mercury*'s words, in his editorials at this time Smiles tried, not very successfully, to hide his frustration with what had happened, while at the same time trying to pass it off as some sort of success:

> Were we to judge by the great meeting of Thursday week, we should say that the Chartists have by far the largest amount of faith in the efficacy of their own principles. The believers in Household Suffrage were tongue-tied; they lacked utterance, and even those put forward to advocate their principles conceded the main point contended for by their opponents. However this may be, the grand object has been accomplished – the middle and working classes have made a joint declaration of the insufficiency of the Reform Act.[16]

Though household suffrage may have seemed a shrewd idea – extension of the Reform Act by compromise rather than confrontation – it had been exposed as lacking clear principle. The decent men who had formed the Leeds Parliamentary Reform Association, tongue-tied and lacking utterance, were forced to concede. From the wreckage of the Great Festival they salvaged the 'unity' theme as the only basis for continuing. An idea so unthreatening could be accepted by everyone. It became the pretext for continued meetings, together with the equally unthreatening proposal for 'a large and commodious reading room ... for the use of the middle and working classes' included in the report to the annual general meeting, read by the secretary, Dr Smiles. But Dr Smiles knew the score – 'It was like flogging a dead horse to make it rise and go. It would neither rise nor go.'[17]

Edward Baines, no doubt enjoying the opportunity to show magnanimity, stopped baiting the Association. On too many issues he and the Marshall-Stansfield camp were on the same side: anti-Tory, anti-Corn Law, anti-Physical Force Chartism. Gradually the Corn Law issue re-entered the deliberations of the parliamentary reformers. By May the mood in Westminster had changed. At last the appalling condition of the poor forced the Whig ministry to look again at the Corn Laws, and to propose the reduction of some duties, and a fixed rate on wheat of eight shillings a quarter.

The proposal was voted down in Parliament. In a general election in the summer of 1841 the status of the Corn Laws was a major issue. Peel retained his place as Prime Minister but supporters of Corn Law repeal lost ground. Only the relentless Cobden refused to blink. His Anti-Corn Law League fundamentalists demanded repeal, total repeal and nothing but repeal. Any other reforming movement, even when sympathetic to the League's objectives, was guilty of heresy, by diverting public attention from the one true cause. After the election Cobden wrote to Smiles, chiding Leeds for lack of anti-Corn Law intensity, and urging Smiles's leadership in rousing the faithful. Though flattered by the attention of so famous a man ('If he wrote such letters to me – a comparatively unknown person, both as regards position and influence – what must he have done to others in all parts of the country, who possessed a much greater amount of both'),[18] Corn Law fatigue had set in. Over the next few years Smiles remained involved, but in a more detached way, with all the reforming movements. But the fate of the Great Suffrage Festival and the intransigence of Parliament on Corn Law reform turned his mind more and more to the problems he could see every day as he walked about Leeds – the problems of poverty, starvation, and sub-human housing in a country with the resources to create great wealth.

This disconnection was succinctly made in the words of an unemployed operative called James Rattray, 'That Great Britain is possessed of elements calculated to secure the nation's greatness and its people's happiness – yet a vast amount of destitution exists.' Rattray was Secretary of the newly formed Leeds Enumeration Committee of the Unemployed Poor. Smiles had remarked on it when writing to Cobden in September about arrangements for a proposed anti-Corn Law meeting in Leeds. His letter shows clearly that by then he was more excited by this new, much more grass roots development.

> I was waited on the other day by a committee of operatives, who have engaged in a most important investigation ... Their object has been to ascertain the actual condition of the operative classes in Leeds ... Every house will be visited, and the means of subsistence and the condition of the dwelling etc will be accurately ascertained.[19]

From the Committee's first meeting on 8 September 1841 the *Leeds Times* gave unequivocal support to its objectives and to the operatives who led its work. The picture emerges of a group of men living every day in the conditions other reformers only talked about, deciding that facts rather than rhetoric must be placed before the authorities. Their aim was a form of statistical survey, primitive but thorough, unbiased and double-checked, to put numbers on misery. They would do the work themselves, record and tabulate the results themselves, and bring them to public notice themselves. They were on the path of self-help, not falling in behind any leader from another class, but running their own project and welcoming the support of any who offered. Smiles was enthused: 'Few of all the associations which have sprung so abundantly on all sides', he said, 'are more novel in their character, more important in their objects ... than the Leeds Enumeration Committee of the Unemployed Poor.'[20] They provided him not only with an example of barely educated men showing their innate worth and wisdom, but also with an opportunity to compare them with their supposed superiors:

> It is impossible to look on the working men of England without feeling proud of one's fellow countrymen. Suffering appalling destitution, goaded with insults from aristocrats gorged with spoils, mocked by one on whom they had heaped honour and wealth, palaced, pensioned and titled servant of their own, they still preserve, unbroken, the peace and order of society ... Urged by the consideration [of the plight of the unemployed] the working classes of Leeds have set themselves to enlighten the deplorable and disgraceful ignorance of the higher classes to their condition ...[21]

Smiles could write like this because he had been in the dark places with the enumerators during their survey work; he and others had been invited as independent observers to confirm that no exaggeration had coloured their reports. He saw whole families huddled together in a dark cellar, twelve feet by nine, with little or no furniture and a few shavings for a bed. But this sort of anecdotal evidence was not the Enumeration Committee's object. Henry Mayhew, ten years later, would astonish the polite world with his accounts of metropolitan low life in his multi-volume *London Labour and the London Poor*. But the Leeds project was concerned with facts, not with sensation, though when the facts emerged they were sensational enough – 20,000 people in Leeds trying to live on eleven pence per head per week. James Rattray believed that the power of his information was instrumental 'when the tariff wedge was put in that was to dislocate the entire fabric of monopoly'.[22]

Rattray exaggerated the ultimate importance of the Committee's work, and in old age Smiles was happy to quote him. But the findings of the Enumeration Committee were undermined by a concerted attack on the validity of their figures. For Smiles, the lesson lay yet again in a contradiction, between the inspiration of seeing ordinary men working to help themselves, and the disillusion of watching their efforts subsumed in factional squabbles and political cynicism. It was another step in his loss of faith in institutions, and his growing conviction that potential for good must rest with individual commitment. The voice of Rattray and his enumerators was drowned in the crossfire between the Chartists, the government, and local lobbying by overseers, who suggested that 'mere operatives' were unqualified to produce accurate figures.[23] The Enumeration Committee, one of its leaders commented, 'being connected with neither party, had had the misfortune to be suspected by both – the Tories suspecting it to be an electioneering trick, the Liberals, that it was got up to injure the overseers'.[24] So on 19 March 1842 the *Leeds Times* reported, with a note of regret, that six months after its origin, 'the Operatives' Enumeration Committee had 'closed their valuable labours on Wednesday last by dining together at John Airey's Old George Inn'.[25] In the spirit of the original members, John Airey had refused to accept any payment for the weekly use of his premises.

By then estimates of the means of the poor had shrunk from eleven pence to amounts varying between nine pence and three pence a week, with some suggesting a national average of barely a penny per head. As the *Leeds Times* declared on 12 March 1842, 'Distress cannot go on thus increasing without leading to the most disastrous results for society.'

A month earlier, in an address to the Bradford United Reform Club, Smiles had made what, in the light of his subsequent career, can be seen as a *valete* to his former political associates. Indeed in his *Autobiography* he marked 1842 as the year in which 'I leave politics'. In that 1842 Bradford address, on 'The Diffusion of Political Knowledge Among the Working Classes', he effectively stepped away from formal involvement with political movements, and declared his belief in the need for a more profound solution to society's evils. In *Self-Help*, seventeen years later, Smiles wrote that 'The noble people will be nobly ruled, and the ignorant and corrupt ignobly. Indeed all experience serves to prove that the worth and strength of a state depend far less upon the form of its institutions than upon the character of its men.' This argument – for the essentially organic nature of government, for nourishing the individual plant rather than designing the landscape – was signalled in his Bradford address. 'We consider the only safe guarantee for the functions of Government being well administered is to be found in the entire responsibility of the governors to the governed,' he told his audience, 'and we therefore aim at basing the representation on the whole of the people ... while we aim to improve the Government, therefore, we must take care that we improve, by all the means in our power, the individuals who compose the nation.' Education, 'knowledge', an increasingly pervasive Smiles theme, was, he said, the key to this virtuous constituency.

And he must have alarmed his Whig friends in Leeds by citing Chartism as an example of what knowledge could achieve. 'I hail Chartism as one of the most noble steps in the march of civilization' (the 'noble people nobly ruled').

> I cannot look at it with the trembling that some people do; but consider it to be one of the most hopeful of all the signs of the times. It is the result of knowledge – political knowledge, if you will – flowing in upon the minds of men who find themselves in the midst of wealth and civilization a degraded and oppressed class.

Chartism was, in his view, entirely natural: 'It is the result of that desire which the creator has implanted in every human bosom – the desire after increase of individual happiness.'

But Chartism, he admitted in his Bradford address, was characterised by many 'imprudencies'. And soon they appeared, literally from the sky, in late June 1842, when Feargus O'Connor paid a messianic visit to Burnley.[26] There, before upwards of two thousand adoring followers, his speech was marked by the appearance in the grey sky above the platform of a balloon bearing the device 'FEARGUS O'CONNOR' in glowing colours. 'Tyrants, look and tremble', the banner said. 'Better to die by the sword than perish of hunger.' After his two-hour address, imploring the people to assert their rights by demanding the Charter, O'Connor walked to his inn, and from the great crowd 'the rattle of clogs was so loud ... that he could hardly hear his own voice'. The near-hysteria surrounding

O'Connor (on arrival 'the masses, anxious to get a hold of his hand, literally besieged the carriage')[27] was generated by their craving for a saviour, from the desolation described by the Enumerators of Leeds.

A few weeks later their stirrings were more menacing. A meeting of mechanics in the Carpenter's Hall in Manchester on 12 August pledged that 'We cannot exist with the present rate of wages and that we are determined not to go to work until we obtain the prices paid in 1839.' Wages for many men had been cut by half or more, by, depending whom you listened to, falling trade, mechanisation, owners' greed and devious practices. Though they had prefaced their resolution by declaring a wish to preserve the public peace, the whiff of battle was growing stronger. There was no shortage of targets for anger. At the Carpenter's Hall meeting, the power loom weavers condemned masters who 'refuse to give employment to MEN in their factories but instead employ women, over whom they can tyrannise with impunity. We are therefore determined that this cruel and unjust system shall be abolished before we go to our work.'[28] Many reasons were given for the proposed stoppage, but determination was universal. The next week, in a series of delegate meetings representing all the trades of Manchester and the surrounding villages, the strike was debated. Was it to be 'a trades or a political contest', in other words was it about wages or about the Charter. In the end the resolution was for 'extension and continuance of the present struggle until the PEOPLE'S CHARTER becomes a legislative enactment'.

In the days that followed, the authorities showed an iron fist: proclamations were posted banning all meetings. Soldiers, hussars and Coldstream Guards, armed police and special constables, bayonets and artillery pieces, poured into Manchester and other manufacturing towns. At first things were eerily quiet on the streets until, inevitably, a stone thrown here, a shot fired there, led to violence on both sides and the reading of the Riot Act. Smiles wrote in the *Leeds Times* of 'a servile war, of which symptoms have so long been showing themselves ... now openly raging'. Everywhere the 'disturbances in the manufacturing districts' made headlines, and in London good people shuddered. But in fact, considering the numbers involved and the depth of their grievances, it was a quiet and rather sad revolution – broken windows, work-place invasions to disable machinery, spats with the soldiery – but no fires, no pitched battles; just starving men and women asking to be heard but finally forced by hunger to trudge back to work having gained nothing.

In spite of his well-established horror of violence, Smiles was on the workers' side. Even while he warned that if the Lancashire strike went on 'war, destructive war must inevitably break out,'[29] he described the plight of the crowds with no food or the means of purchasing it. 'Take any wise man,' he added, 'even a philosopher, and keep food from him for a week, at the end of that time you will find him a savage.' When the strike ended he defended the strikers against denunciation, seeing their actions as the inevitable outcome of social inequality, political injustice and intense competition.

What Smiles may have regretted most in all of this was the threat to his long cherished hope for union between the working and middle classes. The protest of the people, and its failure, would, he feared, make the division wider. He tried to straddle the fence, between the anti-Corn Law League, so reviled by the Chartists as a front for the 'millocrats and the shopocrats', and the universal suffrage camp, regarded with such suspicion by the Liberal establishment. It may have been the frustration, exhaustion even, of watching so many interest groups shouting at each other without listening, that made Smiles at this time start to hold them all at arm's length. Or it may have been something much more personal. He fell in love.

8

Many More Strings

How did they meet? Shy glances across a crowded lobby at Mill Street Unitarian Church after Sunday service? Or perhaps at a soirée of the Leeds Mechanics and Literary Institution – where ladies paid one shilling, gentlemen one-and-sixpence, and tea was on the table at five – she had admired the confident, eloquent young man who had given the lecture. Whatever the circumstances, the outcome is certain: nineteen year-old Sarah Anne Holmes and Samuel Smiles, ten years her senior, fell in love some time in 1842, and by the end of the year pretty much everything in Smiles's life had changed. 'I had got engaged to be married', he says in his *Autobiography*. 'I leave political life – I cease to be editor.'

Well, yes and no. It is unlikely that Sarah Anne and Samuel ever became officially engaged. Neither did he abruptly 'leave' political life, nor cease completely to be editor of the *Leeds Times*.

Engagement, other than as a secret between the two, seems unlikely because, although not quite Romeo and Juliet, these were undoubtedly star-crossed lovers. Sarah Anne's father, John Holmes, otherwise John Holmes Dixon, a moderately successful small businessman surrounded in Leeds by examples of immoderately successful big businessmen, had high hopes for his beautiful only daughter. Mr Holmes had worked hard to raise himself from his trade as plumber to the status of 'contractor' in plumbing, glazing and copperwork, with premises in Little Templar and a polite home in St George's Terrace, with sofas, card tables and a piano.[1] He had married a woman of mild gentility in Jane Dixon, taken her

name, and allowed her to send Sarah Anne to Miss Martineau's boarding
school in Liverpool. Correspondence between Sarah and her mother,[2]
and between Miss Martineau and Mrs Holmes, suggests a girl groomed
for improvement – a little French, a little music – 'send me a word if you
dance. I should think there will now be sufficient for quadrilles' – the
avoidance of 'foolish and idle books' and the adoption of fine needlework
and fine emotions – 'I am glad you have learnt the happy outcome of
controlling your feelings, as well as exercising your patience' – and above
all, superior companions, as advised by Miss Martineau, 'if they can
be found, near her own age and above her, somewhat, in talents and
attainments ...'

Miss Martineau probably did not mean *materially* above, but Mr
Holmes did. His expensively schooled daughter, able to mix with families
of solid prosperity, was not to be allowed to waste everything on a
Scottish journalist with not much more than £100 a year and few
prospects, however popular he might be in progressive political circles.
Not that Smiles was unwelcome as a friend. He was received often at the
Holmes house, sat with their friends at the card tables, probably played
his violin to Sarah Anne's accompaniment on the cherished piano. After
more than a year of this solicitude he believed he was seen as, in his own
words, '*the* one'. But he was deceived. When he approached Sarah Anne's
father for her hand he was given the Yorkshire brush-off. Rankled, Smiles
recorded the scene in a later note:

> I put the question plainly but respectfully. The answer was,
> 'No, you shall not have a farthing of mine.'
> 'I do not want a farthing of yours: I want to marry your daughter.'
> 'No, you shall not have her.'[14]
> The words were accompanied with something rather contemptuous,
> which need not be repeated ... Well! I now wished to be married. I put
> the whole question to herself – to give it up, or be married. The answer
> was 'Don't on any account give it up.' There was consequently the other
> alternative.

This was the 'engagement', a secret pact between the lovers to defy her
stern father – all gloriously romantic; but Samuel Smiles was too realistic
to flee to Gretna Green. The snub from Mr Holmes was provocative,
prompting a determination not just to go ahead and marry Sarah Anne,

but to show that Samuel Smiles had many more strings to his bow than might be suspected by the bourgeois plumbing contractor.

The sabotage of the Enumeration Committee had been a bitter disappointment to Smiles. Now a more personal view of political questions, as suggested in *The Diffusion of Political Knowledge*, loosened his attachment to political activity. The *Leeds Times* editor's job was limiting, interesting though it had been. 'I was introduced to good society, was invited out a good deal, and made many friends. But it seemed to lead to nothing.'[4] Add to this his growing boredom with the day-to day editorial duties and the weekly grind of turning out leading articles – 'the threshing of straw that had been a thousand times threshed' as he put it – and it is easy to see how he concocted the plan for the next stage of his career – the ceasing to be editor, without completely ceasing, and the leaving of political life, without completely leaving. His plan was for what would now be called a portfolio career. The Smiles portfolio would contain part-time editorship, freelance journalism, medical practice, and book writing.

So at the end of December 1842 the Hobson-Smiles partnership at the *Leeds Times* was dissolved.[5] Smiles, in his own words, 'ceased to be editor', though his name went on bearing the title 'editor of the *Leeds Times*' well into 1845. At the same time he planned to re-launch his career as a doctor. On 25 March 1843 an advertisement appeared on the front pages of all the Leeds papers: 'A CARD – Dr S. Smiles, Surgeon &cetera, Springfield Place, Mann's Field, Holbeck.' Smiles, 'with the assent of my affianced', had taken a house in this small community on the edge of the town and put up his surgeon's plate. Hardly pausing for breath, he accepted a commission from Mann & Co, a prolific local publisher of almanacks and guidebooks, to write a series of guides and pamphlets. And soon he would start work on another book.

The rationale was clear: eggs were to be prudently distributed in several baskets, professional respectability asserted, and greater personal freedom gained – all contributing to a riposte to his future in-laws and, more importantly, boosting his sense of self-worth. It was a tough year, but rewarding: 'I think 1843 was my heaviest year of work. I was well and healthy, took plenty of exercise, and my mind was always alive and active. I found work, plenty of work, necessary for my happiness and welfare.'[6]

With such a densely packed surrounding population to serve, Smiles managed to attract more patients in Holbeck than he had done in Haddington, though the practice, on its own, would not have kept him. In his *Autobiography* he paints a picture of unrewarding struggle:

> It used to be said of doctors that they rarely got bread enough to eat, until they had not teeth to eat it ... They are regarded as friends and even angels by people when they are ill; but when the debt has been incurred they are regarded as something very much the reverse. They often get neither money nor thanks.

In the meantime he persevered, and in fact created a practice apparently strong enough to be passed on and be still in operation well into the next century.[7]

But writing, any writing, was his best-loved occupation. So while he gathered patients for his Holbeck practice he went on writing regularly for the *Leeds Times*, and following his own agenda. All through his life, like most writers, Smiles hungered for the financial independence that would allow him to write what interested him rather than what a publisher might prescribe. Much later, when his books had started to sell in large numbers, he turned down many commissions for biographies, and when he stopped contributing to the *Quarterly Review* he explained that 'in writing for a Review you hand over the fruit of your brain and diligence to another ... I afterwards preferred writing for myself, at my leisure; I found it more satisfactory.'[8] That was in 1875, by which time the Smiles name on the spine of a book meant big sales. For now, any relief from the straw that had been a thousand times threshed was welcome.

So he produced a stream of guides for local bookseller Mann's,[9] some of which, he modestly boasted, 'had an immense circulation', especially his *Guides* to America and to the English Colonies. Mann's also co-operated with him to produce a book on Ireland – not a guide, but a history. Many of the poorest and, in Smiles's view, the most exploited workers in Leeds at the time were Irish. The *Leeds Times* opposed government policies on Ireland and saw parallels between the plight of the poor on both sides of the Irish sea. 'Nothing can be clearer than that the interest of those who are tyrannised over both in England and Ireland is the same,'[10] the paper declared. ' – if there be a gain to be made by a fraud or an oppression practised on his weaker neighbour, the enemy cares not on which side of the Irish channel it may be.' Smiles's inherent concern for the poor and exploited, and his hatred for aggressors, those same 'robber barons' he had previously railed against, bred in him a persistent though equivocal sympathy for the Irish. The title of his book flagged up his position: *A History of Ireland and The Irish People Under The Government of England*. It was advertised on the front page of the *Leeds Times* on 2 September 1843, as a part-work:

> price three pence (to be continued every succeeding Saturday) till finished ... to be published also in monthly parts, price one shilling. The whole to be concluded in about twenty-four numbers ... The object of the work is to depict the sufferings of the Irish people from cruel misgovernment – to show what the country has been, what it is now, and what it is capable of becoming under a better system ... stated with boldness, firmness, and impartiality.

These instalments were published anonymously.

A 'review', published a week after the first part went on sale, did little more than quote from the text, acknowledging that 'A first chapter can no more be regarded as a specimen of a work, than a brick can be of a house.' But in that extract the Smiles agenda of the time is apparent – anti-aristocracy, anti-military, warning that England's greatness is being put at grave risk by the blind and selfish policies of a small, unrepresentative clique: 'Ireland has been, for nearly seven centuries, the slave of England. Her soil has been looked upon merely as a hunting ground for our aristocracy, with soldiers for their bloodhounds.' And was there a subconscious echo of the anti-imperialist voice of the Irishman Edmund Burke fifty years earlier, over English behaviour in India? In a sub-Burkeian burst of anger, Smiles wrote:

> Coercion, oppression, extortion, treachery, confiscation, plunder, and massacre, have been the principal instruments used by the English aristocracy in the government of the Irish people ... England stands arraigned at the bar of the world's opinion, for her treatment of Ireland.

By December 1843 Smiles had finished writing all the instalments for the *History of Ireland*. On Monday evening, the 4th, he gave a lecture on

'The Social Condition of Woman' for the Youths' Guardian Society, in the huge new schoolroom provided by Marshall's, with 'upwards of a thousand persons being present'.[11] Perhaps Sarah Anne was among the thousand. Perhaps she remarked afterwards to the speaker, her *fiancé*, on her own social condition. At any rate three days later, on Thursday 7 December 1843, Dr Smiles took a morning off from his schedule of doctoring, writing, editing and lecturing and, armed with a special licence, 'went quietly to the parish church in Leeds, with my wife's cousin, who gave her away, and we were happily married. I never regretted it. It was the best day's work I ever did.'[12] There was no holiday or honeymoon. Less than a week after his wedding Smiles was on the platform at an Anti-Corn law meeting with Cobden, Bright, and his hero Colonel Perronet Thompson, who had been one of the earliest parliamentary supporters of the People's Charter.

Smiles talks in his *Autobiography* about his 'once solitary home lighted up with love and cheerfulness'. His later correspondence shows that he was deeply, sometimes extravagantly, attached to his family. But during his early marriage those days and evenings of attending to patients, of newspaper work, and writing, lecturing, and chairing committees, would have given little time for domestic bliss. Christmas had hardly passed before he was on a platform in Leeds Bazaar supporting the radical Irish MP William Sharman Crawford's plan for disrupting government business. Smiles was in rollicking form that night, imagining 'the noble Lords out at the elbows [laughter] ... Prince Albert himself going about with a shocking bad hat [renewed laughter]'. Behind the jokes his wrath at an unrepresentative system was as fierce as ever:

> Let them cast their eyes abroad over England, Ireland and Scotland, and look at the condition of the people. They found great masses of them almost starving ... were we not justified in stopping the wheels of government that inflicted such injuries on the people. What confidence could they have in a House of Commons when in England about 8 out of every 9, in Scotland 11 out of 12, and in Ireland 19 out of every 20 were unrepresented ... was that a government for the people?[13]

Throughout 1844 and 1845 Dr Smiles appeared on platforms, was co-opted to committees, and delivered lectures. Though less politically com-

mitted, his name was still clearly valued in support of every radical Whig-
gish cause, from temperance, church reform and children's employment
conditions, to Corn Law repeal and universal suffrage.

Very soon Sarah Anne became pregnant, and a few months after their
wedding the Smiles's moved from Springfield Place into Leeds town, to
Wellington Street. There, on 28 August, their first child was born, named
Janet, a salute to her Smiles grandmother, still shop-keeping in distant
Haddington. Smiles did not slow down, but he had started to re-balance
his energy and re-order his priorities.

In April *A History of Ireland* had been published in book form in Leeds,
London and Dublin, 500 pages in thirty-two chapters, price ten shillings.
A small advertisement appeared in the Leeds papers on 14 April
announcing the event. On 15 June a much larger notice followed, eagerly
quoting from the reviews. 'We strongly recommend it to our countrymen'
declared the *Dublin Post*. The *Athenaeum* approvingly noted 'his sympathies on the side of the oppressed; and his opinions the result of careful
examination.' (When, thirty years later, his son William became a leading
figure in the industrial success story of Belfast, and a strong supporter of
Ulster Unionism, Smiles's views on Ireland showed some revision.
Though, in an echo of his own attitude to Chartism, he would warn his
son against association with violent demonstration, Smiles deplored
Gladstone's Home Rule proposals for Ireland.) He had high hopes for
the book, at least as a decent supplement to the income from his medical
practice, but the equivocal tone of some of the reviews confirmed his
lurking fear that it would not be a winner. The *Athenaeum*, though kind,
had commented that 'the author has made but little use of the documents published by the State Paper Office' and Smiles acknowledged in
his *Autobiography* that 'no one could be better aware than myself of the
imperfections of the work, arising, in a great measure, from my having
to work at a distance from the best authorities'.

He tried again a year later to generate sales of the part-work version,
now in thirty-two threepence-ha'penny instalments, with advertisements
in the *Leeds Times* on 24 and 31 May 1845. But by then, as far as financial
reward was concerned, the game was up. Smiles had had his first brush
with the commercial realities of being an author when his Irish distrib-
utor for the *History* failed: 'the arrangement with the publisher was half

profits, but so far as I was concerned, I received nothing'. This bruising experience didn't put Smiles off writing, but it did change his view about the role writing should play in his life: 'I had given up the idea of living by literature. I liked to regard it as my staff and not my crutch.'[14]

At the same time, after more than five years as cheer leader for Leeds's radical-Whig industrialists – Marshall, Kitson, Stansfield and the others, whom he increasingly came to regard as politically motivated – he turned towards the working out of his own personal philosophy. From now on the public 'Dr Smiles', previously on call for every radical cause in the West Riding, would be replaced by a man stripping himself back to the issues and interests which engaged him most. His contributions at the Leeds Mechanics' Institution and Literary Society concentrated, during 1844 and 1845, on six major lectures on *Men and Times of the Commonwealth.* This period in English history had an obvious fascination for someone devoted to Milton, and to dissent at every level. Smiles was an instinctive Roundhead. He would have liked, he said later, to have written a book on the subject, but now his more realistic view of life discouraged the idea: 'It is only men of sufficient means and fortune who can devote themselves to the pursuit of any branch of history.' So he contented himself with adapting the original six lectures given in Leeds to a set of four, which he delivered at the Manchester Athenaeum and to the Mechanics' Institute in Liverpool.

Mechanics' Institutes – with their minglings for tea at five and dessert at eight o'clock, their one-and-sixpence entry tickets, their reading rooms for members, and their well-stocked libraries – were not everywhere, in spite of their name, the haunt of men from the factory floor or the work-shop. Dr Smiles could find it perfectly congenial to take to the platform at meetings of (in Leeds's case) the now combined Mechanics Institution and Literary Society, and to share his general cultural interests with the well-dressed gentlemen, and ladies, in the audience there.[15] But, in his 1842 lecture on the Diffusion of Political Knowledge, he had made his opinion clear about their limitations. Now a sharper, more visceral interest concerned him, and a different audience.

9

Seeds of Self-Help

Y EARS LATER, when he had left Leeds, left newspaper work, and left the public platforms of the West Riding, Smiles wrote the Introduction to his new book, *Self-Help*. In it he offered a picture touched by the sentimentality of a Victorian genre painting. A group of roughly dressed 'young men of the humblest rank' are seated together in a garden, near 'a little boarded hut'. From the slates they hold on their knees we can see that the purpose of their gathering is instruction – 'improving themselves by exchanging knowledge with each other', until a summer shower starts to 'dash the sums from their slates'. But they will meet again, their appetite for self-improvement unquenchable, by rain, or shortage of books, or lack of accommodation. Nothing will thwart the mission of these working lads to help themselves.

This vision may seem idealised, but it was based on Smiles's experience and direct involvement with just such young men in Leeds in the 1840s, and on a conviction about their worth, and how they might realise it.

'How,' he asked, in the *Leeds Times* in September 1844, 'are the people to be educated? ... the church has failed them ... the state has failed them; Dissent cannot educate them ... The answer is – they must educate themselves.' He pointed out not only the lack of practical help, but perhaps more importantly, the presence of bias in education. He was deeply suspicious of the manipulation of minds by government or church. He went on to suggest that young men of the working classes might 'form themselves into Education Societies, or if they choose to call themselves so, Mutual Instruction Clubs'.

A month later the *Leeds Times* carried a letter, strongly endorsed by the editor, from the reforming journalist William Howitt (to whose short-lived but influential *Howitt's Journal* Smiles later became a regular contributor). In his letter Howitt enthused about the new 'People's Colleges' as

> the grandest and most triumphant step yet made in this glorious cause [popular education]. Imagine a people *thus* educated; a people who have paid for their own education; who have devoted the few hours of their leisure to acquire it ... They will look back ... on no party tools who have been insidiously warping their spirits and feelings to the wishes of a sect or a class ... What an honest, healthy, unconquerable, incorruptible sentiment must fill and fortify such men ... and when such men have grown to a population! – what a magnificent object of contemplation![1]

The ideas which had worked William Howitt into such a state of excitement were part of a spreading interest in 'self education'. A correspondent in the *Leeds Times* a week later described how

> a few operatives in Lockwood, resolved on self-improvement, commenced a mutual improvement society ... they have lately been able to establish a library, which now contains 150 volumes [compared with the 4,000 in Leeds Mechanics' Institute library], besides about 30 class books. The classes at present established are – Reading, Writing, Arithmetic and Grammar.

Similar groups were appearing in many other towns at the same time. Smiles's young men of humble rank, seated round the boarded hut in Leeds protecting their slates from the rain, were not alone. And just as they came to be evoked in *Self-Help*, they were described, fifteen years before that book was published, by the chairman at the meeting to mark the first anniversary of the Leeds Mutual Improvement Society, held in their room in St Peter's Square Leeds on 19 March 1845. Mr Jackson, the meeting's chairman, described how they had at first 'assembled in the house occupied by the mother of one of the members, then moved (foretaste of *Self-Help*) to the garden house at the top of Richmond Hill.'[2] The numbers grew so fast that after six months they had to find a larger room, 'the one now occupied'.

This 1845 account gives a wonderful sense of grass roots energy, of the purity of small means and the potency of small beginnings. The principal classes were 'chemical and elementary'. Pupils in elementary class were taught reading, writing and arithmetic. Charges varied from one half-penny to two pence per week. Outside teachers (including Smiles, who had for some months been giving lessons to a group meeting in Zion school) gave their time free, and all the money paid by pupils ('now almost a hundred') went towards books and furniture. 'All this must,' the chairman told the meeting, 'be regarded as gratifying proof of success.' He then handed over to Dr Smiles for the evening's main address.

Of the hundreds of talks, speeches, lectures and contributions to meetings that Smiles made during his twenty years in Leeds, this was the one which most explicitly represented a Smiles manifesto and a re-direction of his energy. The scene was very different from the great room filled by carefully-dressed ladies and gentlemen at the Music Hall, where soirées of the Leeds Mechanics' Institution and Literary Society often took place. On this night candles flickered against the bleak walls of a space in an abandoned cholera hospital. The rows of young men facing him seated on their wooden benches, of the humblest rank and humbly, but no doubt 'respectably' dressed, didn't represent the prosperous classes of Leeds. But they did, Smiles believed, represent the true wealth of the country. He talked directly to them, urging them with real force to understand their own value and to recognise the nature of their opportunity. This address was the counterpart to his 1842 lecture on the *Diffusion of Political Knowledge*. That had been addressed to those who might influence the education of the poor – a plea for help for them. This was addressed to the poor themselves – a declaration of how they might help themselves.

The idea of self-education and mutual improvement was not, as we have observed, new, or confined to this group in Leeds. But that evening Smiles used the idea to focus on more than the lack of means for the education of the working classes. He returned to his 1842 warning against government or church 'stereotyping the national intellect', unrolling a graphic picture of what he saw as the danger of the wrong sort of education, delivered for the wrong reasons – a conspiracy by the powerful to use education as a corral rather than a gate to freedom.

He returned to his earlier warning against government or church 'stereotyping the national intellect'. He would deplore, he told his audience,

> the day that saw the young mind of England put in the leading strings of any ascendant sect or party in church or state. I should fear that then education would be employed as a kind of stereotyping process – to mould the public mind ... to produce a Lethe-like torpor and a non-resistant compliance with the demands, as it might be, of an arbitrary power.

Smiles's support for the idea of self-education was hardly surprising, but his enthusiasm for his listeners' particular approach was delivered that night with a new passion. Their mutual improvement society was, he said,

> one of the most gratifying signs of social progress ... that men who have worked a hard day's work should come together, night after night, – to seek instruction – to gather knowledge – to cultivate each others' minds – to expand their intelligent gaze – to find pleasure in science, literature, and art – is a most delightful and gratifying sight – more gratifying to me than all the other signs of development and progress in the age we live in.

And more than this, his careful laying-out of a philosophy for such education underlined both his growing disillusion with 'politics' as a way of achieving progress and his reservations about merely 'useful' education, as advocated by such movements as The Society for the Diffusion of Useful Knowledge. Poor mechanics, he had written in the *Leeds Times* in 1839, 'scarcely needed such lessons in economy: poverty has been, in this respect, a better (as well as a more bitter) teacher than the Society for the Diffusion of Useful Knowledge'.[3]

In his 1845 lecture Smiles made no reference to the political movements – Corn Law abolition and extended suffrage – which he had previously advocated as essential precursors to better education. *No* government, he now suggested, should be trusted with the education of the people, for factions, especially the church, would distort it to their own ends.

> Should we ever obtain a National System of Education it must be under the control of *the people*, and not of the government ... free and open to all,

and not exclusive and sectarian ... For what is the great worth and value of education? Is it merely to read, write, and cast accounts? To settle down in a state of contented stupidity? ... never to venture out of the beaten tracks prescribed by the schoolmaster? No! no! ... It is the freedom of the mind – mental self-dependence – the free and unshackled use of the human faculties – earnest self culture and development, so that the whole nature of man becomes stronger, better, freer, happier ... If education has not given men greater power to overcome wrong, to resist evil, to work out good, to unfold the highest elements of character, and to liberate the intellect and the conscience, I say that Education has failed of its great purpose ... The mind that passively submits to the will of others ... that cowers to fashion and habit, and has no will of its own – that has resigned its individuality, this is not an educated, but a trammelled and degraded mind ... It is not governments then, but THE PEOPLE, who must educate the people.[4]

Victorians gorged themselves on speeches and speechifying. Sermons on Sundays routinely lasted for over an hour. One of the peoples' favourite recreations was to listen to each other talking from platforms. So Smiles's address to the Leeds Mutual Improvement Society, at over six thousand words, would not have dismayed his audience by its length. It was, according to a contemporary newspaper report, 'throughout loudly applauded'.

This report was, of course, in the *Leeds Times*, where Smiles still held the title of Editor. The other Leeds papers ignored it – the *Leeds Intelligencer* because it always ignored the radical 'Mr Miles', the *Leeds Mercury* perhaps because Smiles's educational agenda, as became apparent later, diverged significantly from the policy of the Baineses. But this lecture was talked about throughout the district, and soon requests came in for repeat performances, to the Mechanics' Institution at Woodhouse, at Thirsk, even to a working men's group at Leeds Roman Catholic Church.

In the following months Smiles gave versions of the first lecture at meetings all over the West Riding, extending and adapting it from week to week. He enjoyed the reaction, the direct contact with young working people, the light in their eyes as they listened, their spontaneous response. The chemistry was exciting, energising. It seemed to confirm his faith in the value and potential of every individual, his rejection of workers as a commodity, his vision of man's essential nobility, regardless of place in the world's hierarchy:

> there is a greatness in him, more than in the whole material creation beside. The elements of nobility are in him – far above the titled nobility of man's creation. Manhood is greater than Kingship; and the name of Man is greater than that of King or any other of earthly dignitaries.

The key to this nobility was Education, properly understood – something immensely richer than a path to mere worldly success:

> the highest object of Education is *progress*, and that Education is only to be valued in so far as it makes a man wiser, better and happier ... that knowledge is the best and the noblest, which quickens the mind in the pursuit of truth, supplies strength for renewed exertions, and impels the intellect onwards in its majestic career.

But it was not all majesty. The grit was at least as important:

> To achieve progress it is important that each individual should be *industrious* and persevering with himself. Every intelligent man must be mainly self-educated, and that portion of his education which he gives to himself is by far the most valuable. The main use of instruction in schools, and in societies such as this, is to enable men to become their own teachers. It is to give them the means of working out their own development. They are helped to help themselves.

The foundation stone, not just for *Self-Help* but for all the Smiles books, was well and truly laid in this address – and industry, perseverance and self-reliance were its aggregate. He hammered home the point, not just in principle, but in the heart-warming stories of real people. Smiles had realised the power of biography to make a point. He chose his subjects with skill, giving example after example – Arkwright the barber, Brindley the day-labourer, Smeaton the watchmaker, George Stephenson the Newcastle pit-boy ... Realising how their stories resonated with his audience, stories of men like themselves, he extended the list as his series of talks rolled out across the country. All the examples he used in the 1845 lectures reappeared, with others, in *Self-Help,* fifteen years later. He made notes about many more: 'I kept adding to the examples,' he wrote later, 'and entered into correspondence with men of influence and action. Some of my best illustrations were obtained in this way; and I endeavoured to work them up into a sort of continuous narrative.'[5]

In the language and style Smiles used in his address, in the targets he chose to attack, and the exemplars he chose to hold up, he sensed that he had found that most intoxicating of visions for a speaker or writer – a direct connection with his audience. The content of the lectures, and of the pamphlet that grew from them, with its deeply unoriginal title, *The Education of the Working Classes*, held little that was new in the way of educational theory. Henry Brougham, an eloquent advocate of mass education, had been a driving force in the spread of Mechanics' Institutes twenty years earlier and had already proposed many of the ideas Smiles now put forward. 'It is no doubt manifest,' Brougham had said to a gathering in Glasgow in 1836, 'that the people themselves must be the great agents in accomplishing the work of their own instruction.' In his 1825 pamphlet Brougham had told the working classes that

> this is the time when by a great effort they may secure the inestimable blessing of great knowledge ... what higher achievement did the most sublime philosophy ever aspire after than to elevate the views and refine the character of the great mass of mankind ... their skill will thereby be increased, their taste improved, their character exalted, and their happiness augmented.

As a twentieth-century commentator observed, 'By 1839 ... such phrases had already achieved the status of cultural clichés.'[6] Smiles had questioned the effectiveness of mechanics' institutes back in 1839, when he wrote of 'the Mechanics' Institutes set in operation some years ago by Dr Birkbeck, Lord Brougham, Dr Lardner and others ... dragging out a painful and melancholy existence'.[7] He blamed this on their middle-class perspective. They had 'been formed on too narrow a basis, and have failed in attracting the class for whose improvement they were originally intended ... It yet remains for the working classes to take the matter into their own hands.'

In fact much of the ground covered in Smiles's 1845 lecture – an

extremely wide ground – had in one way and another already been
covered by Brougham and the earlier reformers. What they lacked was
not the substance but the presentation. What Smiles had discovered was
the voice, and the instinct for story-telling – the realisation that the real
lives of real people were the most potent teachers of all. The cultural
clichés may have been echoed, but they had found a new expression, and
Smiles had found a new career, even if for a time he was forced into a
diversion.

Smiles gave his talk to the men at the Leeds Mutual Improvement
Society on 19 March 1845. Sarah Anne and their seven-month-old
daughter Janet were by then settled in the Wellington Street house. As
he said, 'My wife and I were altogether united through life. I obtained a
cheerful and affectionate companion, and I hope that she obtained |a
devoted and equally affectionate husband.' The affection and devotion
were beginning to clash with lecturing, editing, writing and doctoring,
and the costs of family life were beginning to exceed the patchy income
from Dr Smiles's patchy career.

The medical practice depended on being in the town centre, hence the
original move to Wellington Street. But it was now apparent that this
raucous area, surrounded by the Court House and prison, the building
work on the new railway station, and the clanging of the Cloth House
bell, was, in the honoured phrase, no place to bring up a family. Besides,
it was on the bank of the river Aire which, colourful though it may have
been, was by now filthy with a mix of industrial waste and sewage – a
cholera threat that Smiles, remembering his father's death, must have
been especially sensitive to (in the event, a cholera epidemic in 1849
caused over two thousand deaths in Leeds). Every practical consideration, in fact, suggested that Samuel Smiles, aged thirty-two, and a father,
needed to find work that would allow him to spend more time with his
family and provide enough money to allow him to move them to a more
congenial area.

That is one argument for the change that happened. The other is that
the writer in Smiles needed the full-time day job and steady income
that would allow him to go on writing in his spare time. The man whose
slogan might have been 'Persevere!', seemed to feel later that all this
change needed an apology, or at least a rationalisation:

I hope the reader does not think that I was too fond of making changes. I could not help it. I had tried to make a living by physic, but failed. I tried newspaper editing; and though it kept me, I found it would not maintain a wife and family. I tried book-writing, and failed there too, so far as income was concerned. Another change was therefore necessary.[8]

And so, 'now having a wife and family to support, I ... applied for the position of assistant secretary to the Leeds and Thirsk railway'. But a doctor, a journalist, a political activist – is this the perfect CV for a corporate administrator? The directors of the Leeds and Thirsk Railway obviously knew their man. Most of them, including Henry Marshall of the great Marshall manufacturing company, and Edward Baines senior, were men Smiles had dined with, addressed meetings with, served on committees with, campaigning on the side of new industry against old landed property, opposing the Corn laws, providing assistance for the poor. They were from the Leeds powerbase of prudent radicals and radical Whigs – solid, nonconformist businessmen, often Unitarians, quite unconcerned by the doctor-journalist's more extreme pronounce-ments. If Samuel Smiles had seemed at times to flirt with republicanism (in early editorials he had praised 'transition from despotism to repub-licanism'),[9] even with Chartism, or to advocate working-class control of education, these were surely just signs of the robust free-thinking on which they had all been raised. All in all, they could see Smiles as a sound man.

Besides, at that time the railway industry was growing so fast that experienced staff were thin on the ground. In Smiles the directors of the Leeds and Thirsk had a man they knew to be hard-working, honest and unusually articulate – a priceless asset in a new business where success so often depended on powers of negotiation and persuasion. They autho-rised their Secretary, Mr Fenton, to invite Smiles to apply for the position of Assistant Secretary and, at the end of 1845, as he passed his thirty-third birthday, he was duly appointed. Fenton himself moved to another job a few months later, allowing Smiles to step up to the Secretary's role.

Accepting the job with the railway company was, in many respects, the hinge in Smiles's career. The idealistic twenty-three-year-old who had arrived in Leeds ten years earlier had evolved into a more prudent, worldly-wise man, a family man who recognised the problem of the pram in the hall[10] but decided, instead of rebelling against it, to adapt his career to it. For the next twenty-five years Samuel Smiles led a tightly disciplined two-part life – as a conscientious company employee in the company's time, as a writer, thinker and campaigner in his own. The result was a sort of triumph, and almost a tragedy.

IO

Twin Tracks

I N THE ROLE of full-time railway executive Smiles now moved his family to their new home in Woodhouse Cliffe, a hamlet on the greener, higher side of Leeds. Beyond lay the quiet village of Headingley, home to the Marshalls, the Stansfields and other luminaries of Leeds business society. The move in their direction hardly made Smiles a member of their social group, but it did signal a change in his view of how he hoped his family might live. This was becoming more significant because on 24 January 1846 Sarah Anne gave birth to their first son, William Holmes Smiles.

Each morning Smiles reported to the offices of the Leeds and Thirsk Railway Company at 5 South Parade where, under the supervision of Mr Fenton, he learned the duties of a company secretary – hardly the most stimulating occupation after life as a newspaper editor. But the choice had been conscious. He was now, in his own words, free from the turmoil of politics, with his evenings his own, to be spent with his family in 'reading and quiet thinking'.

At the railway company office, as he had done in his early weeks at the *Leeds Times*, he learned the basic needs of the work quickly, which was just as well. A few months later Fenton retired and Smiles became company secretary, with full responsibility to the Directors and Share-holders not only for keeping proper records of Company affairs, but also for the great matrix of legal and statuary obligations involved in opening any new stretch of railway line. For every section planned, and for its financing, a separate parliamentary committee resolution was needed.

For every formal meeting an advertisement had to be placed in the local press. For every transaction or resolution of directors or shareholders a full account had to be recorded. This seems like tedious stuff. Smiles described it as regular plodding business, for which, with faux modesty, he claimed to have some talent: 'It was steady, routine work, requiring application, judgment, power of organisation, and trustworthiness. In none of these, I hope, was I found wanting.'[1]

But this bureaucratic scene belies the brutal drama of creating a part of Britain's first railway system. In fact, Smiles had entered a world of high-risk investors and buccaneering entrepreneurs who were prepared to drive through their plans regardless of opposition from either commercial adversaries or the forces of nature. In the case of the Leeds and Thirsk Railway Company, the obstacles on both fronts were peculiarly intimidating.

Their proposed line, with its declared objective of connecting Leeds with the northern ports and with Scotland, was in direct conflict with the interests of the most ruthless railway baron of his time, George Hudson, chairman of the Great Northern Railway and associate of George Stephenson. By 1844 Hudson had built up a network of more than a thousand miles of line, dominating the areas where the new Leeds and Thirsk planned to operate. Breaking the Hudson monopoly, and freeing Leeds from dependency on his lines, was a principal objective of Henry Marshall, chairman of the new company, of Edward Baines senior, main spokesman for the company at Westminster, and their co-directors.

Hudson was not their only problem. Like a scene from George Eliot's *Middlemarch*, the railway had to deal with objections from the people and the landowners in the countryside where the line would go. Money, as ever, had to be the promoters' main response. In just one of many cases taken against the company, Lord Cardigan claimed in May 1845 that the proposed line would damage his land and harm his tenants. The matter was settled by compensation of £10,000.[2]

Though men like George Hudson and Lord Cardigan tried to thwart or exploit the Leeds railway adventure, their opposition was dwarfed by the landscape itself. The new railway, to follow its preferred route, would have to go over, round or through a high ridge between the rivers Aire and Wharfe at Bramhope, and across the valleys on either side. In the spirit of the time, through-and-over was the only acceptable option, whatever it took. It took over two miles of tunnelling and the building of five great viaducts spanning the valleys.

The records of the Leeds and Thirsk Railway from the time are thick with references to calls on the shareholders and scripholders for more money or permission to increase borrowings, and to Parliament for the right to raise more funds, and more funds, and yet more funds.

These records, signed by 'Samuel Smiles, Secretary',[3] and no doubt drafted by him, seem calm and considered, even romantic in places, conjuring a vision of Leeds joined to gleaming harbours on the northern coast, and on across the sea to the distant Baltic. Opposition is dealt with lightly: 'Although the Great North of England Company, or other parties having management of that line, have strongly opposed us, we have reason to believe that they will give reasonable facilities to our traffic.' In fact George Hudson acted as though he had nothing to fear, gloating over his competitor's problems at the Bramhope tunnel and declaring that they would bankrupt the Company.

In Leeds the impression of calm was sustained. George Grainger,[4] Chief Engineer on the project, advised the proprietors on 28 February 1846 that

> the Leeds contract and Bramhope contract have been let to James Bray, the works on the latter being the heaviest and most important on the line, were commenced in the month of November last year, and are being prosecuted by him with great energy. The shafts required for the tunnel have all been commenced ... the driftway is in progress, and is being carried on night and day, three sets of men being employed.[5]

In May that year, to further steady shareholder nerves, Smiles minuted a report reassuring them that

> considerable progress has already been made with some of the heaviest works. We say this much in order to satisfy the minds of those share-holders as may have been alarmed by the false and altogether unfounded reports industriously circulated by interested parties, hostile to this line of the railway.

In fact these 'heaviest works' involved almost two and a half thousand men, working in the dark and damp, forcing a way through the Bramhope ridge for over two miles using picks, shovels, and their bare hands. All big infrastructure projects have a tendency to take longer than planned and cost more than expected. The Bramhope tunnel works dragged on for five years; the cost approved in 1845 of £800,000 rose by completion in 1849 to £2,150,313.[6]

Most railway work in the nineteenth century was nasty, brutish and badly paid. Henry Mayhew recorded an old navvy telling him of his days working on the Manchester and Liverpool line, sometimes digging, sometimes shovelling, paid 2/6 to 3/6 a day, forced by the company to rent a company house, to shop in a company shop (the notorious tommy-shops) to drink over-priced company beer, and often suffer the loss of his wages to unscrupulous sub-contractors.

There is no evidence of this sort of exploitation among the Leeds and Thirsk workforce. Mayhew's informant told him of working on the new lines in Lancashire and Yorkshire, 'and we did much better when our pay increased ... and there were no tommy-shops that summer, for the company wouldn't have them on that line'.[7]

By some contemporary standards the Leeds and Thirsk Railway Company may have been enlightened employers. But the Bramhope tunnel and its associated works involved death, injury and exploitation by sub-contractors. Sometimes workers were driven to sue for unpaid wages. Usually they lost. When they were injured, even killed at work, little attention was paid. When John Taylor fell to his death from the bucket lifting him up a shaft after he had placed a charge of gun-powder, the incident merited just three lines in the *Leeds Times*.[8] When a nineteen-year-old labourer was killed by a stone falling seventy feet down a shaft, the inquest found 'that death was accelerated by his own incompetence'.[9]

These were works that took five years and involved nearly two and a half thousand men – navvies, quarrymen, stonemasons, carpenters, as well as four hundred horses. A population of over three thousand, including families, lived for these years in two hundred wooden bothies in a field opposite Bramhope cemetery, or in a hundred other bothies strung along the line. Many were poor Irish immigrants, unemployed farm labourers from as far away as East Anglia and Scotland, and weavers thrown out of work by the factory slump. Navvies were paid one pound ten shillings for a seven-day week, working a twelve-hour day. They were lowered down shafts, deep into the floor of the tunnel, to work in dark and often water-logged ground. Estimates suggest that one-and-a-half billion gallons of water had to be pumped out during construction. The number of men injured is unrecorded. A plaque near the site was later erected 'as a memorial at the expense of James Bray Esq, and the Agents, sub-contractors and workmen employed there, in memory of the unfortunate men who lost their lives while engaged in the construction of the Brampton tunnel of the Leeds and Thirsk Railway'.[10] Twenty-four were thus remembered. The only record of welfare for the workers was a motion 'read by Dr Smiles, Secretary: That the sum of one hundred pounds be devoted for the religious instruction of the workmen along the Leeds and Thirsk Railway.'

It is hard to believe that Smiles himself was more concerned with the well-being of the men's souls than of their bodies, but his job demanded a dispassionate response. Though his work was at his desk in South Parade rather than in the dark shafts of Bramhope, it makes uncomfortable reading to see this apparent detachment by a man who had been writing for the last eight years as the workers' friend and a self-described radical.

Deserter or hypocrite? Neither is necessarily true. Smiles had already demonstrated his moral dilemma between the human benefits of progress and its human cost. He was certainly capable of feeling concern for workers' well-being (and as remarked, the Leeds and Thirsk was relatively enlightened in this respect) and at the same time of being excited by the conquest of an apparently immovable obstacle like the Bramhope ridge. He judged health and safety issues through the eyes of his own time.

Smiles had a pattern for his life in these years. He thought of himself as someone whose calling was 'literature' and whose duty was 'business'. He had little patience with the either-or school of thought: 'It is a favourite dogma of some,' he declared,

> that he who courts the muses or indulges in composition, must necessarily be unfitted for the practical business of life ... Some of the most successful men in business at the present day, are men who wield the pen in the intervals of their daily occupations.[11]

To succeed, the writer must be a Smiles man: 'Generally you will find the successful literary man a person of industry, application, steadiness, and sobriety.'[12] In this self-image he pursued his career in the Leeds and Thirsk Railway while at the same time taking every opportunity to sustain his still fragile career as a writer.

A set of recurring ideas and attitudes had dominated Smiles's previous work, from *Physical Education* to his articles in the *Leeds Times* and his 1845 pamphlet, *The Education of the Working Classes*. Smiles was a radical, in an apolitical sense, in his impatience with the status quo and in his belief in the possibility of progress, not by any cosmic force or by élite leadership, in the Carlyle mould, but through the innate possibility for progress in each man and woman. It was, in the Smiles view, the equal right of each to be accorded this possibility. Equally it was their responsibility not to ignore or misuse it. The original sin, and the deadliest, was idleness of spirit. From it all, others sprang.

Smiles styled himself a 'literary man', because he valued literature as the art of communicating useful and morally robust ideas. These were the ideas he wanted to communicate. He would have deplored Sam Goldwyn's remark that 'messages should be delivered by Western Union'.[13] Smiles's devotion to literature was a devotion to delivering messages, and though the context often changed, the message stayed essentially the same. While he settled in to his job with the Leeds and Thirsk Railway he found his next writing opportunity through his involvement with the benefits society movement, and specifically with the Society of Oddfellows.

The Oddfellows had started in 1810, when a group of twenty-seven working men in Manchester got together to form a society to do something about the financial distress caused to families by injury, illness or death. Every member of the society would contribute a small amount weekly to a general fund which they could then call on for help when disaster struck. It was a cooperative assurance society which developed with some of the trappings of a medieval guild. Later supporters from the wealthier classes, initially put off by the Oddfellows' apparently secretive rites and ceremonies, expressed surprise when they discovered that the Society's work was so practical. By 1845, when Smiles encountered it, the Society had spread across England, and internationally,

with 300,000 members, invested capital of £720,000, and support
from peers, Members of Parliament and wealthy men and women of all
backgrounds.[14]

The ethos of the Oddfellows was of pride in their equality and
independence. Members benefited as a right, when the need arose. This
was not a handout but a hand-back. Moreover, they allowed 'no allusion
to politics and no religious disputes ... Whilst they exhorted piety they
had no companionship with sects.' The appeal of such an organisation
to Smiles was irresistible.

On 21 December 1846 the Leeds District (membership 5,725) of the
Manchester Unity of Oddfellows held a grand soirée in the Leeds Music
Hall.[15] Proceedings, in true Yorkshire fashion, started with tea, 'and when
the attack upon the edibles commenced, there was not a vacant seat to
be found'. Cups away and crumbs swept from the tables, speeches began.
Among the distinguished speakers were William Beckett, a Leeds MP,
George Goodman, ex-Mayor of Leeds, and Dr Samuel Smiles. The
first speakers referred to the purposes of the Society – 'for a body of
individuals to relieve each other in sickness and distress' – praised it for
its rich history and spectacular growth, and paid tribute to eminent supporters like the Marchioness of Hertford, Lady Gordon, and Lord de
Grey. When Smiles's turn came he went, after the mandatory spoonful
of praise, straight to his message:

> there was a lesson of self-respect and self-help in this conduct ... men must,
> to a great degree be their own elevators ... not cast like straws on the strand
> of time, merely to mark the direction of the current, but each of them had
> the powers to will, to do, to overcome difficulties, to achieve progress, to
> improve their condition, however adverse that might be.

The force of Smiles's contribution to this meeting prompted his old
adversary, Edward Baines of the *Leeds Mercury*, to commission him to
write and report in that paper on the benefit society movement. Smiles's
enthusiasm for the ideals of the Oddfellows eventually led to his taking
on the editorship of the quarterly magazine of the Grand United Order
of Oddfellows, published in Leeds. This re-entry into published work
was important to Smiles.

*

Through the late 1840s and early 1850s his twin track career achieved a delicate balance. His enthusiasm had always been for the modern and progressive, the possibility of a better world. He saw practical, mechanical enterprise as one part of the answer, moral and intellectual enterprise as the other. His railway job kept him in touch with the first, his occasional journalistic work with the second. But though the idea of the 'man of business wielding the pen' may have been attractive to him, Smiles was always a writer before anything else.

At that time a magazine press was emerging in London inspired by the same ideas, and supported by some of the same people, as the *Monthly Repository* of the 1830s. Originally a Unitarian magazine, the *Monthly Repository* had by 1845 come under the editorship of W J Fox and then of Leigh Hunt. Though under Fox the magazine had moved from a religious to a secular agenda, the spirit of Unitarianism – of 'prioritising reason and toleration over tradition'[16]– was still a powerful influence. Fox's *Monthly Repository* was the meeting place of two sympathetic ideas, Unitarianism and utilitarianism, and of writers sympathetic to both.

This circle of reforming intellectuals, including Southwood Smith, John Bowring, Mary Leman Gillies, Guiseppe Mazzini, and William Howitt – many of whom Smiles had encountered in London on his way back from Leyden ten years earlier – were now engaged with a new publication, the *People's Journal*. A magazine involving them would be a natural home for Samuel Smiles. In the past he had sat at their feet; now he was an experienced newspaper editor with a reforming reputation who would be welcomed to their circle. It is likely that during visits to London on the business of the Leeds and Thirsk Railway, Smiles re-established contact At the time of his high profile support for the Working Men's Mutual Improvement Society he had had some contact with William Howitt, now editor of the *People's Journal*.

Soon Smiles was writing regularly for the magazine. His first articles in the *People's Journal* were prompted by his work with the Society of Oddfellows, and discussed the importance of benefit societies. He went on during 1846 to write about a wide range of topics, from 'Factory Women' to 'Popular Amusements and Recreation', but his instinct that exemplars were the best teachers moved him more and more towards the genre that was to make his name, biography. Among his last contributions to the *People's Journal* were short biographical pieces on Richard Cobden and St Vincent de Paul.

When Howitt parted company with its co-owner John Saunders, to start his own *Howitt's Journal of Literature and Popular Progress,* Smiles followed him. In the larger world of London publishing, the Saunders-Howitt split was a minor scandal, but for their idealistically-minded contributors it created the sort of divided loyalties that follow a marriage break-up. Like Smiles, most of those he knew best stayed with Howitt, now co-editing *Howitt's Journal* with his wife Mary. 'Assisted by Samuel

3 Mary Howitt: 'We sought in the pages of Howitt's journal to urge the working classes to be their own benefactors...'
(The Mary Evans Picture Library)

Smiles, a most able defender of the rights of industry and the benefits of self-culture and other gifted and popular writers,' wrote Mary Howitt, 'we sought in the pages of Howitt's Journal, in an attractive form, to urge the labouring classes, by means of temperance, self-education and moral conduct, to be their own benefactors.'[17] These writers helped to make Howitt's new magazine a publication to watch (if not necessarily a commercial success).[18] He liked to include in each issue a list of contributors, declaring that 'The Editors are happy to announce that they have secured the assistance of the following eminent writers ...' The list would include Dr Bowring, E Elliott, Mary Gillies, Leigh Hunt, Douglas Jerrold, Joseph Mazzini ... and others later more famous: 'Hans Christian Andersen of Copenhagen ... J Whittier, American poet' and of course 'Dr Smiles (Leeds)'.

In the new publication Smiles's contributions were faithful to the Howitt agenda. In 1847, in the first issue, he provided a piece on one of his favourite subjects: free public libraries. He was able to use the model of his old hero Samuel Browne of Haddington and the itinerating libraries, to illustrate their feasibility. The article provided a platform for his educational theories: 'The most important part of education has to come when school days are over ... but knowledge itself has yet to be gained ... opinion matured, morals formed, character strengthened, and education perfected in a noble and manly character.'[19]

Then the trajectory towards biography was resumed. For his first biographical piece Smiles chose a most unlikely subject, the French novelist George Sand. In Victorian Britain French novels were equated with dirty books, though at this time the law was less watchful than it became following Lord Campbell's 1857 Obscene Publications Act.[20] Later in the century Henry Vizetelly, publisher of Zola's work in English translation, was jailed for outraging public decency. Smiles himself was outraged by what he described as the Ultra-Tory stigmatisation of George Sand's work. The *Quarterly Review* had described it as an 'infamous cargo'. This assault, Smiles argued, was because Sand had identified herself with the French ultra-Democratic party, though she came from an aristocratic background.

Her crime was to have escaped from a cruel marriage of convenience, and to have written 'of that feeling or passion which forms the key to the social happiness of the great majority of human beings'. However insensitive her early works may have seemed to the English, 'for we are a marvellously moral people, great worshippers of propriety', Smiles praised her later works for their 'faith in the true and earnest devotion to the cause of human progress'. This was the real message of Smiles's mini-biography[21] – the rising of Amantine-Lucile-Aurore Dupin (Sand's original name) above her plight, but more significantly, above her aristocratic origins, to become a promoter of 'the co-operative efforts among working classes for the improvement of their general condition'. She would make labour 'the commander instead of the slave of the world. She honestly and eloquently preaches the great gospel of work'.

Smiles closed his article by identifying himself with Sand/Dupin's moral position: 'Good men are the only men I would esteem', she pronounced '... and whom I would register in the calendar of human greatness ... Those lofty men who build for their glory, and not for our happiness ... I disown them; I erase them from my tablet; I inscribe our curé in the place of Napoleon.'[22]

Then Smiles moved on to more predictable subjects, in a series on 'Poets of the People', which ran in *Howitt's Journal* during 1847 and 1848. 'Poets of the People' was in itself almost a mini-self-help thesis, with its themes of triumph over poverty by self-belief and perseverence, and its placing of personal achievement above inherited status. Smiles's first Poet, touchingly, was his predecessor at the *Leeds Times*, Robert Nicoll, in whose life Smiles surely saw some self-image. Nicoll demonstrated that 'intellect is of no class, but even in abodes of deepest poverty there are warm hearts and noble minds... Every spare moment of his time was devoted to self-improvement.' He read Milton, Locke, Bentham, and with special attention, Smith's *Wealth of Nations*. 'He declared his radicalism, his resolution was to 'stand by the order, that of the many'.'

Other subjects included Samuel Barber, 'a hand-loom weaver of Lancashire, a true specimen of the poet of the working classes'. Again there is that hint of mirroring – 'His mother, like the mothers of most men of strength of character, was a remarkable woman' – and of foreshadowing his own approach to biography – 'Barber's 'Life of a Radical' gives a greater insight into the life and political condition of the English people in recent times, than all the lives of political leaders that we know of put together.' There could hardly be a better summary of the Smiles creed than the postscript to Barber's volume of poems with which Smiles ended his article: 'The salvation of a people must come at last from their own *hands* and *hearts*.'

Smiles chose Victor Hugo as another Poet of the People, demonstrating that a poet could be of the people without necessarily being from the people. With Victor Hugo, as with George Sand, Smiles portrayed the possibility of conversion. Though Hugo had a noble mother, 'in the course of numerous poetics and other works ... he has gradually abandoned the Royalist ground, and rested not, till he had reached the opposite extreme'. Smiles used the Hugo piece to mock men 'schooled in the "practical" business of money-making. For this the smallest modicum of brains, as everyone knows, is sufficient.' Smiles admired the ideals of the French republicans. He liked to use them to scorn the English aristocratic system: 'The men who have taken the lead in

the great social system of the French people ... are not born legislators –
they have not been destined from the cradle to be the wearers of coronets
and the leviers of taxes.'

Smiles's acceptance by the London circle of dissenting intellectual
journalism was important to him, not just for its access to publication,
but for its enrichment of his personal life. The bond these people felt in
pursuit of a common ideal gave them a sense of familial comradeship.
In 1847 the Howitts came to Leeds to support one of Smiles's favourite
causes, the Leeds Redemption Society. William Howitt took the chair at
a soirée in the Music Hall. He read letters from others in the group –
W J Fox, Douglas Jerrold, Mazzini. About five hundred attended, 'a fair
proportion female' according to the *Leeds Times*, with Mary Howitt and
Sarah Anne Smiles no doubt included. Young Mrs Smiles, with three
children to look after (Edith was born that year), and a husband who
spent all day at his office and every evening at his desk, must have been
especially at risk from that familiar Victorian condition, the woman's separate sphere. The Howitts and the Smiles's were to become lifelong
friends. The affection of Mary Howitt and involvement, however peri-
pheral, with a publishing world where women ranked equally with men,
was like some sort of escape for Sarah Anne, and gave considerable
satisfaction to Samuel. In fact Sarah Anne remained throughout her life
in the role of helpmeet, but the embrace of Mary Howitt, and soon of
other 'liberated' women, eased the dreadful sense of entrapment felt by
so many of her contemporaries.

William Howitt was a man of great commitment and energy, with that
Victorian capacity to turn out, seemingly without pause, thousands of
words on every idea or experience he encountered. But he was not a good
businessman, and just eighteen months after its launch *Howitt's Journal*
failed. William and Mary Howitt were to rise again, and the Howitt-
Smiles friendship was to survive. In the meantime another aspiring
magazine publisher, another woman of reforming zeal, had joined the
communion of saints, and she quickly adopted Samuel Smiles as her
mentor.

II

A Very Productive Quiet

SMILES MET Eliza Cook in unlikely circumstances. It started with Charlotte Cushman, a high-voltage American actress, who visited England in 1848 in a bid to burnish her American reputation with success on the London stage. Among her letters of introduction to London's liberal intellectual circle was a note to the Howitts. Through them she met, among others, Matilda Hays, part-time actress and writer who had translated some of George Sand's novels into English, and Sand's latest champion, Samuel Smiles.

The Cushman-Hays relationship has been chronicled as a 'Boston marriage' – one of those deeply sentimental friendships between women to which polite Victorian society turned a blind eye, on the premise that women were incapable of physical passion.[1] Elizabeth Barrett Browning wrote of Cushman: 'I understand she and Miss Hays have made vows of celibacy and eternal attachment to each other ... it is a female marriage.' Of the affair, Cushman's biographer has said that 'the two were living as romantic partners, off stage as well as on'.

Hays was not, however, Cushman's only conquest in England. She also became a close friend of the poet Eliza Cook. Cook was well known for her defence in her poems of the poor and the marginalised and was very much in sympathy with the views of the Howitt circle, where both Cushman and Cook were welcomed. Smiles in his *Autobiography* described Charlotte Cushman as his friend, one welcomed in his home. Some time in the summer of 1848 she visited the Smiles household in Leeds, accompanied by her friend, Eliza Cook. The two were warmly

4 Eliza Cook: 'would you be willing
to do any part of the matter for
the projected journal?'
(The Mary Evans Picture Library)

received, as the Howitts had been, by both Samuel and Sarah Anne. Cushman and Mrs Smiles became, according to Aileen Smiles, 'cronies'.[2]

Eliza Cook had made her name as a poet, free-thinking, compassionate, a torch bearer for the under-privileged. She was also a determined and ambitious woman – her ambition centred on starting a periodical for the promulgation of her ideas – a venture which she saw as 'a woman's declaration of independence'.[3] In all respects – her views on equality, privilege, and education, her spirit of independence, and her obvious commitment to hard work – Eliza Cook was likely to strike a chord with Samuel Smiles. So when she used her visit to his home to enthuse about her plans and pick his brains on publishing and editorial practice, he was happy to co-operate. Eliza had found a mentor; Sarah Anne had found more friends in her husband's writing life, and Samuel Smiles (post Howitt) had found a new outlet for his writing urge.

In the pre-launch phase of her new journal Eliza pressed and flattered, writing to him from Torquay on 14 October: 'would you be willing to do any part of the matter for the projected journal? ... I should like you to make your own choice as to the work ... will you also tell me what would be the duties of the "practical man".' Smiles had obviously talked to her about the Howitt-Saunders split and warned her about the problems of partnerships. 'I find plenty of men ready to share with me,' she told him 'but I am shy of 'Saunders', as you say ...'[4] Anyway she was determined to counter the belief that women were unequipped to succeed in the practical world outside the home. She could, she told Smiles, 'see no reason why a woman should not possess sufficient brains to be allowed to try her luck in the world, with kindly help, as well as these "almighty lords".'

Eliza and Charlotte continued their travels that month; it must have been a fine October. Eliza wrote again a few weeks later, from Greenhythe in Kent: 'My kindest regards to Mrs Smiles in which our "American Ally" heartily joins ... this coast is indeed beautiful and I am charmed with it ... I feel like a child full of happiness and wonder.' Eliza was an enthusiast, an optimist, undeterred by the challenge she had given herself. It was an attitude Smiles would have related to. Back in London in November, she wrote to him again, on a wave of excitement about her journal. She thanked him for his 'kind advice on all points of my project', wanting to share each step of the way – her hiring of a 'sub', 'who writes well and has had practical knowledge of all sorts in getting out a Journal!', and the help of her brother 'who is somewhat versed in business matters'. She asked for Smiles's advice on choice of publisher, on copyright, on the pricing of the magazine. On all questions she flattered him, constantly assuring him of the value of his advice: 'What do *you* say? ... You can decide this for me ... I need not say how highly I estimate your mind nor how proud I shall be of your name.' Most importantly she wanted him to write for the new publication, in which, she assured him, he would be in good company,

> for I find facilities of various kinds opening to me, and literary help that promises to make the thing respectable. May I trust to you my dear sir for three or four articles on any popular subjects that you may think best, by the end of January or middle of February, I leave it to your own choice and shall be truly obliged by your valuable services.[5]

This was the call he wanted, the call he needed, to energise, amid the greyness of his daily work, his ambition as a writer – the yang of literature to balance the yin of business.

The 'three or four articles' suggested by Eliza before the launch were punctually provided. They were the advance party of a horde. Over the life of *Eliza Cook's Journal*, published weekly for five years, Smiles contribute several hundred articles (most of them anonymously).[6] In his *Autobiography* he remarks that in the first year he sent her an article weekly, but the pace quickened until, 'in the fourth and fifth volumes of her journal I must have contributed at least half of the articles in each number'.[7]

Smiles was, as both Alex Tyrell and Adrian Jarvis[8] have pointed out, diligent in re-using his own material, so that *Eliza Cook* articles often included material recycled from previous work (new material from *Cook* was even more often resurrected for use in subsequent books). His first piece, given pride of place, immediately under the banner on the first page of the third issue – 19 May 1849 – offered readers of *Eliza Cook's Journal* his thoughts on Young Men's Improvement Societies. In this he also referred to his other most recent interest, the Oddfellows Societies. As before, he widened the argument beyond the movements' practical advantages, to their moral and spiritual power, but now with more rhetorical flourish: 'how much more glorious is it, without show, or noise, or barbarian clangour, to go quietly and perseveringly onward in the work of developing and improving human faculties, and opening them to great truths and principles ... every man possesses a free activity in himself; he has a power of *will*, an innate energy and means of action which enables him in a great measure to act the part of his own educator, his own emancipator' – the old message with a new shine seemed to be the new message.

Of course the sheer number of contributions Smiles made to *Eliza Cook's Journal* led inevitably to a wide range of topics – from the nature of a gentleman, or the role of competition, to phrenology, temperance, or the pleasures of travel (he even experimented with fiction). The same earnestness of purpose pervaded them all, the same lessons of individual responsibility and its role in responsibility towards others – and seeded throughout, the ingredients for the book that would make him a global celebrity. This had already been in gestation for some years, at least since his 1845 lectures on mutual improvement societies: 'I endeavoured to work them up into a sort of continuous narrative. Then I arrived at the title by which my assemblage of facts became afterwards known – *Self-Help*.'[9] Smiles's vast output for Eliza Cook, while at the same time applying himself to his duties in the Leeds and Thirsk Railway and to his family responsibilities, was his own form of self-help – and of duty, thrift, and character. It certainly added to his assemblage.

In his later writing life Smiles was able to find an idea for a book, devote himself to collecting the material, and move straight into creating the manuscript. By then he had a publisher and an audience in waiting. But in these Leeds years he was compelled to be a watcher and waiter, discovering ideas, trying them in journalistic form, and storing the seeds, perhaps subconsciously, for possible later development.

At the same time as Sarah Anne was entertaining Charlotte Cushman and Eliza Cook in Woodhouse Cliffe, the army in the dark finally broke through the last cruel yards of the Bramhope ridge. On 31 May 1849, welcomed by banners, bands, and cheering crowds along the line, the first locomotive passed through the tunnel. Smiles shared with the directors the excitement, and the sense of both triumph and relief. The completion of the tunnel, and of the towers and viaducts flanking it, had been a feat of will-power. It had started five years earlier, derided by George Hudson, stalled at every step by huge natural obstacles, blighted by injury and death, and as each year passed, increasingly questioned by shareholders and banks. The need to keep cajoling them for more money never stopped, but once the tunnel went through, the value was clear.

All of this had added immeasurably to Smiles's work. The documents to be prepared, resolutions for raising capital, visits to London to give evidence before Parliamentary sessions, all kept him fully engaged with railway business. Now the new line needed a new station, in Leeds town, which would be a joint enterprise between four companies. Smiles records in his *Autobiography* that 'at their first meeting they appointed me secretary of the "Leeds Central Station".' He was, one suspects, proud to accept the added burden.

Smiles was not prepared to be a grey functionary in an organisation. He was too curious, too exercised by possibilities, not to be excited and involved. He interested himself in details of engineering, in coupling screws and multi-tubular boilers. And he saw in action the qualities that he could applaud in men of business – 'It was a treat to observe the quickness with which they saw the points of a case, and the rapidity with which they did their work – brushing away everything that was immaterial and subsidiary.'[10] Smiles admired effectiveness, thrifty use of time, concentration on objectives, and humanity. He had seen these qualities in some of his teachers in Edinburgh. He had held them up to the young and the poor as ways out of their entrapment. Now he saw them in operation in his daily work. In his *Autobiography* he gives a fascinating sketch of his ideal man of business. Beckett Denison sat on the board for the development of Leeds Central Station.

> When he was there he was always appointed to preside. He made an excellent chairman. He kept discussions closely to the point, allowed no gossip to interfere, saw that the heads of the minutes taken were accurate; and when the business was dispatched ... he was as cheerful and gossipy as the rest. It was like a breath of fresh air to get Beckett Denison to appear among us. He was a fine, tall, jolly man – full of fun; and yet an excellent man of business.

In much of his own correspondence, and in the recorded impressions he made on contemporaries, Smiles, too, seems to have had much of that amiable nature.

By the summer of 1849, with the completion of the great tunnel, a renewed air of expectancy pervaded the Leeds office. The vision of a rail network spreading across the north-east, to the coalfields of Newcastle and those magical ports on the coast, at last seemed a reality. And not just trade, but people, would be freed by the extension of the railway. Smiles felt part of it, shared the excitement, and wanted to convey this to the readers of *Eliza Cook's Journal*.

In much the same way as enthusiasts talk in the twenty-first century of the unifying power of the internet, of its social and democratising influence, so Smiles enthused about the transformative power of the railways: 'They have made of England and Scotland, as it were, one large city, with green fields, hills and dales, rivers and lakes, stretched out in their midst ... serving to unite mind and matter, and to draw the ends of the earth together.'[11] He conjured up a picture, rather like the railway posters of the nineteen twenties and thirties, of a beautiful life opened up for everyone: 'wholesome exercise and enjoyment ... bringing the populations of crowded towns in touch with the healthful force of nature, where they may breathe the breath of a new moral life, and give free play to the higher feelings of their inner being'.

Faced with the reality of black towns and primitive villages, this was a cry of hope, that the railways might ride to the salvation of both, of 'how the natural and the cultivated may become one; how the benefits of town and country are to be combined, how the city may be rescued from its squalor, and field and forest from their ignorance'. Smiles had come a dozen years earlier from the smiling country of East Lothian, and his quiet walks through Holland and Germany, into the heart of England's industrial adventure. The change had shocked and excited him, and forced him to confront a moral dilemma, between the price of progress and the price of denying it. Convinced of the ultimate virtue of progress, Smiles attempted a balancing act between idealism and pragmatism. The future *could* be victimless, if only the potential victims could be shown how.

And so he shared, at least for the time being, Eliza Cook's optimism, expressed in her remarks to her readers in the first issue of her *Journal*: 'There is a stirring in the mass, which only requires steady and free communion with Truth to expand itself into that practical and enlightened wisdom on which ever rests the perfection of social and political civilization.'[12]

Smiles had given time and energy in the past to politically framed reforms, to Corn Law abolition and extension of the franchise. His experience had disillusioned him. He had, he said, left political life when he left the *Leeds Times*, but he never gave up on the cause of practical and enlightened wisdom for the masses. Ignorance, not industrialisation, made victims, and if political action was needed to combat ignorance he would return to politics.

Though he had written in the past of his suspicion of the role of either church or state in education – that tendency to mould minds to the needs of others – Smiles the pragmatist understood that without some part for both church and state, little could be done. 'The only flourishing schools at that time were the schools established by the Church and by Wesleyan congregations.'[13] He had come to believe that, whatever the virtues of self-education, a national system of day schools, locally controlled, funded from the rates, was the only way to make proper schools and proper teaching available to the masses. 'It is admitted on all hands that the people of the poorer classes are not educated – that they are not in the course of being educated – and that there is no prospect of their being efficiently educated without a large and reliable provision being made for that purpose.'[14] A Bill to promote 'the secular education of the people of England and Wales' was currently before Parliament. Liberal church-men supported it, arguing that each sect could provide its own religious instruction outside the day-school curriculum. But for many traditional dissenters independence was more important than public money, even though their voluntary schools, suffused by evangelical religious teach-ing, were slowly dying for want of funds. In Leeds only one remained, even though, Smiles said, Leeds was 'the capital of the voluntary educa-tionists and the headquarters of the voluntary movement'.[15]

The voluntarists, led by Edward Baines, still pronouncing from the editorial chair at the *Leeds Mercury*, determined to mount a campaign against the Bill and against anyone supporting secular education. Smiles was equally determined to oppose him. In this he worked closely with his brother Robert, then Secretary of the National Public School Asso-ciation in Manchester, leading the campaign for the Secular Education Bill.

In this campaign all the old techniques were to be used – public meetings, resolutions, articles and letters in the newspapers, canvassing of prominent people – and Samuel Smiles, hard-worked secretary of the Railway Company, principal writer for *Eliza Cook's Journal*, conscientious husband and father, took on the battle. His letters to his brother Robert at that time show Samuel Smiles as a man relishing the fray, almost redis-covering his youth. In public and written debate he might seem formal, respectful, even gracious ('It is but fair to give due credit to the sincerity and conscientiousness of men of all parties in the discussion of this ques-tion'),[16] but privately he shows a gleeful vindictiveness. In April 1850 he told Robert: 'I should like to make Baines swallow the dose, and cram the 'Godless' bill down his anti-papist throat.'[17] He was delighted with the force of his own arguments and convinced of ultimate victory. A few weeks later he was writing again:

> The dissenters here are fit to eat me. Yesterday I smashed their Voluntary Education back and side, and showed up the magnificence of their efforts – namely one voluntary educational school for 150,000 people! I must take up the fact and send it back in their teeth ... 'Neddy', as we call Baines here, cannot have slept very soundly last night.[18]

Through the rest of 1850 Smiles sustained his campaign for secular education, and his derision of the Bainsites. He wrote to his brother almost every week, sometimes every day, with a stream of advice, questions, and very little modesty – 'We have beaten Baines by a large majority at a meeting of about 10,000! Glorious. I spoke for about an hour and a half!'[19] – again, on 24 April, writing to Robert about a meeting the previous Tuesday: 'I am told the facts I mentioned are thoroughly choking to Baines, and cut him up far more than Barker's speech.'

5 Edward Baines: '"Neddy" as we call Baines here, cannot have slept very soundly last night.'
(The Mary Evans Picture Library)

The national education debate, like the debates over extending the suffrage, started with the sort of snap and vigour communicated in Smiles's letters at this time. But by the end of 1850 little real progress had been made. In the following year an air of resignation had started to creep into Smiles's comments. The urgent responses of the previous spring had changed to a certain weariness with the subject: 'My dear brother, My wife tells me that a parcel of circulars has arrived from you ... I shall not be able to look into the contents for a week or so. I suppose you are still pushing ahead.'[20] The 'Humbug Whigs,' he suggested, would waver, and the Stanley administration 'might not choose to take up a subject which could give rise to a good deal of contention throughout the country'.

Smiles's cynicism with politicians may have hardened, but he would not yield on the fundamental principle – that sectarianism had no place in schools. In February 1852 he issued 2,000 copies of an open letter to Edward Baines, declaring:

> I object to the teaching of doctrinal religion in the common day-schools.
> Were the nation of one mind on the point of religious belief, there could
> be no difficulty about the matter. But we are not of one mind, for the diver-
> sities of religious opinion now-a-days are endless ... secular knowledge
> and morality can be taught without injury to man's conscience.[21]

Here again is a hint of the influence of Emerson and the New England transcendentalists, and their plea for the exclusion of the church from education.

In his *Autobiography* Smiles wrote that 'during the last three years that I lived in Leeds I remained quietly within my shell. I took no part in public meetings of any sort.' Was Smiles sulking in his tent during those years? Certainly they did not end happily for him, and when the time came to tell Sarah Anne that their life in Leeds was over, some disappointment clouded their departure. But that was later. In the meantime anything that smacked of loss of self-belief was not the Smiles approach. Difficulty fuelled ambition – 'it might almost be said that early encounter with difficult and adverse circumstances was the necessary and indispensable condition of success.'[22] He may have given up public meetings, but he had not given up the cause.

His 1852 letter to Baines, already cited, was his last comprehensive public statement of the case for national secular education. But it did not signal an end to his commitment to the work of the national Public School Association. When a deputation from the Association was received at Westminster in June 1853 by Lord John Russell, Smiles was a key member of the group. Much of the case put to his Lordship was based on the points already featured in Smiles's dispute with Baines:

> the deputation expressed a very decided opinion as to the value of a good
> system of secular instruction, and maintained that the numerous sectarian
> differences in the country rendered it impossible to provide, with equal
> justice to all parties, a system of public instruction [publicly funded],
> unless such system were divested of religious character.[23]

Russell listened politely and promised the deputation 'his best considered action', but he was no longer a government minister, and, though sympathetic, had little power to help.

Perhaps the fate of the public education campaign confirmed Smiles's fear that government would never rise above party interest. Increasingly he concentrated on his conviction that social progress – the happiness and well-being of the people – depended on individual attitudes. Writing drove Smiles, and the character of men drove his writing. It would of course be disingenuous to represent Smiles as a man who wrote selflessly, driven only by conscience and conviction. He was ambitious, combative, and arrogant enough to be believe in the material as well as the social value of his work. In later years he showed no lack of hardheadedness in his dealings with John Murray, his book publisher.

If Smiles really believed that he remained quietly in his shell at this time, it was a very productive quiet. In London *Eliza Cook's Journal* was a success, selling up to 50,000 copies a week.[24] Because he was responsible for so much of its content, his journalistic earnings must have been worthwhile – worthwhile enough for him to suggest to his brother that he might 'work the mine' by submitting material based on his educational writings. 'You may add a little to your income by so doing ... I have written to Mr Ryall, Miss Cook's manager, and told him you could write him some such article.'[25] Confident in his own professionalism, Smiles offered to check his younger brother's work before sending it on: 'If you have any tales or poetry, or scraps of any kind "fit to be seen", send them over to me here and I will look them over before going.'

Through 1852 and 1853 Samuel himself worked the mine, often using old notes, like his youthful journeys – those Dutch idylls and the walks in the Lammermuir hills – to feed the demand. A series of 'Dutch Pictures' appeared almost weekly through the autumn of 1852 and into 1853, and a series on 'The Scottish Borders' in the early months of 1854, just before Eliza Cook's illness forced her to end her *Journal*. In the five years of Eliza Cook's publishing adventure she and Samuel Smiles had come to depend on each other – she for his professional support, he for an outlet for his writing. Since 1849 he had been prolific, with 'stories, novelettes, reviews, travels, articles on domestic life ... and a large number of brief biographies'.[26] When all this ended it could have created a dispiriting emptiness, especially when it coincided with a threat to his other career. Things were changing quickly at the Leeds Northern Railway Company (its name had been changed after line extensions in 1848), not particularly in Smiles's favour. His opportunity to confront difficult and adverse circumstances had arrived with a bang.

12

Double Act

T WELVE YEARS earlier Smiles had sat among the guests in the saloon of the Leeds Music Hall at what the *Leeds Times* called 'an intellectual feast ... a galaxy of men of science'.[1] Over five hundred diners had gathered there to celebrate the union of the Leeds Mechanics' and Literary Institutions. It was another night of elaborate toasts, of long speeches and mutual praise. Smiles did not speak, but he listened with particular acuity to the speaker introduced, late in the evening, as 'the first engineer in the world', George Stephenson. Stephenson visited Leeds occasionally and Smiles had been introduced to him before, but they were not acquaintances.

Stephenson's address that night was probably a refreshing change from the other, more lofty contributions. He spoke 'with great simplicity of style and manner, and a strong provincial accent'. He spoke of the priceless value of education, and of his struggle to overcome his own early lack of it. 'He gave some useful advice to young engineers, and above all he counselled them to perseverance – never to believe in such a thing as difficulty which they could not conquer.' Stephenson was in his sixties at the time, white-haired, energetic, still driven by the fire of curiosity (he talked about his vision of an electric wire circling the globe so that men could talk to one another 'at nearly the same time'), still with his 'strong provincial accent'. Smiles stored away that image, consciously nourished by Stephenson, of a man of simplicity and grace, a man who had started with nothing and achieved everything, a man who had never contemplated a difficulty he could not conquer.

When George Stephenson died in 1848 Smiles was stepping into his own career as an independent journalist. In *Howitt's Journal* he had experimented with biographical sketches. After Howitt, when Eliza Cook offered him a new opportunity, his memories of Stephenson were still vivid. He was able fill out the picture by talking to his friend and colleague, John Bourne, the Leeds Northern Railway's senior engineer, who had worked with Stephenson. The resulting profile of George Stephenson appeared on the front page of the fifth issue of *Eliza Cook's Journal* on 2 June 1849. Smiles praised Stephenson's straightforwardness and openheartedness. He pictured 'a zealous self-cultivator, always observant, always improving, always advancing ...' None of this, Smiles implied, was for personal glory. It was for a higher good: the invention of the locomotive 'was to bring cities together, nearly annihilate space, and confer on man as much new power and enjoyment, as if he were endowed with wings'.

A few weeks later he developed the same theme – the social, almost spiritual contribution of railways – in his article on 'Railway Travelling', when he wrote of 'the really great services which they have rendered to the cause of human progress'. In that article he also confronted the worst side of the railway mania of a few years earlier. He argued that, while the fate of dupes and greedy speculators was a passing evil, 'the enterprise was grand, was truly noble'. He was filled by admiration for the true entrepreneurs, men like his own employers: 'They were generally far-seeing and strong-headed men ... capable of inspiring confidence and mastering difficulties.' Now, in 1854, the railway companies' pride was beginning to fade. Shareholders, even in the established lines, were suffering falling dividends. Although more and more people wanted to ride on the trains, there were too many companies operating on the same tracks to make commercial sense of the noble enterprise. So while Samuel Smiles was coming to terms with Eliza Cook's illness, and the closing of that journalistic mine, the directors of the Northern Railway Company in Leeds were considering the future of their business.

Smiles was very aware of his Company's problems, and of the futility of several operators trying to win business from the same area. Throughout the country rail companies were implementing rationalisation and merger. For over a year Smiles had been working on background planning for an amalgamation of his own company with the York, Newcastle & Berwick, and the North Midland Railways, with the common aim of extending the line as far as the Tyne, and the profitable business of carrying coals from Newcastle. The 1853 plan stalled because the proposed line, passing Durham, might shake the lenses in the Durham Observatory's telescopes. In Parliament the necessary Bill was refused. A new plan, reassuring the astronomers of Durham and the directors of the three companies, was agreed and the appropriate legislation passed early in 1854. Even then the terms of the deal had to be approved by the shareholders of all three companies, and of course each group thought the other was getting some advantage. Months of negotiation followed, generating vast paperwork. Smiles had to keep control of it all, and was charged with putting together the final document detailing the terms and recommending acceptance.

Its completion should have been a moment, if not of triumph, then at least of great satisfaction for Smiles, and anticipation of the gratitude of the directors. But in view of what transpired, he recalled later only that he felt 'when signing the final report, as if I were driving the last nail into my own coffin'.[2]

The Leeds Northern would be no more, its need for a secretary no more, but there was plenty for Smiles to do. He was sent over to Newcastle to have the new shares registered there and to help administer the changeover. The directors in Leeds indicated that an interesting new job in the amalgamated company would soon become available, and encouraged Smiles to apply. It might mean relocating to the new head office in York, but so be it. Progress carried a price. He sent a letter, as suggested, expressing interest in the new position. Meanwhile he was asked to stay on in Newcastle and make himself useful.

It was a humiliating experience. He took lodgings in Elswick Road and reported each day to Newcastle Station, where he had been given a cramped, windowless room beside the secretary's office. The work was cramped too, insignificant he called it, with no access to the board and, in the months he was there, only once invited to attend a committee meeting of the directors. Life could have seemed bleak, away from his family, adrift in a strange town, with only his engineering colleague John

Bourne for a friend, and a fruitless, monotonous job to fill the working hours. But at least it was summer, with long, clear evenings entirely at his own disposal. With the prospect of the York appointment in mind he travelled over there one weekend to look at houses that might be suitable for a family with five children (by now Janet and William had been joined by Edith, Sam junior, and Lilian). In his Tyneside surroundings he went in search of George Stephenson. He saw the pitheads, the miners' cottages, the old colliers' road, the pumping engines and sheds and disused locomotives, and imagined the presence there of the penniless, illiterate boy who had made the whole railway miracle possible. Smiles's dead-end job and lonely evenings became an opportunity. He had been delivered to the place where he could bring the young George Stephenson to life.

John Bourne (who had been his main source for the Cook article in 1849) helped with suggestions about where to visit and whom to interview. At Bewley Burn, where Stephenson's father had worked, he talked to ancient colliers and enginemen who had worked with Stephenson, and who remembered Geordie, as they called him. At Newburn he found George Stephenson and Fanny Hindmarsh's marriage registered, and made a tracing of the entry. One Saturday afternoon – 'that being my holiday and the only day on which I could conveniently leave Newcastle'[3] – he visited Edward Pease in Darlington. The eighty-eight-year-old railway pioneer had been Stephenson's first backer, the one who had seen the young man's first working locomotive, had believed in it and had appointed Stephenson as the engineer of the Stockton and Darlington Railway. When Smiles, having dined with him, left Pease late that evening to take the last train back to Newcastle he was, he said, 'freighted with valuable information'.[4]

His working days, stranded outside the secretary's office at Newcastle station, continued, as did the silence from the directors in response to his letter. All through that summer, in the face of frustration and anxiety, it was the Stephenson project which sustained him – both the thrill of the chase and the constant reminders of difficulties overcome. From these expeditions, and his hours in his room in Elswick Street surrounded by his notes, he knew that he was gathering something substantial, treasure for the book he had so long wanted to write.

Some years earlier, prompted by the response to his *Eliza Cook's Journal* article, he had contacted Stephenson's son Robert, also a railway engineer, about writing a biography of his father. Stephenson's reaction had been cool. He had had other approaches, but nothing had happened, probably, he suggested, because of reader apathy. 'If people get a railroad they do not care how or by whom it is made.'[5] He pointed out that a recently published *Life of Thomas Telford* had flopped. Smiles argued that the Telford book had been badly done, devoid of human interest. 'If I decided to write the life of his father, I would endeavour to treat of his character as a man as well as an engineer.' Robert Stephenson was unconvinced, but kind. 'I thought it better to warn you against losing your time, your labour, and your money.' But he had left a door open. If Smiles ever did decide to go ahead, Stephenson would help him. That had been four years earlier.

With the research riches gathered in his Newcastle summer Smiles decided to approach Robert Stephenson again. This time the answer was quite different: 'I am glad to hear that you have not given up the idea of writing a memoir of my late father; and now that I have more leisure it will afford me pleasure to assist you in many points which are only known to myself ...'[6] In October Stephenson came to Newcastle, took a room at the Queen's Hotel, and devoted himself to giving more help than Smiles could ever have hoped for. He showed him his father's cottage, the sundial with the settings Stephenson had calculated, the room with its rough earth floor and the old oven, still there, where on cold days his father used to put his pitman's watch to make it go, by melting the oil. As they stood in the room, George Stephenson stood with them.

Smiles went back to Newcastle that evening bright with excitement about the book he was now determined to write. Stephenson returned to London, but before leaving he sent a note to Smiles at the Central Station encouraging him to go ahead, and suggesting he use the earlier *Eliza Cook* article as a starting-point. 'You cannot do better than keep that excellent article[7] in which the sketching of my father's biography contains the heads of all that is wanted ...' On parting, the two agreed that they must keep in touch. Now no one was better equipped, or more eager, to write a biography of George Stephenson than Samuel Smiles. All he needed was a stable family life and a steady job.

In the meantime another project turned quietly in his mind. Ever since his teaching experiences at the Zion School in Leeds and his talk to the young men of the Leeds Mutual Improvement Society, he had kept his notes and outline for the book to which he had given the working title *Self-Help*. There would be time now to tidy up the manuscript and possibly offer it for publication. A Leeds printer, Walkers, did show an interest, but Smiles decided to hold it back and perhaps try in London when he was next there.

Early in October he was called over to Leeds. He had waited so long for news of a proper position with the amalgamated company that he was by now ready to accept anything reasonable, and a modest salary, for the sake of a settled life, for the sake of his family, and for the sake of the Stephenson book. At the Leeds office he was told that all the new staffing arrangements had now been made, and that for him there was nothing. Smiles was angry and hurt, not just because he had been made jobless, but because he was the only one. 'Places were found for all the old officers, excepting myself.'[8] He put the rejection down to lobbying hard by one of the new directors for his own man to fill the position originally earmarked for Smiles. In Smiles's view, his few friends had failed to push hard enough for him.

Other factors may have been involved. Did his employers resent his second career as a journalist? Were they anxious about his sometimes controversial political views? Had Edward Baines, riled by the voluntary education debate, lobbied against him? Whatever the full story, Smiles was determined to learn from it.

He had spent a decade working for a growing company and, as far as he could see, had achieved nothing. He knew newspaper work, loved journalism, and hungered for independence and for a forum for his ideas. He had seen how William Howitt had started a periodical and had failed only through the Saunders factor. Even with that, Howitt was back on his feet again. Eliza Cook, with no previous experience, had made her *Journal* a prominent feature of the London publishing scene. Surely a London newspaper published and edited by Samuel Smiles must have a good chance of success? So he thought, and so he canvassed opinions from men he respected, including Richard Cobden. They warned him off. 'If I were bent upon speculation in Cockney journalism, I would reserve myself till the compulsory stamp duty is abolished,'[9] Cobden replied. Another correspondent, the poet Gerald Massey, told him: 'I was somewhat surprised by what you had in contemplation. I had a taste of that some time ago. A friend of mine bought O'Connor's *Star of Freedom* ... he spent 700 or 800£ and it failed.'[10]

While Smiles mulled, an advertisement appeared, for Secretary of the South Eastern Railway Company in London. Smiles didn't want to leave Leeds, but he needed a job. This time he did not leave things to a well-worded letter of application. He planned a comprehensive Smiles-for-Secretary campaign, invoking the help of powerful Leeds figures like Henry Marshall of the great spinning company, his former chairman at the North Eastern, William Beckett, banker and political heavyweight, and George Goodman, local MP. With their support, and the backing of his many contacts across the rail industry, he submitted his application. The selection process, as he discovered, was not straightforward. Nevertheless, on 18 November 1854 the *Leeds Times* announced that 'Mr Samuel Smiles, formerly Secretary of the Leeds Northern Railway company, has been elected Secretary of the South Eastern Railway Company.' His sponsors had obviously done a good job, for the Directors of the South Eastern later recorded that out of fifty candidates, 'they selected Mr Smiles, because of his experience and the high character of his testimonials'.[11] Smiles was quick to write to Robert Stephenson with news of his move. Stephenson, ever polite, wrote to congratulate him on his success. In his letter he included, however, a note of warning: 'I fear you will find the South Eastern a very difficult concern to keep in train satisfactorily. More of this when I have the pleasure of seeing you.'[12]

Robert Stephenson lived in lonely widowhood in London, where his house in Cambridge Square was a convenient walk through Hyde Park to his office in Great George Street, Westminster. There he practised, in partnership with George Bidder,[13] as one of Europe's most sought-after engineering consultants. As George's son and collaborator, and as consultant-on-call to rail companies across the world – Robert Stephenson knew the workings, and mis-workings, of his industry more thoroughly than any man alive. He was a quiet, studious man, absorbed by his profession, with little of the charisma or entrepreneurial flamboyance of his father. Though hugely respected by his peers, in the public eye he had never come out from under his father's shadow, nor did he want to. His dearest ambition now was to ensure George Stephenson's place in history.

He knew that there could be more than one version. In his own, his father had been a plain man of startling genius, who by selfless application had overcome his humble origins to give the world the first railway locomotive and all the benefits that flowed from it. Other versions hinted at arrogance, personal ambition, and the taint of dirty dealings in the underworld of railway mania. But there was worse – a suggestion that George Stephenson was not the inventor of the steam locomotive, but the plagiariser and exploiter of other men's ideas. If a Life of George Stephenson was to be offered to the world, Robert wanted none of these speculations, but a reflection of his own sincere conviction of his father's worth.

In his dealings with Samuel Smiles he had recognised someone with a similar vision, concerned with the positive lessons of the George Stephenson story, with lessons about life, and work, and the profound value of British engineering. He liked Smiles. He wanted him to write his father's biography. He was glad Smiles's railway career had survived, that he had come to London, but feared that the notorious board of the South Eastern might overwhelm him, and drown the project. Soon Smiles shared his fears.

The process of Smiles's appointment as Secretary had from the start suggested antagonism among board members, including rows over whether the existing Secretary, G S Herbert, should stay or go, and whether a director-nominated candidate should be handed the job. When the question of Herbert's successor was discussed some directors had asked why Mr Herbert 'had been dismissed, and no reason having been assigned, that he be requested to resume his duties'.[14] And all this was after the job had been advertised, forty applicants considered, and six, including Samuel Smiles, interviewed by the board. The resolution for Herbert's reinstatement was eventually defeated by five votes to three, and it was resolved that 'on Mr Smiles giving satisfactory security to this Company for his fidelity to the amount of £4000, he be appointed Secretary to the Company with a salary equivalent to £600 per annum' (this was a hundred pounds less than Herbert had been paid). A suburban bank manager's salary at the time was about £90 per annum.[15]

In the Leeds office Smiles had always been busy, but it had been orderly, business-like busyness. The London Bridge office of the South Eastern Railway turned out to be more like a war zone. Robert Stephenson had warned him:

> I was aware also that you had had a struggle against a section of the Board when you obtained the appointment. When you succeeded I knew that you would have many serious difficulties to contend with – a divided board – a reduced income – increasing expenses, and as a temporary consequence discontented shareholders.[16]

As with many other rail companies, the South Eastern had survived by a mixture of aggression and amalgamation. In the process it had created an atmosphere of antagonism with other operators in the south-east, particularly with the London, Brighton and South Coast Railway. Herbert Spencer described the railway business as beset by 'Feuds perpetually prompting boards to make aggressions on each other's territories – every attack on the one side leading to reprisal on the other.'[17] Such battles often damaged profits and worried shareholders, though they had given the South Eastern a monopoly of rail transport in Kent. The man credited with this or, depending on where you stood, blamed for its clumsiness and inefficiency, was the Chairman and Managing Director, James Macgregor. For a decade Macgregor had presided over a board split by their loyalty or otherwise to him, and by their representation of various groups of shareholders. One clique had recently mustered enough strength to vote Macgregor out office as Chairman, though he remained on the board and was still the dominant presence among the directors. Behind all their other discussions now lay the question of who might succeed him.

Smiles, by nature a quietly mannered and orderly person, was appalled by the behaviour he saw in the South Eastern boardroom. He had been used to decorous and constructive discussion, to men who would meet round a table 'for the purpose of getting through their work'.[18] In the South Eastern boardroom he found directors jumping to their feet, shouting at each other, set on points scoring, on attacking

Macgregor or defending him, rather than on business. It was, Smiles said, 'a fruitless waste of time'. In the Smiles litany of sins, none could have been worse – and it even extended to forcing him to waste his own time.

The recently elected MP for Berwick-on-Tweed, John Forster, was one of the most vocal members of the board, and hostile to Smiles. It was he who had put forward his own candidate for the Secretary's job, and lost. Now he was taking it out on the new man. 'I soon found,' Smiles said, 'that Mr Forster was ready to trip me up about the composition of the minutes.' Smiles's practice at Leeds had been to make a complete and accurate record of boardroom decisions. Now Forster demanded that the minutes should include a verbatim account of all discussions leading to decisions. By consulting the company's solicitor and invoking the legal requirement for 'minutes and proceedings', Forster forced Smiles to include the chaff as well as the wheat. Smiles put this down to spite, though he acknowledged in his *Autobiography* that Forster had a deeper purpose: to create a record he could later use to influence shareholders in the election of a new chairman.

It was all dispiriting stuff, far from the shiny new beginning Smiles had hoped for when he travelled south. In his dead days in Newcastle there had at least been summer, long hours of daylight, the search for Stephenson, even the hope of a recall to head office. Alone in January in London, living in lodgings at 40 Trinity Square Southwark, adjusting to the tensions of a strange job, spending dark evenings hunting for a home for his family still in Leeds, the prospect of writing the George Stephenson book faded by the week. He had sent, without much optimism, the manuscript for *Self-Help* to a new London publisher, George Routledge & Co.

Then, at last, he found a house where he was sure Sarah Anne would feel happy. Number 8 Glenmohr Terrace in Blackheath was a decent suburban villa with enough room for Mr and Mrs Smiles and their five children. By the turn of the year family and furniture had been translated from the smoke of Leeds to the high open spaces of Blackheath. The South Eastern had a line to Lewisham, so Smiles had an easy journey to work each morning, and back each evening to a reunited family and a place that felt like home. Even the disappointment of a letter from Routledge turning down *Self-Help* did not spoil his sense of life improving. That book was not his main interest. The notes for George Stephenson were safe in his desk drawer in Glenmohr Terrace, and some time, if the pressure at the South Eastern lifted, he might return again to that work.

Smiles's *Autobiography* suggests that at this time he was under almost intolerable pressure. He describes the relentless demands of the directors, the correspondence he took home, the overlapping meetings and minutes to be written. 'Sometimes I found it difficult to accomplish this work; and sitting long at my desk, either at the office or at home, often gave me a splitting headache.'[19] He might almost have given up: 'I began to think that there might be some difficulty in carrying the work further.' Robert Stephenson sent grim messages:

> Since you undertook your new situation, you have frequently passed through my mind, and I began to feel that your new engagements would be far too numerous to admit of your giving the biography any attention. Moreover I felt that if your board found that you were not giving your full time to their business, it might cause dissatisfaction ... as I take rather a gloomy view of the future prospects of the South-Eastern, I fear your troubles are not at an end.[20]

That was in October 1855, less than a year after Smiles had taken up his post at London Bridge. He had arrived with his career on two broken legs: his living dependent on a highly unstable company, his writing future on one book which had been rejected and another which he could find no time to write. He stayed at the South Eastern for another eleven years. When he resigned in 1866 he was a highly valued officer of the company, on warm terms with his directors, and one of the most famous authors in Britain.

It is tempting to see in this dramatic turnaround a mirroring of one of his later 'Illustrations of Character, Conduct, and Perseverance' from *Self-Help* – Smiles as hero in the face of overwhelming odds. But then another other perspective is offered, of quick relief from most of his problems, and considerable satisfaction and interest in his job. He was publicly praised for his skilful management of the shareholder poll for Board elections in March: 'They [the scrutineers] desire especially to acknowledge the labours of the Secretary, Mr Smiles, and Mr Randal, the traffic clerk, whose arrangements could not be improved.'[21] He was able to hire a shorthand assistant to ease his clerical chores. Elections led at last to a new Chairman, James Byng, with whom Smiles 'maintained a pleasant and agreeable intercourse ... during the twelve years that I remained with the company'.[22] In fact the two stayed good friends long after Smiles left the railway business. Other directors came in at the same time as Byng, and the in-fighting seemed to stop. But the South Eastern was never an easy place to work. The tensions of fierce competition for routes and the recurring need to raise new capital for expansion, led often to strained board meetings and consistent pressure on operations. The golden days of the railways were past. Smiles noted the pressures on expenditure: 'the pay necessarily scanty. The number of good berths in a railway company becomes more constricted from year to year,' he told an ex-colleague looking for employment, 'and the high salaries concentrated in fewer hands ... it is the true policy of railway companies'.

To the outside world, however, Smiles chose to portray a more satisfying working environment. He became almost light-hearted in telling the story of the miracle by which a number of sealed boxes of gold bullion, carried from the South Eastern's London depot to Folkestone, were found, on reaching Paris, to contain lead shot. It took a year to solve the puzzle, of detective fiction complexity, in which crooked staff conspired to make the switch. Coincidentally with the disappearance of the gold, Mr Tester, passenger superintendent at London Bridge, had shaken hands with his colleagues before leaving to take up the post of General Manager of the Royal Swedish Railway. Smiles had happily provided him with a character reference for his new employers. Of course it turned out that Tester had been an essential player in the bullion robbery and had received a third of the booty. When he foolishly returned on holiday, the English constabulary was waiting for him. The Royal Swedish Railway had to find a new general manager. Smiles, we presume, was not asked for a reference.

Being secretary of the South Eastern Railway was not, in spite of an unpleasant start and Robert Stephenson's doleful predictions, the job from hell. Smiles was beginning to enjoy himself. The demands were no less, but under the new board the work had its own integrity. However hard he had to apply himself, it was application for a practical purpose, and not simply to serve the interests of one or other faction. The directors were non-executive; they came in for fortnightly meetings, agreed strategy, fulfilled their statutory obligations, and left the running of the business to the management. Increasingly Smiles felt valued by the board and respected by his fellow managers. Work stopped being a chore and became an interest.

His good humour at this time is apparent from his personal correspondence. The Smiles home in Glenmohr Terrace was close enough to Greenwich Park and the wide green spaces of Backheath for his children to be able to run free, fly kites, and wonder at the stately buildings on the river below, and the views over London, misty in the distance.[23] The Smiles were a two-stage family. Janet, William, and Edith (11, 9, and 8 respectively) formed the first cohort, Sam, 3 and baby Lilian the second. Sarah Anne wanted to show them off in their wonderful new surroundings, to her mother, who still lived in Leeds. The old lady may have been reluctant to travel but her son-in-law (close enough to address her as 'My dear mother') was determined to share his family's happiness.

> I ... formally wish and urge, implore and entreat, supplicate and beseech, that you will do us the favour of a visit ... I promise you a most cordial and hearty reception, for the sake of Sairy Ann, for your own sake, for my sake, for 'Dear Leeds' sake and for the sake of our small squadron of infantry, all of whom love you much (including myself).[24]

He invited her to come and admire their carpets and their stucco woman on the upper lobby, the rosy cheeks of the children, the heath and Greenwich Park and the pensioners with their cocked hats. Clearly he delighted in it all. The joyful, skittish tone of this letter reveals a man at ease with himself. Whatever the pressure at work, it was positive. He could deal with it – by starting early, using his shorthand assistant efficiently, finishing each day's work before leaving so that nothing half-done presented itself in the morning. He describes his routine with a certain self-righteousness: 'I was always there first ... always before the bulk of the clerks, and the example had, no doubt, its influence.'

With such discipline he could, he believed, be both conscientious secretary and productive writer. 'I know' he protested, that there are many people who think that a man of business who devotes his leisure to writing is in a measure lost. He ought to devote his whole time to business or to literature; and literary men are not considered business men ... What has a railway secretary, who is paid for his work as such, to do with writing books?

His answer? 'I was at liberty to do with the leisure of my evenings what I thought proper, provided the results were not at variance with my other duties.' These defensive words were written thirty years later, when, although by then a hugely successful author, Smiles seemed still to feel that he had not been accepted as a 'proper' writer (or as he would have put it 'a literary man') – because writing was not his full-time occupation. How could he be an artist without devoting himself wholly to his art?

Yet Smiles always believed in the valuable coin bearing the proud profiles of the business man on one side and the writer on the other. It was in his mind even as he was setting an example to the clerks in the South Eastern Railway. *Self-Help* had already been written, though still unpublished. The book expands at length on the businessman-artist double act: 'It has, however, been a favourite fallacy with dunces of all times, that men of genius are unfulfilled for business, as well as that business occupations unfit men for the pursuits of genius.'[25] He goes on to cite examples: Plato selling oil to fund his travels, Shakespeare as theatre manager, Chaucer as Commissioner of Customs; and

> We have abundant illustrations, in our own day, of the fact that the highest intellectual power is not incompatible with the active and efficient performance of duties. Grote, the great historian of Greece, was a London banker. And it is not long since John Stuart Mill, one of our greatest living thinkers, retired from the Examiner's department at the East India Company.

Samuel Smiles saw himself in good company. It was time to put aside the disappointment of *Self-Help's* rejection and Robert Stephenson's forebodings. 'There was that old Life of George Stephenson that had been hanging over my head for so many years. Could I not proceed with it now?'

13

'A Successful Author!'

I T IS instinctive now, a century-and-a-half after Smiles's book on Stephenson was published, to see George Stephenson as a figure from history, a side-burned ancient in a black frock coat. For Smiles, of course, he was a near-contemporary, someone at the leading edge of modern technology, someone he had met. Many of the readers of his proposed biography would be people who had known Stephenson; some would have worked with him; most would feel they had, in some way, shared a world with him. Smiles knew that back in 1849, researching his Stephenson article for *Eliza Cook*, he had made the mistake of believing all he was told. 'I did not know at the time that these stories were apocryphal.' For a full biography he would have to be a good deal more careful. However, the most valuable message he took from the 1849 article was not its errors, but its impact. It had been copied and republished in newspapers and magazines all over the country and stirred up a deal of interest. This reaction suggested a hidden appetite for the story of a man widely, but vaguely, perceived as a national hero. Smiles was sure that for the proposed biography he had, so far, no competition. Certainly Robert Stephenson knew of none, and any aspiring biographer of his father would have needed to approach him.

Setting out to plan the work, Smiles was open to a rich mix of aims and impulses. He needed to get on with it quickly, before anyone else had the idea, and while the people who had known George Stephenson were still alive and available to be interviewed. He needed to be authoritative, to be sure of his ground on engineering detail and on anecdote, and at the same time avoid the 'Telford trap', of dehumanising his subject (he later wrote his own biography of Telford). But there was an over-arching question. As a railway insider Smiles knew enough to realise the ambiguities in Stephenson's life – his sharpness as a business operator, his association with George Hudson (the Railway King now dethroned and disgraced), his unacknowledged debt to other engineers – counteracting the image of the honest genius. But Smiles knew that, in spite of imperfections, he had a star waiting to stride on stage. The audience was agog. The curtain was still down. What sort of man, when Smiles raised it, did he want them to see?

He had no doubt. He and Robert Stephenson were already agreed: the world must be shown the unpretentious man who, by combining unique engineering brilliance with strength of character, had overcome every difficulty to give humanity the immeasurable gift of rail travel. Moreover, his life, from the humblest start, must show the rest of the world how deep was the seam of national genius; Stephenson stood for England. It was the story Robert Stephenson wanted. It was the story the nation wanted, and it was the story Samuel Smiles wanted to tell – because he believed it told an essential truth, not just about George Stephenson, but about the nature of humanity.

For the first time since his rejection by the directors of the North Eastern Railway, Smiles was excited. His greatest dread, of space in his life not usefully filled, need no longer haunt him. His days at work and his evenings of leisure were under control: 'My health was restored; I could clear away my work for the day; and I went home with my mind clear and unfagged. I recovered my evening's leisure, and could spend it in amusement, recreation, or the pleasure of social intercourse.' When Smiles writes like this, of evenings idled away in domestic cosiness, one can almost see a dismissive smile, a quiet shake of his head. This, he implies, is for others. For a man of purpose 'The question then occurred, what was I to do with the leisure time thus set at liberty? My object always was – for indeed it had become a habit – to turn my spare minutes to some account.' Now, driven by George Stephenson, the habit was resumed, and never again dropped.

Time, for Smiles, was not to be found by rummaging for it through an untidy life. Rather each hour must have its place, like stationery in a well-ordered cupboard, so that there would be no loss through random-ness. He set the boundaries of his 'business' life, starting each day so regularly that 'in passing the window of my neighbour, Wilson of Black-heath, on my way to the station, he declared that he could set his clock by my movements'. Returning home with equal precision (and with Wilson the curtain-twitcher still in place?), family time came first; and then after supper his hours for writing, well used because they were well marked. It was not easy. Samuel and Sarah Anne, the five children, and almost certainly a live-in cook and housemaid (they'd had both in Leeds) filled all four stories of the Glenmohr Terrace house.[1] He had no library or quiet room of his own, and had often to work with the children playing in the room. But he was able to ignore the racket, as he had been able to ignore the clatter of machinery and prattle of people in his newspaper and railway offices. Sometimes, if the evening was fine, he would leave the house and walk on Blackheath, 'preparing a sentence or laying out a subject, and returning home to commit the results to paper'.

The structure of the book was to be simple. He would build it in four parts: 'early life', for which he had done most of the research; history of the development of the railway locomotive, for which Robert Stephenson had already compiled the information; the creation of the rail transport system, of which Smiles, as a railway secretary, had first-hand knowledge; and some coverage of the social and economic background to the railway phenomenon. In his *Autobiography* he referred to 'writing out' the life of George Stephenson, as though it were that straightforward. But of course it wasn't.

George Stephenson had thrust himself to the front of the biggest, fastest-growing, and most financially extravagant enterprise the country had ever seen; also the most successful. In the process he had acquired a vast fortune, a vast ego, and become a household name. This would have been impossible without attracting enemies, detractors, envious friends and jealous ex-colleagues. Only a few years before his death, Railway Mania – hysterical and destructive speculation in railway shares – had cost thousands of ordinary people their life savings. In *Duty*, published in 1880, Smiles described, without naming him, the fall of the disgraced Irish MP, and main investor in the Tipperary Bank, John Sadleir: 'A coronet had seemed to gleam before his eyes. But in this he was disappointed. He had launched into Italian, American, and Spanish railways, and lost heavily.' His fate? The railway speculator took prussic acid and died, and for his greed hundreds suffered: 'What scenes there were on the streets of Thurles and Tipperary after his death was announced! Old men weeping and wailing for the loss of everything; widows kneeling on the ground and asking God if it could be true that they were beggared for ever.'[2] As Smiles was planning his book, Herbert Spencer was publishing in the *Edinburgh Review* a dissertation on *Railway Morals and Railway Policy*, reminding readers of what he called 'That elaborate system of tactics by which companies are betrayed into ruinous undertakings that benefit the voracious few at cost to the many.' George Stephenson, with his mountainous wealth and his lordly mansion at Tapton House had been, in many minds, among those voracious few. The railway industry had its dark side; so, although largely unacknowledged, had George Stephenson. Smiles needed to navigate his hero through some murky waters, while displaying his magnificence. He needed as much evidence, from the most authoritative sources, as he could possibly gather. Robert Stephenson, who knew everyone in the business, was a priceless link. John Bourne, still working for the North Eastern, gave useful pointers.

Two of Stephenson's most significant achievements had been his part in the creation of the Stockton and Darlington Railway – the first public railway in the world to use 'loco-motives',[3] or moveable engines, to carry goods and passengers, and in the Liverpool and Manchester Railway, going further, faster, and over more difficult terrain, than the Stockton and Darlington.[4] Between them, these two projects had broken through scepticism about the performance of steam locomotives and the value of railways as a widespread means of transport. Edward Pease, a Quaker woollen merchant and banker in the North East, had been Stephenson's backer on the Darlington enterprise. Now an old man, he was happy to give Smiles all the help he could. So were men like Thomas Gooch, who had been a principal engineer during the building of the Liverpool and Manchester, Henry Booth, one of its original promoters, and Thomas Sopwith, an engineering colleague of both Stephensons. Most of the men Smiles approached were generous, both to him and to Stephenson's memory.

Only one, Nicholas Wood, disappointed him, particularly as he had been George Stephenson's longest term collaborator and a lifelong friend. Wood refused to answer Smiles's letters, or to answer Robert Stephenson's. Smiles called on the help of his old friend John Bourne, now the chief engineer on the North Eastern, who apparently knew Nicholas Wood. When Bourne called on the old engineer he got a sharp answer. He wanted £3,000: 'if you will put me in for that ... I will give you all the information Mr Smiles wants.' Smiles managed without this extortionate co-operation. In 1825 Wood had written *A Practical Treatise on Railroads*. Smiles found what he wanted there. It was one of the few 'secondary' sources he used, or so he later claimed: 'Little or no information was derived from books or reports, but nearly all from personal enquiry and intercourse.' The number of quotations from official reports and other written sources that ended up in the book makes this hard to believe.

On his desk at home Smiles still had his notes from the old *Eliza Cook* article, and everything from his summer's work in Newcastle in 1854. With the pile of material now accumulating he had a formidable writing task on his hands. All through the autumn and winter of 1855 and throughout 1856 he stuck to his routine, leaving the supper table each evening to devote himself to George Stephenson. The result was a remarkable book, richer and infinitely more vibrant than his earlier bland outline could possibly have suggested.

The effectiveness of the *Life of George Stephenson, Railway Engineer* came partly from Smiles's professional skill as a writer and his awareness of his readers' needs. He gave them a hero they could identify with, in a landscape they could recognise. He took them behind the scenes, played on the layman's fascination with the esoteric, planted anecdotes where demonstration or entertainment demanded. There were good guys and bad guys – the malevolent enemies-of-progress, the greedy parasites; and the virtuous visionaries – with the good eventually triumphing. It was a rags-to-riches story in which the hero wore his rags and his riches with equal dignity.

The book was, however, more than a technical accomplishment, and more than a 'life'. Whether Smiles knew it or not, it represented a personal statement, and was driven by the author's relentless enthusiasm, his joy almost, at finding in Stephenson a real-life demonstration of all that he, Samuel Smiles, most passionately believed. The weighty sentences might seem ponderous to today's reader, but Smiles spoke with the voice of his time. When he wrote that

> There was still wanting the man who should accomplish for the locomotive what James Watt had done for the steam engine, and combine in a complete form the separate plans of the others, embodying with them such original inventions and adaptations of his own as to entitle him to the merit of inventing the working locomotive, in the same manner as James Watt is regarded as the inventor of the working condensing engine

he was not just hauling along, like an engine, a great weight of words. He was preparing the ground for the dramatic claim in the next sentence: 'This was the great work upon which George Stephenson now entered, probably without any adequate idea of the immense consequences of his labours to society and civilisation.'[5] Smiles wanted his man on the same pedestal as Watt, and technology to be recognised as society's great benefactor. Civilisation did not depend on kings, bishops, lords or warriors, but on workmen.

The message was for the 'higher' classes, so that they would understand where the real wealth of the country lay, and for the working people, so that they might look in the glass and see reflected the face of George Stephenson. If Stephenson, with all his disadvantages, of poverty, illiteracy, and social handicap, could do it, anyone could do it.

While Smiles was writing *George Stephenson*, the bundle of notebooks containing the manuscript of *Self-Help* lay ignored in his desk drawer, but the theme of the two books is the same. In *Stephenson* (not afraid to address the reader directly) he comments that

> It is true that he who, by his own voluntary and determined efforts, overcomes the difficulties early thrown in his way, and succeeds eventually in teaching himself, will value the education thus acquired much more than he to whom it has been imparted as a mere matter of duty on the part of parents or society ... it usually also exercises a more powerful influence in the formation of his character, by disciplining his spirit of self-help, and accustoming him to patient encounter with, and triumph over, difficulties.

All through the *Life of George Stephenson* these self-help messages recur like a motif:

> Thrown from the first upon his own resources, he early acquired that habit of self-reliance which formed the back-bone of his character ... The very grappling with difficulty was an education in itself' ... He had risen from a lower standing than the meanest person there; and all that he had been able to accomplish in the course of his life had been done through perseverance.[6]

Honesty, sobriety, thrift, modesty ... Smiles finds opportunities, while describing Stephenson's achievements, to pin all these medals on his hero. Even in the midst of what Smiles called 'the railway saturnalia of 1845' his Stephenson held to the path of practical virtue: 'he had no desire to accumulate a fortune without labour and without honour. He consistently stood aloof ...'[7]

Smiles made no attempt to disguise the didactic or patriotic purpose of his book. Thirty-three chapters deal with steam and iron, gauges and brakes, tracks and tunnels and viaducts and the miracles of modern transport, and with how George Stephenson wrought them. But in his treatment Smiles knew what he was doing. Commenting afterwards, he attributed the book's success to 'my not overlaying it with too many engineering details, and bringing out, as much as possible, the human and individual character of the Man'. The thirty-fourth chapter is simply headed *His Character*. Its first paragraph announces that 'The life of George Stephenson, though imperfectly portrayed in the preceding pages, will be found to contain many valuable lessons. His was the life of a true man, and presented a striking combination of those sterling qualities which we are proud to regard as essentially English.' He reprises, in case his readers may have missed the point, what those sterling qualities are: self-reliance – improvement of time – perseverance – encounter with difficulties – thoroughness – determination – honest thrift – patience – hatred of humbug ... They are carefully listed in the chapter contents. They are not the marks of privilege, but of everyman: 'No beginning could have been more humble than his; but he persevered: he had determined to learn, and he did learn. To such a resolution as his, nothing really beneficial is denied.'[8]

6 Robert Stephenson: 'in a comfortable armchair, settled back to hear what the railway company employee from the suburbs had to say...'
(The Mary Evans Picture Library)

When he had at last finished 'writing out' his *Life of George Stephenson*, Smiles's first call was on Robert Stephenson. With the manuscript in his bag he made his way one dark autumn evening in 1856 to 34 Gloucester Square to seek the blessing of his collaborator. Smiles, ever the anecdotist, re-imagined the scene in his *Autobiography*. Robert's old engineering friend and colleague, Thomas Sopwith, was there. Both men were ten years Smiles's senior, both with the easy assurance of great worldly success, both had 'dined, and dined well'. In comfortable armchairs they settled back by the fire to hear what the railway company employee from the suburbs might have to say. Smiles needed their attention. He picked out 'some of the most interesting parts – his father's early life, and the history of the safety lamp. I read on and on; and when I looked up Sopwith was drowsy, and Robert Stephenson was profoundly asleep!' Or perhaps just relaxing with his eyes shut, for when Smiles had the temerity to stop reading the great man chastised him: 'Oh, I hear you very well. Go on if you please.'

The reading finished, Stephenson was apparently satisfied, but unexcited, by what he had heard. His manner was perhaps a touch patronising. When Smiles said he planned to approach England's most august publishing house, John Murray of Albemarle Street, Stephenson thought he might need help: 'If a few hundred pounds would be of use, for illustrations and such like, let me know.' Smiles responded: 'I don't think that will be necessary, as I have no doubt I can get the book published, without expense to anyone.'

Smiles recorded in his *Autobiography* that Stephenson was surprised by his answer, and understandably so. The publisher of Lord Byron, Sir Walter Scott, Jane Austen – the natural home for most of the distinguished men of letters of the time – was surely beyond the reach of a Scottish journalist with a book about an engineer. But John Murray, for all his firm's literary aura, was, above all, a business-man, and in a professionally presented life of George Stephenson he recognised a business opportunity. Smiles's lack of doubt may have been bravado, but the work, planning and research he had put into the book, and his experience as a writer, convinced him that a good publisher would take it seriously. More importantly, he was a good reader of the spirit of the age. For such a book, he believed, the time was right and he chose John Murray as a publisher who would understand this. More surprising is that in 1854 he had offered *Self-Help* to Routledge instead of Murray. Perhaps he felt it was too slight an affair for the famous house. George Routledge was just starting in business and Smiles may have seen him as more likely to take a chance on a new genre. He was, of course, wrong; so was George Routledge.

By the end of 1856 all that was forgotten. John Murray had the nearly-finished manuscript of *George Stephenson* (Smiles, as his letter below shows, still wanted to add some finishing touches), and he liked it. There would, as Smiles had assured Robert Stephenson, be no expense for the author.

On 10 December 1856, a week after his forty-fourth birthday, he received a formal proposal from John Murray to publish the book on a half-profits basis. Smiles replied the same day, clearly delighted, yet alert to his own interests:

My Dear Mr Murray

I am favoured with your letter of this date, and agree to your proposal with respect to the publication of the Life of Stephenson. I have no objection whatever to the ms being placed in the hands of a competent person, with a view to correction – as my regular associations have to some extent interfered with the proper execution of the work in a literary sense. The collection of the materials has however cost me a good deal of labour as well as expense and I shall be glad to be remunerated by the sale of the

7 John Murray III: 'With a house of your standing, and a man of your
character I believe I shall be safe.' From a portrait by Sir George Reid.
(en.wikipedia.org)

book. My past experience of the division of profits in such ventures has
not been encouraging, but with a house of your standing, and a man of
your high character I believe I shall be safe.

Will you be good enough to place the ms in hand with a view to bringing
it out with as little delay as practical. When you next make your announcement of forthcoming books perhaps you will be so kind as to include it –
as this may possibly have the effect of inducing parties at present unknown
to me to send in further information which may be embodied while the
work is going through the press. Within the last fortnight I have obtained
from Newcastle some information which I wish to include in the first
chapter, and I shall therefore be obliged by your sending this part for the
imprint. I enclose the title, which I wish to stand on the title page, <u>without</u>
the motto from Macaulay.[9]

Already Smiles was showing his life-long habit of getting involved with
both the production and marketing of his books.

Murray was taking a chance with this book – a 'risque' as he described it in later letters. He was dealing with an unknown author working in a new biographical category. But with an editor to oversee the manuscript, a modest print run for the first edition, and a cautious fifty-fifty profits split with the author, he felt comfortable about *George Stephenson*'s prospects. Southey's *Life of Nelson*, published by Murray's in 1813, had been, over the years, the firm's most successful biography and one of its proudest achievements. Murray recognised the people's need for heroes. War, victorious war, had given them Nelson. Peace provided less fertile ground, but in the 1850s Britain's industrial and technical advance seemed its own sort of national triumph, and George Stephenson was surely ready to become its hero. Samuel Smiles was no Robert Southey, but he was a man of his own time, of George Stephenson's time, sharing George Stephenson's field of activity, and the people's enthusiasm for railways. Subject, author and public interest seemed perfectly matched. John Murray was confident of covering his costs, and hopeful of a decent profit. Samuel Smiles was determined that, through his own character, conduct and perseverance, the book would succeed.

Over the next six months he devoted himself to preparing it for publication without, if he is to be believed, any relaxation in his work for the South Eastern Railway. Already he was urging pre-publication notices in the press, seeing this as a way of shaking out additional information. He was still finding material for the first chapter, asking for new sections to be added. In the new year he was chasing a Stephenson fan, 'Mr Bell', to 'be favoured with a sight of any documents he may be in possession of on the subject of the biography'.[10] On 14 February he sent Murray copies of references to the forthcoming book in the *Leeds Times* and *Leeds Intelligencer,* remarking coyly that the notices 'are inserted without my knowledge. I am, however well known in these northern towns, having worked in Leeds in a somewhat public capacity for many years.' His old paper remarked that 'Stephenson well deserves a careful and clever biographer, and we have no doubt our friend Mr Smiles ... will do full justice to the man by contributing to literature a work worthy of his pen and worthy of his subject.' Whatever the truth about insertion without Smiles's knowledge, the *Leeds Times* showed remarkable prescience in suggesting what his underlying theme might be: 'Stephenson was a self-taught man, and the story of such a life as his must – if justice is to be done – be full of instruction and example to others.'

The book grew. In March Smiles wrote asking for the addition of 'an address of Mr Robert Stephenson to be appended to the Life ... Mr Stephenson himself wishes that it should be given and I must defer to his judgement ... the life would not be complete without some such summary of railway results'. The thirty-five-page 'summary' was a transcript of Robert Stephenson's address, a year earlier, to the Institution of Civil Engineers on his election as their President. Smiles, unimpressed by the suggested cuts of the 'competent person'[Sir John Milton, later chief clerk in the War Office] (and by his fee of £30), took what he called 'an early opportunity of restoring' the missing anecdotes, 'as I think that personal anecdotes, when characteristic, greatly enliven the pages of a biography'. At the same time he chafed at delays in typesetting: 'The setting up of the MS still gets on slowly. Only six sheets have been corrected but I infer that some more urgent work is in hand.'[11] By April the finishing touches were being applied, including a likeness of the great man for the frontispiece – an engraving from Lucas's portrait[12] – an extremely shrewd and striking face, as Smiles remarked to Murray. He was right, though 'shrewd' was not necessarily the impression he strove for in the book.

Smiles showed a mix of nervousness and optimism as the sheets from the printer accumulated. He knew that however much research he did, however many contacts he made, when publication day came, much would still be left unsaid. He felt comforted by the knowledge that a number of short print runs were possible, second and third 'editions', so that he could treat the book as a work in progress. It was a point he kept emphasising to Murray: 'It is better to try a limited edition at first [they had agreed on 1,000 copies] as I may be able considerably to improve the book as a second edition is preparing; and I do not doubt that this will be shortly called for.'[13] He wanted to delay advertising until the last minute, 'and just before release I will submit for you a list of papers ... in which I am of opinion you may advertise with advantage'. Smiles was obviously a skilled networker, happy to use his contacts in the press to plug his book. He assured John Murray that he would 'also be able to obtain a number of good reviews of the book, which will probably prove of greater service'.

The *Life of George Stephenson, Railway Engineer* made its debut on 26 May 1857, when Smiles gave the first bound copy to the Institution of Civil Engineers at its headquarters just a few doors from Robert Stephenson's office in Great George Street. Robert Stephenson was the Institution's President. When he wrote to Smiles the following week he reported that 'those who have perused the volume you left with the Institution, not beyond two or three, like the tone and feeling of the Biography very much indeed. They like both the head and the heart that produced it.'

The creation of the steam locomotive had not been an event but a process, depending on crucial contributions from different people at different times, learning from each other, adapting and improving each other's work. The same was even more true of the development of the railway system that gave the locomotive its practical value. But collective credit does not make a good story, or an inspiring hero. Smiles wanted both, and was selective in his use of the material he used to create them. This was not cynical, but driven by a belief in George Stephenson's unique vision and in the character he needed to make it a reality. Other wonderful men had played their parts, but there was only one giant. Inevitably, advocates of other claimants were upset by this approach. Smiles knew it would happen, and was both combative and realistic enough to arm himself – thus his eagerness for successive editions, allowing him to process new information and criticism as it arrived. One of the earliest and most significant changes from the first edition was the removal, after pressure from the Institution of Civil Engineers, of references to engineers attaching their names 'to the most daring and foolish projects'. This was an echo of Spencer's much blunter accusation that 'the morality of railway engineers is not greatly above that of railway lawyers. The gossip of Great George Street [home of the Institute, and, of course, of the office of Robert Stephenson and George Bidder] is fertile in discreditable revelations.'[14] Over the years Smiles made many revisions to the book,[15] but never strayed from the central narrative.

This was the version accepted, and welcomed, by most reviewers. Like Robert Stephenson's friends at the Institution they went for tone and feeling, and for the combination of head and heart that had produced the book. *The Times* was so overcome that on successive Wednesdays,

9 and 16 September, it spread its review over a full page of the day's news-paper – a combined dissertation of almost fifteen thousand words. Smiles must have been thrilled. Not only was the sheer scale of these notices a massive advertisement for the book, but *The Times* reviewer played back to its readers some of Smiles's most cherished ideas – about the underestimation of men who have risen from the ranks compared to 'the claims of lineage or the privilege which inherits', and the paper's description of what was to become the archetypal Smiles hero, 'with his noble simplicity and energy, his zeal for his kind, his native born gentleness and indomitable tenacity'. When *The Times* stated 'that by Mr Smiles, who has performed this office [of providing a life of GS] with eminent success, a considerable void has been filled up in modern history', Smiles knew he need have no fear of such begrudging critics as the *Spectator,* which commented that 'Mr Smiles is not devoid of that zeal for his hero which is often observed to characterise the biographer ... George Stephenson neither discovered the principle of the railway, nor invented a locomotive, nor even first applied it to practical use.' Even then the magazine's reviewer accepted the value of the biography, and others received it with enthusiasm. George Eliot wrote to a friend: 'The "Life of George Stephenson" has been a real profit and pleasure ... he is one of my great heroes; has he not a dear old face?'[16] Thanks to Smiles, the George Stephenson myth was given the power to last a hundred years, and thanks to George Stephenson, Samuel Smiles was given the designation he craved: 'Behold me', he rejoiced, 'at last, at the advanced age of forty-five, a successful author!'

14
Enthusiasm on All Fronts

SMILES scarcely dared to contemplate his good fortune with the publication of *George Stephenson*. He had no mind or time for other half-finished projects, like redrafting the self-help book, though he was always happy to beat the self-help drum:

> People wondered how a person so utterly unknown in the literary world should have been able to write a successful book, especially on the topic of an engineer. But they did not know the long training I had had for the work, and the difficulties I had overcome – the encounter with which, indeed, had educated me – nor the reading, thinking, observation and perseverance, which are about the sole conditions for success in anything.

In the months after the sell-out of the first print run of *George Stephenson*, John Murray's concern was with keeping up production, minimising amendments, and agreeing plans for further editions. There were three between June and September – a total of 4,500 in those months, all hardback copies at 16 shillings each. Smiles played his role avidly, writing almost weekly to Murray with acknowledgements and suggestions. The *Examiner* published an enthusiastic review on 22 August, claiming Stephenson as 'the peculiar hero of the working man, and on behalf of working men we are disposed to petition for a cheap abridged edition'. Smiles told Murray he thought that 'the same size and price should be adhered to so long as the book sells freely'.[1] But he passed the *Examiner*'s idea on, asking Murray for his views. In fact no cheap abridged edition appeared until 1859.

In the meantime, Smiles afterwards asserted, 'literature occupied a very small portion of my thoughts, and a still smaller portion of my working faculties ... for months together I did not set down a word for the printer'. If this gives the impression that he was disengaging from the book, or from other writing projects, the impression is misleading. He was consistently in touch with John Murray, sending additions and amendments for new editions, and dealing with comments and criticisms from readers. He answered many readers' letters himself, often acceding to their wishes. When Macadam's grandson complained of the way the book treated his grandfather, Smiles promised to remove the offending passage, 'as I have no wish to give anybody offence'. These intrusions, like 'old Herepath calling to complain that I had not given him credit for having exposed the fallacy of the atmospheric system', gave Smiles encouragement. He welcomed reaction, critical or flattering. 'All this shows that the book is being extensively read.'[2]

And of course soon he saw the finest of all compliments to an author – his imitators. Having created the genre, Smiles felt able to patronise followers. A year after the appearance of Stephenson he picked up news that Sir John Rennie had been working on a life of his own father, and had already written eight-hundred pages. Far from fearing competition, Smiles was dismissive. 'I do not know that the materials will be very interesting, or that Sir John will make much of them.' He was always comfortable, even smug, about his own particular ability as a writer: 'I have no doubt the success of "Stephenson" has set many writers at work; but engineers generally are not interesting subjects in themselves and books about them can only be made interesting by skilful treatment of the accessories.'[3]

The tendency to puff up his authorial status was probably no more than the understandable bid of a newcomer for self-confidence. But in his dealings with Murray's, Smiles showed signs of a tougher self-belief. John Murray had generously, after the sell-out of the first two editions, offered to improve terms for future publication. 'With regard to the Life of Stephenson,' he wrote,

> its success is now so thoroughly confirmed, and the risque [sic] of publi-
> cation is so reduced, that I am enabled to state that on completion of the
> second edition, I shall be happy to publish future editions in consideration

of one third of the profits instead of one half, and from that time forth account for two thirds to you after deducting all expenses.[4]

Nine months later Smiles was writing to Murray demanding even better terms:

of course the arrangements with the fifth edition will be on the same footing as the previous editions – you taking a third of the profits in respect of your risk in the publication. But with reference to future editions, will you be good enough to state what could be arranged in event of my taking all the risk.[5]

Murray's response was swift and indignant. 'Considering that I have born [sic] all the bother and brunt of the day in respect of your Life of George Stephenson,' he protested,

and that I myself volunteered to sacrifice no small part of the emoluments to which I was entitled by our original agreement made, be it remembered when there really was a risk whether your work would meet with failure or success. I find it rather hard that you now suggest making other and what you consider more advantageous arrangements.[6]

On this occasion Smiles backed down, and agreed to continue as before, but he returned to the point in the future. His upward trajectory as a Murray author would ensure that eventually he won improved terms.

Compared with the disillusioned figure who had limped into London three years earlier – dismissed from his job in Leeds, bereft of his magazine publisher in London, his manuscript rejected by Routledge and his self-esteem undermined by his employers at the South Eastern, Smiles was now bursting with confidence and enthusiasm on all fronts. As the widely praised author of a book on George Stephenson, and a friend of Robert Stephenson, engineering legend, his employers at London Bridge had to see him in a new light. Their Secretary, whom they may have regarded as an occasional scribbler, had revealed himself as an author whose work commanded attention from the most revered publications in the country. Their employee was a celebrity. He certainly expected them to listen to his views on their business.

The operation of the railway company was very much the responsibility of its excellent General Manager, C W Eborall, and of its Secretary, Samuel Smiles. The Directors concentrated on capital decisions and on lobbying Parliament to support any plans for extension. As far as Smiles was concerned, they lacked ambition, having neither the will to press their case hard enough at Westminster nor the vision to appreciate their opportunity.

The most profound strategic decision facing the company at this time concerned its London terminus. This was at London Bridge Station, on the south side of the river, while the bulk of the capital's growing population and commercial activity was on the northern side. The South Eastern's rail network, all across Kent and south as far as the coast, and on to the continent, would be of immensely greater value if it could stretch an arm across the Thames, and offer a hand to the huge market which lay on the northern side.

The booming middle and clerical classes were setting up homes in the new suburbs and beyond. Days out, at the seaside or in the country, were becoming the rage. W P Frith's painting of a crowded beach – 'Ramsgate Sands' – had been the sensation of the 1854 Royal Academy's summer exhibition. It was the railway that made such scenes possible. Mrs Beeton, soon to become high priestess of the suburbs (the first instalment of her *Book of Household Management* appeared in November 1859), was the voice of a generation expecting easy rail travel, to work and to play. London, billowing into 'Greater London', was the world's largest market for rail travel, but the South Eastern, though poised on its perimeter, was cut off from its centre. Eborall and Smiles recognised the problem, but though the directors agreed in 1857 to promote 'such a scheme as will effectually supply access to the West End of London, and so complete the system of railway accommodation for Kent and the Continent',[7] nothing was done.

Smiles, in spite of his need constantly to give attention to his publisher, his readers, and his authorial future, was determined not to see the South Eastern lose such an opportunity. And perhaps in this he was showing more than an employee's conscientiousness. George Stephenson had provided him with a focus for all the ideas he most treasured – the idea of progress, of the power of technology to change peoples' lives, of the great social benefits of a railway system – as well as the idea of success based on difficulties overcome. The timidity of the Board of the South Eastern was in denial of all these. So when Smiles wrote of literature occupying 'a very small part of my thoughts, and a still smaller portion of my working faculties', he was revealing less tension than synergy between the two parts of his life.

So he and Eborall acted. They organised a survey of passengers arriving by train at London Bridge station, and found that more than three-fifths were bound for places to the west of Temple Bar, and especially for the area around Charing Cross. Smiles then prepared a 29-page blockbuster – *A Statement in Support of the proposed London Bridge and Charing Cross Railway submitted for the Consideration of the Directors of the South Eastern Railway*, published on 16 February 1858. The directors would have been brave indeed not to consider it, and not to be hammered into agreement, as Smiles and his aides piled statistic upon statistic, survey upon survey, and calculation upon calculation to make their case. No movement of people or traffic in London escaped examination, creating a picture of a metropolis doomed to gridlock if the proposed railway and its new terminus did not go ahead.

The directors were invited to reflect on the fact that 'the journey by cab or omnibus from Paddington to London Bridge occupies the same time as the journey by railway from London Bridge to Tunbridge Wells'. For Londoners modern life had arrived. The time occupied by the journey to and from the station, through the packed streets, was greater than the railway journey itself. And what about London Bridge? The traffic which passed over the bridge 'in one day between 8am and 8pm was 60,080 persons on foot, and 11,498 vehicles.'

Of course Smiles did not rely on facts and figures alone to make the case. He knew too well the power of a human story to back up an argument. If no real-life biography was available for the job, Smiles was happy to invent one. The *Statement* includes

> The case of 'Paterfamilias', who wishes to give his wife and family the benefit of country air for a month at Reigate or Dorking or Tunbridge Wells, or perhaps the sea air at Hastings or Folkestone ... he contemplates running down two or three times a week to see his family, and with that object proposes to take a season ticket for the period. Suppose him to live in Regent Circus or Oxford Street.

Then the plight of Paterfamilias is laid out for all to see. At the weekend, stuck in the traffic between his west-end home and London Bridge station, PF cannot reach his family, pining for him in Reigate, 'even if he put himself to the objectionable expense of a cab ... perhaps he may be caught in a block in one of the only thoroughfares ... or on London Bridge at about four o'clock when the pressure is the greatest, and miss his train.' But in one bound Paterfamilias, blockaded in Oxford Street, can be free – if the new line and new station at Charing Cross go ahead. 'For the case would be altogether different. He could take his carpet bag in his hand, as City passengers now do to London Bridge, and walk from his place of business to the station, able to depend on taking the train to a minute.'

Highlighting Paterfamilias's difficulty in running down to Reigate for a few days, the *Statement* took little account of the poor families whose pathetic homes stood in the way of the proposed new line, except to note with satisfaction that 'for the greater part of its course, [it] passes through some of the worst property in the metropolis, and therefore the cost will be not nearly so great as might, at first sight, be anticipated.'[8]

In February 1858 Smiles submitted this blueprint for railway heaven to the Directors of the South Eastern Railway. They did not argue against its findings, but refused to provide the capital necessary to make the scheme possible. Smiles and his allies would not be defeated. They proposed raising the money through a new company, with a board of four from the South Eastern and four representing other interests. Smiles prepared the prospectus.

While all this was going on he was managing the publication of the fourth edition of *George Stephenson*, looking again at the idea of a cheap version, and discussing with John Murray ideas for other biographies. Only months after the launch of his first Murray book he was already working on the next one:

> I have for some time been working on a companion life of Watt ... there are a thousand interesting topics arising out of the industrial history of the last century – with which Watt was intimately identified which should render such a life, if fitly executed, of considerable historical interest.[9]

In the meantime the campaign for a rail link over the Thames, and a grand new station at Charing Cross, was not allowed to slacken. Smiles's prospectus attracted the necessary investment in the new company. Parliamentary approval was the vital next step and, although opposed by the Brighton Rail Company, it should not have been a problem. Unfortunately, however, the proposed line, just as it approached the south bank of the river, would touch the grounds of St Thomas's Hospital. The hospital's trustees lobbied Parliament to reject the application. Helped by a brief prepared by Smiles, the company's counsel, W J Alexander, made a case powerful enough to persuade the Parliamentary committee, and both Houses, to approve the Charing Cross scheme. They imposed, however, a very expensive condition: the company must buy St Thomas's Hospital – buildings, grounds, and all attaching property – at a price to be set by an independent arbitrator. After two weeks of court hearings the arbitrator delivered his decision: the rail company might proceed with their scheme on payment to St Thomas's hospital of £290,000 – the equivalent today of about £80,000,000,[10] but in the context of the amounts involved in nineteenth-century railway construction, apparently acceptable.

St Thomas's was demolished and eventually a new hospital arose, in some magnificence, on its present site opposite the Houses of Parliament. The new railway was able to start its progress across the former hospital's grounds and over the river towards its new station. Samuel Smiles took great satisfaction from these events. Whether or not his treatment in his *Autobiography* of the Charing Cross project is seen as boastful, certainly it reveals his abiding belief in the value of industrial progress (even, in this case, at an extra cost of £290,000), and in the reward of obstacles overcome. The new rail link, and its Charing Cross terminus, did not come into service until 1864, but by that time Samuel Smiles's parallel career had moved on to a completely different level.

The balance of Smiles's preoccupations had changed significantly since his arrival in London. In Leeds, in spite of declarations about 'leaving politics', he had always been engaged. His place there had been accurately described to John Murray when he said he was 'well known in these northern towns, having been working there in a somewhat public capacity for many years'. But London's power to stretch, to divide and isolate, made that sort of 'public capacity' for Smiles both impractical and unwanted. The campaigning journalist and committee-joining activist had been left in his northern past; but not necessarily the ideas that had driven him. From now on those ideas sustained their life in his books, through the lives of his heroes: the best beginnings were the humblest, the greatest achievements the most difficult, the finest education the self-acquired. Anything could be reached by anyone who followed the golden path of perseverance.

So convinced, Smiles had taken on the double task of helping to transform his company's place in London's railway system, and of becoming the chronicler of his country's industrial achievements, both at the same time. Following his 1857 note to Murray about a Watt biography, by the summer of 1858 excitement was gathering in his mind for something more ambitious: a sweeping history of England's engineering legacy, based on the lives of its creators. 'I am still getting up information about Brindley, Watt, & the others,' he wrote to Murray in August,

> and am still of opinion that an interesting series may be written – illustrating the industrial history of England, and indeed of the modern history of England, which may be said to have commenced with the Engineer, for the Engineer has been largely instrumental in providing those internal communications – canals, roads, & steam engines etc – which have conferred so much wealth and strength on this country. When I am ready with a first volume I will confer with you further on the subject.[11]

So already, while successive editions of *Stephenson* sped through the press, Smiles was planning the multi-volume work that he believed might be his greatest achievement.

He spoke to Robert Stephenson about the idea. Stephenson had been as surprised as Murray by the success of his father's biography, and admired its author. 'Still, he doubted whether I could rely on the same element of success in the lives of departed engineers, who had died and left scarcely a trace of their history.' But Smiles saw the value of the departed engineers as more than their works; he saw the drama in 'their noble efforts, their temporary defeats,' in their triumphs based on strength of character and moral courage.

In spite of Smiles's eager prompting on the subject, Murray seems not to have reacted. The long-discussed short, 'popular' version of Stephenson was at last almost ready for publication. Standing alongside the full volume, and bringing the Stephenson story to a much wider market, it was of more commercial interest to Murray than a speculative giant group biography. Smiles's undoubted skill with engineering subjects could, Murray hoped, be better used in the short term and without risk, by contributions to the Murray-produced *Quarterly Review*. Articles appeared in January 1858 on Iron Bridges, and in July and October on James Watt. The *Quarterly Review* played a continuing part in Smiles's writing life for the next twenty years.

For now, these articles helped to add to his income, already greatly boosted by his share of profits from sales of *George Stephenson*. In July Murray's had sent him a cheque for £694-2-5.[12] This would have more than doubled his total income, given that his salary as railway secretary was £600 a year. In fact Murray's had underpaid him. In his letter acknowledging the amount he politely but firmly reminded them of the change, after the third edition, from half to two thirds of profits. Three days later he received another cheque for £121-5-3.[13]

These comparative riches provided Smiles with the confidence to plan a move for his family from Glenmohr Terrace to something a little further up the hill, a little closer to his beloved heath, a little grander. Number 6 Granville Park Terrace would give him the space, appropriate for a successful author, to have his own study, where he could work undisturbed, for as many hours as he wanted. In tidying his desk for the move he took the opportunity to review again the *Self-Help* manuscript rejected by George Routledge five years earlier. Though he had little time before the move to give attention to it, he wanted to sound out John Murray on the idea for the book.

There had been other books on a similar theme. In his youth Smiles had read George Craik's *Pursuit of Knowledge Under Difficulties*, but he had in mind something more practical, concerned with 'the ordinary business and pursuits of common life',[14] drawn from his own observation and experience. It would not, of course, be of the same stature as *Stephenson*, or of the big biographical series he had already suggested. This was something slight, which would take only a few months to have ready, and provide, perhaps, a useful filler between *George Stephenson* and other major engineering biographies. 'I expect to see you shortly,' he remarked in a letter to John Murray on 5 January 1859, 'about a small book to be published about June'. But he was so much occupied at the time with other things 'that I am prevented from getting on with it in the evenings as steadily as I would like'. He did not believe it would add value to his name as an author; it might best, perhaps, be published anonymously.

John Murray, when he saw the manuscript, agreed to publish the book. His terms again, given the risk in producing something so different, would be for a fifty-fifty split of profits.[15] Smiles, however, having learned from the argument over Stephenson, decided to reverse the contractual obligation, take the production risk of the new book himself, and go for the maximum profit. After all, it was to be only a small book, with small expectations. The credit balance on Stephenson would more than cover initial printing costs (Smiles suggested 1,500 copies).[16] John Murray seems to have seen no reason to disagree. Risk-free, he could be as bullish as he liked about the book. In the event he persuaded Smiles to publish under his own name, and to double the suggested print run. A little flattery helped to smooth the agreement: 'I think with your name on the title-page you may venture to commence with the printing of 3,000 copies.'[17] (In his subsequent research for a memoir of the House of Murray, Smiles unearthed the fact that Jane Austen had done a similar deal with John Murray's father in 1815 for the publication of *Emma*. Murray had offered £450 for the copyright, which she declined.)

In the weeks before the launch of *Self-Help* Smiles's main interest continued to be the progress of *Stephenson*. Robert Stephenson had died on 12 October, and was buried at Westminster Abbey on the 21st in a service attended by 3,000. His father had been quietly interred in his own home town of Chesterfield. The much greater public attention paid to Robert's passing has been attributed in part to the impact of Smiles's book, 'that powerful biography which made George Stephenson loved by thousands'.[18] In any event, Smiles, never willing to miss an opportunity, suggested to John Murray a further edition of the original, 'embodying also the Life of Robert Stephenson ... I think the subject can best be treated by working up the career of the two men together'.[19] But nothing was done at the time. Three weeks later the first signals were coming through that *Self-Help* might be doing something exceptional.

'I am exceedingly gratified to learn that *Self-Help* has gone off so well', Smiles wrote to John Murray on 26 November. 'What was the number

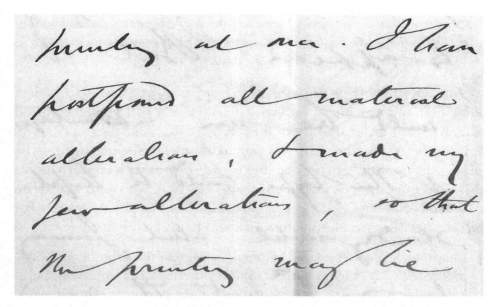

8 Smiles's letter to John Murray, December 1859: 'I have postponed all
material alterations, so that the printing may be proceeded with at once...'
The adrenalin flows across the page...
(National Library of Scotland, John Murray Archive (Ms.41099))

sold? I see the Athenaeum gives 3200, and the Critic 6000, but the latter
must be a mistake. I presume the type is still standing, as arranged. I will
at once set about making corrections and additions.' *George Stephenson*,
which had made Smiles 'a successful author', had sold about 4,000
copies in its first three months. *Self-Help* was surpassing that in its first
three weeks. But even then neither Smiles nor Murray had any idea of
the publishing success that was thundering towards them. Smiles seems
to have been at least as much concerned with his contributions for the
Quarterly Review. He really didn't want *Self-Help* to get in the way of his
next article: 'I am now busying myself with an article on Mills and Spinning Jennies for the next Quarterly and should like to be informed
whether the forwarding of proofs of *Self-Help* be urgent.'[20] Nor did his
interest in the Stephensons fade. He returned, in the same letter, to the
idea of Robert being added to the book on George:

> about the story of Stephenson, it occurs to me that I might now proceed
> with writing out the story of Robert's life to be appended to the other ... I

have contributed a short article on the subject of R Stephenson to Fraser's for December, but have kept in reserve the more interesting matter relating to him which can be served up in the book itself.[21]

With a reprint of *Self-Help* already in hand Smiles conceded a few days later that he must hurry with his corrections: 'I will make few or no alterations in order that there may be no delay, and they may go on printing off by Monday.'[22] By now Smiles was clearly feeling the pressure of keeping up with both the demand for *Self-Help* and his concern for his other, 'serious' work on engineering subjects. Writing to John Murray on 1 December about *Self-Help*, the adrenalin flows across the page – big writing, fast, excited, hardly time for space between the words:

I have postponed all material alterations, so that the printing may be proceeded with at once. You may safely order a large impression, but I leave that to you. The most important notices have yet to appear, but it would be an advantage if the type could be kept standing until about January, to see what the demand may be.

And yet on the same day Smiles was off to the north in pursuit of infor-mation for his article on spinning jennies – 'I go down to Manchester this evening to see some Crompton accounts and look at some cotton factories.' He was so little aware at the time of the significance of *Self-Help* that he 'tore up the manuscript as waste paper'.[23] At the year's end, with the reprint of *Self-Help* now on its way through the bookshops, Smiles's gratification lay mainly in his other work: 'I am in hopes that the article [on cotton spinning, for the *Quarterly*] may be read with much interest,' he wrote to John Murray on 29 December. 'Without vanity I may say that it will be the most complete thing of its kind that has yet appeared – and a good deal of it has been the result of personal enquiry and research.'

The small book, meantime, was spreading in its thousands to readers for whom the *Quarterly Review* was largely invisible. The People, not just in England, but across the world, were discovering Samuel Smiles.

15

The Enticing Warmth

ALTHOUGH Smiles had realised, as soon as the scale of early demand for *Self-Help* became apparent, that the book was headed for popular success, his attitude towards it was ambiguous – almost as though he saw it as a distraction from his more important work. If he had fathered a monster, was it a monster he could learn to love? He must surely have understood that he had designed an overtly populist book, directed at a different readership from *George Stephenson* or any of the other biographical projects he planned. If he did not, press reaction would soon give him plenty of hints. His own *Leeds Times*, unsurprisingly, was one of the first out of the blocks, on 26 November, tagging *Self-Help* as a book for the young, particularly the working-class young with little access to formal education: 'Every young person should read "Self-Help" – and no Mechanics' Institution or Educational Society should be without it ... Mr Smiles writes for the million.'[1] His style, too, was for the million: 'what the French call naïveté – a certain kind of exquisite simplicity'. Smiles's Introduction to the first edition identifies the book at once with the young and unsophisticated, tracing its origin to those same 'young men of the humblest rank resolved to meet in the winter evenings, for the purpose of improving themselves and exchanging knowledge with each other'. Though he refers to the link between *Self-Help* and his life of George Stephenson, he points out that 'The illustrative sketches of character introduced are, however, necessarily less elaborately treated – being busts rather than full-length portraits.' *Self-Help* comes in bite-size pieces, undemanding of its readers' time. This pick-and-mix quality was a gift for reviewers and editors – reviewers able to select examples which most supported their point of view, editors able to extract ready-packed snippets to brighten their columns. This quotability was also a gift to Murray's and to Smiles, by ensuring that word of their book spread quickly and widely.

Self-Help has something of the nature of a reference book, without a reference book's detachment. It is a sourcebook for instruction and inspiration rather than, like *George Stephenson*, a continuous inspirational narrative. As might be expected from a man with Smiles's love of the mechanical, it is carefully constructed to meet its purpose, in his own words: 'citing examples of what other men had done, as illustration of what each might, in a greater or less degree, do for himself'.[2]

Each of its thirteen chapters, which average about ten thousand words, opens with a short homily setting out the chapter's theme, then moves seamlessly into biographical examples illustrating and expanding on the theme. Often this involves some fancy semantic, and syllogistic, footwork. Smiles was, as an obituarist remarked, 'Happy-go-lucky in his premises [but] ever confident in his conclusions.'[3] For instance Chapter Two, headed 'Leaders of Industry', opens with the assertion that 'One of the most strongly marked features of the English people is their spirit of industry', goes on to slide from 'industry' meaning work, through the same word meaning industrial manufacture, to the role of inventors in creating industrial progress, and back to the 'industrious' character and lowly origins of the inventors. 'A steady application to work is the healthiest training for every individual, so is it the best discipline of a state. Honourable industry travels the same road with duty; and Providence has closely linked both with happiness.' Thus set up, examples follow: of Watt – 'one of the most industrious of men' – through Arkwright, William Lee (inventor of the stocking frame), John Heathcoat (inventor of the bobbin net machine), and many others – their careers all used as examples both of the rewards of application and of the way great industrial success can grow from the humblest beginnings.

Newspaper editors are moralisers, and *Self-Help* gave them an inexhaustible source to feed from. They were happy to keep on citing the book, and the book kept on selling. Its time was right. Britain's triumphant industrial surge had brought wealth to many, intimations of prosperity to many more, and a greater awareness to both of the corrosive effects of mass poverty. A country that had gained so much had an equally heightened sense of how much it had to lose. The world's greatest economy was ashamed, and afraid, of its poor, so brutally classified by Henry Mayhew 'under three separate phases, according as they will work, they can't work, and they won't work'.[4] Society's ambition was to move the last two categories into the first. Conscience, compassion, self-interest and self-protection combined in an urge to improve the left-behind. This urge had been apparent for some time in the encourage-ment of culture through public art galleries, exhibitions – as far back as the Great Exhibition of 1851, with its low-priced tickets, some as low as a shilling – and the Manchester Art Treasures Exhibition of 1857. Museums, cheap magazines of an improving nature like *Good Words* and *Leisure Hour*, and of course the spread of moral, cultural and practical education through movements like the Mechanics' Institutions, all moved in the same direction. *Self-Help* and its message must flourish in ground like this, and Smiles be aware of the rich seam he had opened. Now he had created two new genres – industrial biography and self-improvement biography. The overarching moral message may have been the same in both, but their audiences were different. Early sales clearly indicated which market was greater. Smiles, however, was in love with his engineers and convinced of his mission to show their historical significance.

His initial reaction to the success of *Self-Help* was to see it not as a prompt to produce others like it, but as evidence of the scope for more industrial biographies. In January 1860, a few months after the publica-tion of *Self-Help*, he told John Murray, 'I have been surprised to find how extensive a field of unworked biography has been opened up to me by the publication of the little book; and it is more than ever clear to me that the men of industry, who have made this country what it is, have been too much neglected. I shall be glad if I can do somewhat to rescue from forgetfulness a few of the more distinguished of these honourable men.'[5]

None of this meant any blunting of Smiles's sharp eye for publishing opportunities. He was too eager and excited, his mind alive with ideas for books, spin-offs, and articles – even when he might not write them himself. 'By the way,' he wrote to Murray in November 1859, speaking of Quarterly articles, I would suggest one which, though I could not undertake it myself, you might find some writer to undertake and it would be extremely full of interest – I mean a review of the work of Leech, a second series of whose pen and pencil sketches is about to appear. Comparison might be made with Gillray and Cruikshank, and the other humourists in that art.[6]

It seems that he also had in mind some sort of *Self-Help* follow-up book, or more likely an article, on books and publishers. He asked John Murray about including

your 'forbears' ... among my list of self-made men ... there must be a great deal of curious facts you can supply me with respecting successful and unsuccessful books – the detection, by the quick-sighted publisher, of the merits of books – in short a large amount of literary anecdote of an entirely original character.

(It was an idea taken up by John Murray almost thirty years later, but in a quite different way.) He was also still alert, as noted, to the possi-bilities available from the Stephenson story. His obituary of Stephenson junior, in *Fraser's* December issue, although it purported to be in praise of Robert, was yet another paean to George, 'the inventor of the passenger locomotive, and the founder of the now gigantic railway system of England and the world'. Robert was then cast as no more than the shadow of his father: 'the honours which George Stephenson failed to receive during his life and at his death, and which in the strength of his self-dependence, he would have been the last to seek, have at length not unworthily been reflected on his eminently meritorious son'.[7]

Smiles did return to the Stephensons, but not until 1862, when their joint biography appeared as the third volume of his *Lives of the Engineers*. *Lives*, rather than *Self-Help*, was the great work on which Smiles hoped to build his reputation. Smiles was a railway man, a participant. His natural interest was in railways and transport – how the development of transport communication had shaped the modern world and how the men behind it had overcome such intimidating difficulties. This was his larger view, an integral part of the *Self-Help* theme. That book he saw at the time of its publication as simply a pleasant lay-by in the greater landscape. In spite of its astonishing success he would not write another in the same mode for almost ten years.

By now Smiles was a significant author in the Murray list. He and John Murray had grown closer, on both a professional and a personal level. As bookmen and Scotsmen, both Edinburgh graduates, of about the same age (Murray four years the older), they had much in common. But Murray's background was very different from Smiles's. As John Murray III he was heir to a famous name and a flourishing business. He had been educated at an English public school – Charterhouse – and sent his son to Eton. As a student he had enjoyed life in the upper echelons of Edinburgh society. His family home was a grand house, Newstead, in its own grounds overlooking the lake in Wimbledon Park. He was a staunch conservative and publisher of the *Quarterly Review*, which Smiles had once characterised as 'ultra-Tory'. Yet Murray was keen to have Smiles write for the magazine, and Smiles was, for the present at least, equally keen to contribute.

He disliked being silent. *Self-Help* and various manifestations of *George Stephenson* were in the bookshops, and *Lives of the Engineers* was still in its research stage. In this lull the *Quarterly Review* gave him a voice, as *Eliza Cook's Journal* had done ten years earlier. But between Miss Cook's soul-searching liberalism and the no-nonsense conservatism of the *Quarterly*, the ethos of the two magazines could hardly have been more different. The interesting question is, how different was Samuel Smiles?

On the evidence of the series of articles he wrote for the *Quarterly* during 1860, very different. Not since his *Leeds Times* days had he published anything so overtly partisan as *Workmen's Earnings, Strikes and Savings*, published in the Quarterly in 1860 (No.215) and reprinted as a pamphlet in 1861 (a considerable 'pamphlet', running to 165 pages). How, without changing his political stance, could a man who had written in 1841 that 'It is impossible to look on the working men of England without feeling proud of one's fellow countrymen. Suffering appalling destitution ... the working classes of Leeds have set themselves to enlighten the deplorable and disgraceful ignorance of the higher classes to their condition' – how could he write twenty years later that 'they [the working classes] do not tell themselves that they are themselves parties to the "process of degradation" which they are described as undergoing ... the

chief evils from which working people suffer are those which only themselves can cure'. Poverty, he claimed, was most commonly 'the offspring
of individual vice and improvidence; and it is to be cured, not so much
by conferring greater rights, as by implying better habits'. Smiles's
Belfast-reared granddaughter, writing in 1956, quoted *Workmen's
Earnings* with relish and applauded what she saw as her grandfather's
conversion: 'You can hardly call Samuel Smiles a radical now. Idiots
never change, sensible men change for the better.'[8]

The problem with *Workmen's Earnings* is not with the remedies it
proposes for working-class poverty – these are consistent with everything
Smiles had been saying for decades – diligence, thrift, temperance,
education, and moral fortitude. The change is in the ills now diagnosed.
In the past he had cited bad government, aristocratic greed, and lack of
education as the roots of society's ills. Now the people's own extravagance, shiftlessness, and wilful ignorance, seem to be the enemies. Not
only did Smiles feel compelled to lecture the poor about how to deal with
their poverty, he seemed determined to scold them for ever having
become poor in the first place: 'improvidence is unhappily the defect of
the class'.

What brought about the change? He was turning fifty, past the normal
mid-point of life. He had moved from Leeds to London, from Mrs
Gaskell's North to Mrs Beeton's South.[9] He was starting to feel the
enticing warmth of prosperity, and of family life at last without financial
strain. And not only were Smiles's circumstances changing – those of
whole swathes of the population were changing too. He was witness to a
real improvement in national prosperity and in the condition of large
numbers of working people. Britain, they were told, was the richest, most
powerful, and best-behaved nation on earth. Everyone could share in the
British dream, if they were well-behaved. Millions did, and were. In this
mood of self-congratulation they often resented rather than pitied the
poor, seeing them not as fellow workers fallen on hard times, but as a
different species, the 'dangerous classes' – those, in Mayhew's terms, who
won't work.

This was the condition of society, and England's perception of itself,
when Smiles wrote *Workmens' Earnings, Strikes and Savings*. However, in
its repositioning of Smiles's argument, and its unpleasant, hectoring tone,

the pamphlet focused on a specific group of workers. Though Smiles spread his fire hither and thither – 'happy-go-lucky in his premises' – *Workmen's Earnings* was prompted by the strike and lock-out of building workers in London in the summer of 1859[10] and the speech in which their leader, George Potter, claimed that 'life to a working man is a ceaseless process of degradation, a daily martyrdom, a funeral procession to the grave'. Compared with the plight of Leeds mechanics in the 1840s Smiles thought contemporary workers had little to complain about.

Enraged both by Potter's words and by the strike's ineffectiveness and waste, he quotes Potter in the opening sentence of *Workmen's Earnings*. In the ensuing 165 pages he seeks first, to dismantle Potter's argument by a historical analysis of employment figures and wages, and from there to make a case that it was not the level of wages that caused distress but the uses to which those wages were put – mainly, he feared 'in ardent spirits, beer and tobacco'. The usual Smiles tropes run through the pamphlet, but it returns most often to thrift as the lesson the working man needs to learn. Having wagged his finger at the improvident, Smiles in the end acknowledges that 'such being the diligence, the dexterity, and the ingenuity of English workmen, it is meet that they should be liberally remunerated', and he calls on employers

> not to stand too strongly on their rights, nor to entrench themselves exclusively within their own order ... were there more trust and greater sympathy between classes, there would be less disposition to turn out on the part of the men, and a more accommodating spirit on the part of the masters.

Although this was an echo of earlier *Leeds Times* appeals for reconciliation, there is a note of resignation, and certainly of weariness with factional conflict, in these closing lines. Smiles seems frustrated by the futility of the argument. If he changed in these years it was not so much a change of sides – from radical to reactionary – as a change away from side-taking. In future his commitment would be even more to his original belief in individual responsibility based on moral character: 'happiness' was not to be found in adherence to political party, or class, or mob, or trade union, or church, but in the moral fibre of the individual, spun from hard work, honesty, self-education, and thrift. A man's battle was not with other men but with himself, and providence had decreed that it was winnable. And if his catalogue of virtues seemed unexciting, Smiles wanted to prove that they were the most exciting, inspiring ideas ever to have occurred to mankind. Look at George Stephenson, look at James Watt, at Brindley, at Smeaton, Rennie, Telford ... Unexciting? Read the lives of the engineers.

Smiles defined his ambition for these books in the preface to Volume I of *Lives of the Engineers*: 'The object of the following pages is to give an account of some of the principal men by whom the material development of England has been promoted.' His enthusiasm spills on to the page. He had opened, he believed, a door to an aspect of British history 'which has hitherto remained largely unexplored'[11] – nothing less than the story of nature tamed to make a vibrant modern nation – fertile land won from the sea ... a country accessible in all directions ... roads, bridges, canals and railways ... lighthouses, breakwaters, docks and harbours. The 'mere mechanics' of the subject may have put off other writers, deterred by 'the necessity of burrowing through a vast amount of engineers' reports ... the driest possible reading'. But Smiles has seen past the grey tide of data to the beating heart of the story: 'The events in the lives of the early engineers were a succession of individual struggles, some rising almost to the heroic.'

He was on familiar ground. For anyone who had missed George Stephenson, the men who had built Britain were, he declared in the Preface to Volume I,

> strong-minded, resolute and ingenious, impelled to their special pursuits by the force of their constructive instincts. In most cases they had to make for themselves a way; for there was none to point out the road ... there is almost a dramatic interest in their noble efforts, their defeats and their triumphs; and their eventual rise, in spite of manifold obstructions and difficulties, from obscurity to fame.

Smiles, always determined to show Britain as the leader of the modern industrial world, felt bound to acknowledge that this was a fairly recent phenomenon. Until the eighteenth century 'We depended for our engineering, even more than for our pictures and our music, upon foreigners.' But happily all, it seemed, was now well: 'After the lapse of a century, we find the state of things has become entirely reversed. Instead of borrowing engineers from abroad, we now send them to all parts of the world ... all this has been accomplished within the last century, much of it within the life of the present generation.' However far Smiles might dip back into history to set the scene for his story, he wanted his underlying message to be timeless. 'Manifold obstructions and difficulties' would always be with us, but so would the human spirit that could overcome them. From Hugh Myddelton's conquest of miles of marsh, mud and rock in giving London its first water scheme in 1613, to Telford's soaring Menai Bridge opened in 1825, Smiles recognised that real challenge came in big lumps, and was determined to meet his own.

In 1859, with his *Self-Help* manuscript barely settled on John Murray's desk, he put his hand to creating the *Lives of the Engineers*, a work that would run to almost 1,500 pages, dense in information and exposition, with 265 original engravings of landscapes, maps and mechanical diagrams. He would be closely involved with the production details of the three volumes, with the nature and quality of the illustrations (in some cases providing his own sketches for reference), in proofreading, correcting and dealing with the printers. At the same time he would continue to write regularly for the *Quarterly Review*, to cope with the demands created by the success of *Self-Help* – and of course he would attend each day, meticulously, to the affairs of the South Eastern Railway.

*Lives of the Engin*eers offers Smiles's version of Britain's infrastructural history – a term with about as much emotional charge as the material it refers to. He tried to help his readers through the mechanical and geographical undergrowth by frequent recourse to his favourite device of 'anecdotes', but perhaps because the focus keeps changing from hero to hero – from Myddelton (whose New River scheme in 1613 first brought clean water to London) to Brindley, Brindley to Smeaton, Smeaton to Rennie and so on – the magic of *George Stephenson* is missing. The character of the engineers' great works interested Smiles. He knew enough about civil engineering to be a good guide, but the works and their history are just heavy framing for the character of the men themselves.

He was aware of how little could be discovered about the earlier members of his cast. 'Myddelton is rather dry-as-dust!' he complained to

Murray, 'so little of personal interest can now be got up respecting him.'[12] Men nearer to his own time were more rewarding. He could walk on the ground where they had lived, meet their ghosts. 'On Friday I expect to be in Eskdale, going over the scene of Telford's early labours as a stone mason and hope to pick up a good deal of curious information about him.'[13] Myddelton appears as little more than a worthy statue, 'a man full of enterprise and resources, an energetic and untiring worker, a great conqueror of obstacles and difficulties, an honest and truly noble man'.[14] But armed with his 'curious information' Smiles could breathe life into Thomas Telford, see him as a boy, wandering from his mud-walled cottage over the hills where 'you seem to have got almost to the world's end. There the road ceases, and above it stretch trackless moors ...' True to the Smiles model, young Telford ran errands and herded sheep to earn his first wages, five shillings a year for clogs. On this life of 'a common working man, whose sole property consisted of his mallet and chisel, his leather apron and his industry',[15] Smiles strung all the elements of his self-help message, and many of his views about life.

Telford came to London, but unlike

> the weak man who is simply a unit added to the vast, floating crowd ... he was able to strike out, keep his head above water, and make a course for himself ... Diligence, carefulness, and observation will carry a man onward and upward; and before long we learn that Telford had succeeded in advancing himself to the rank of a first-class mason.[16]

These chapters are laced with tales of Telford's humanity, of his care for his mother, writing to his cousin:

> I am not rich yet; but it will ease my mind to set my mother above the fear of want. That has always been my first object; and next to that, to be the 'somebody' which you have always encouraged me to believe I might aspire to become. Perhaps after all there may be something in it![17]

There was, of course, a great deal in it, as Smiles detailed over several hundred pages. But though Telford may have been a great engineer, Smiles wanted to be sure that no reader missed his qualities as a man, qualities that fortified him all his life. When Telford agreed to take on the creation of St Katharine's Dock in London, though now grown old and fast becoming infirm ... he had been engaged upon great works for upwards of thirty years, previous to which he had led the life of a working mason. But he had been a steady and temperate man all his life; and although nearly seventy, when consulted as to the new docks, his mind was able to deal with the subject in all its bearings as it had ever been; and he undertook the work.[18]

Smiles's didactic technique was simple. He had evolved his ideal of what 'a good life' should be, and then searched for examples of those who had shown how it might be lived. It was the case-history principle, used so effectively by business schools in later centuries. But instead of teaching how to run a business, Smiles taught how to run a life, and just as no business is perfect, no life is perfect. Smiles dealt with imperfections either by rationalising them or by using their conquest to emphasise his point. George Stephenson's bad temper and arrogance were part of 'the simple earnestness of his character. No wonder that he should have been impatient of that professional gladiatorialship against which his life had been one long struggle ... who that has made his way through so many difficulties would not be so?'[19]

As to Telford, his main crime (apart from being a bad poet – 'No amount of perseverance will make a poet of a man in whom the divine gift is not born') – was to flirt in his youth with dangerous political ideas. In an untypical burst of irony Smiles recounted how Telford had become tainted by, of all things, reading Paine's *Rights of Man*.

No sooner had he read Paine then he felt completely enlightened. He now suddenly discovered how much reason he and everybody else in England had for feeling miserable ... lo! Mr Paine had filled his imagination with the idea that England was nothing but a nation of bondmen and aristocrats ... If [formerly] Telford could not offer an opinion on politics ... he now had no such hesitation in giving an opinion on a constitution more than a thousand years old.

This was the voice of the writer of *Workmen's Earnings, Strikes and Savings* rather than of the young Leeds editor who in 1839 had mocked the constitution: 'no-meaning is the outcry of "Constitution! Rally round the Constitution!" If this means anything at all it means, in the words of Jeremy Bentham, 'rally round waste, rally round depredation, rally round oppression ... there's your sheet anchor – matchless constitution!'[20]

Smiles recorded with relief how Telford's employer discovered what he had been up to, but 'was forgiving and the matter went no further'. Telford, apparently, 'became wonderfully reconciled to the enjoyment of the substantial freedom which, after all, was secured to him by the English constitution'[21] and was kept so occupied by his forgiving master 'that he found but little time to devote either to political speculation or to verse-making'.

Telford was the last act in Volume II of the planned triple-decker. Volume III, the long-discussed combined lives of George and Robert Stephenson – less a labour of love than a marketing ploy – was largely a rehash of old material, with a final flourish aimed at silencing all pretenders to the Stephenson throne:

> We trust that the explanations thus given will have made it sufficiently clear to the reader that the claims made on behalf of Trevithick, Hedley, Hackworth, and Gurney, of having invented the steam-blast, are without foundation; and that George Stephenson, and no other person, was its sole inventor.

All three volumes were completed and published in 1862. The work involved had been immense but Smiles, now aged exactly fifty, was determined, like his great engineers, not to slow down. He might, however, have been wise to note what he had written about John Smeaton who, 'though naturally possessed of an excellent constitution, and capable of enduring much fatigue ... excited his brain too much'.[22]

16

An Engineering Pantheon

THE MAKING of *Lives of the Engineers* had been for Smiles an affirmation of his role as a serious writer. Like Smeaton, Rennie, Telford, or any others in his cast, the weight of its labour, for Smiles, increased his determination to see the thing through. The greater the pressure, the greater the addiction. His correspondence with John Murray through 1860 and '61 is full of references to the work – 'I hope the books I am now engaged upon will prove as successful as those which you have already published for me ...' He would be going to Eskdale,[1] not just to research Telford's background, but to make sketches for the book's illustrations. His letters were often addressed from his London Bridge office, to such an extent that he asked Murray to be sure to mark his replies 'Private', 'as all letters not so marked are opened'.[2] The pressure was always represented as being positive.

> I have been sticking very close to 'The Engineers' of late, and am getting through very satisfactorily. But it is very dry work to be going through piles of old canal pamphlets and such like. Still I have continued to sift out many points of interest, and to run up a by no means unlifelike portraiture of Brindley and the Duke [of Bridgewater], which I have been last working on.

He regarded it as a badge of honour to do original research on his subjects, spending every possible hour digging through records or visiting locations. During holidays, at weekends, or if railway business took him out of London, he pursued his quarry – whether in Yorkshire, Birmingham, Scotland or Cornwall. Just as in his youth in Holland and

Germany, he never travelled without a notebook. No written source was to escape, and what he could not find himself he employed researchers to root out. He found one so efficient that he recommended him to John Murray: 'a gentleman employed by me during the last month in searching up facts relating to the old engineers ... so efficient he might be able to help you'.[4] In his *Autobiography* he commented on the help he had had 'from some excellent readers and extractors of evidence', who used to work for him at the British Museum and at the City Record Office, though he did not include women in his praise. 'I found that the great defect of ladies' help was incompleteness and inaccuracy. They neglected dates and references. They could not even copy correctly. They had no originality, and could not follow up a track of investigation.' He made his opinion of womens' education clear: 'I hope that Girton and Newnham will do something to educate ladies in attention, accuracy, and thoughtfulness.'[5] As this was before the 1870 Education Act, very few women would have been schooled for this sort of work. But for Smiles, only men could be trusted 'to copy accurately, with correct references down to the exact page and edition of the books copied from'. Smiles drove others as he drove himself.

His diligence was, he believed, rewarded by the publication of the three handsome volumes of *Lives* which appeared, the first two at the end of 1861 and the third in 1862, and by their respectful reception.[6] He wrote to John Murray as soon as the reviews started to appear. Because he took such pride in his research, he was annoyed by what he described as the carping tone of the *Athenaeum*. It accused him of 'merely skilfully working up what has been brought to my door by others'. Whereas, he reminded Murray, 'the fact is the bulk of the lives of Brindley, Rennie and Telford are obtained from ms and from personal enquiry'. However in general the critics' opinions pleased him – 'the reviews are most gratifying'. *The Times*, as it had done with *The Life of George Stephenson* four years earlier, gave almost two whole pages to *Lives of The Engineers* (21 November and 24 December 1861). In an unusual flash of modesty Smiles remarked to John Murray that 'the *Times* is even more interesting than the most interesting parts of the book itself'.[7]

In fact *The Times* said everything that Smiles could ever have wished a reviewer to say. One is tempted to remark that he could hardly have put it better himself (reviews in *The Times* were anonymous at the time). This one so closely reflects Smiles's views that it must surely have been written by someone who was at least an acquaintance. He was credited with having created 'an Engineering Pantheon'. The subject matter was recognised as being of real importance, the author as uniquely equipped to do it justice, and (dismissive of the carping *Athenaeum*), its originality noted. 'Mr Smiles was distinctively qualified to perform [the undertaking] by his literary as well as by his professional experience.' He 'had obtained a mass of original materials'. And surely the most cherished words of all, given Smiles's mission as historian of practical progress – 'It was a chapter of English history which had to be written, and which probably no one could have written so well.'[8]

That was just part one of *The Times*'s coverage. Four weeks later, on Christmas Eve, part two appeared, placing the cherry firmly on top of Smiles's Christmas cake. His engineers' achievements had

in a word, made Britain opulent, and their authors have been public men, more emphatically than politicians proper. The world begins to see where its real interests are involved, and it is not ungrateful in the long run for service truly rendered. It is only greed and pretentiousness which it regards without love, entombs without honour, and is willing speedily to forget. For men such as these, noble in the spirit whence their works proceeded, it approves the effort to commend them as examples to posterity.[9]

This was a notable change in the view taken until then, and most loudly articulated by Carlyle and by Ruskin, that 'the world's interests' lay in a medieval past, and were likely to be destroyed by industrial progress. It now became respectable to praise industry.[10]

For five years, since his breakthrough with *George Stephenson*, Smiles's life had been on an upward curve. He had barely come to terms with the Stephenson success when *Self-Help* added its impetus. Now *Lives of the Engineers* provided him with a true sense of arrival. William Gladstone commended the work while speaking at a public meeting in Manchester. Sir Stafford Northcote, a prominent Conservative politician, welcomed it during a speech in Exeter.[11] This acceptance from both sides of the political divide prompted Smiles to see it as endorsement of one of his favourite themes, that 'Industry is, indeed, of no party,'[12] and men of all

classes could well unite in celebrating the triumphs of British Engineering.' They would also unite, he believed, in welcoming the thoughts of
Samuel Smiles. From the young with new lives to shape, to the mature
with a new world to understand – from *Self-Help* to *Lives of the Engineers*
– he had caught the attention of his age.

In fact this latest display of biographical virtuosity simply emphasised
the long-running ambiguity in Smiles's life and career. Doctor and
journalist, journalist and railway executive, railway executive and author,
and now two sorts of author with two sorts of audience, he confronted a
wider split and a more profound dilemma. In 1857, with the publication
of *George Stephenson*, he had proclaimed himself 'at last, at the advanced
age of forty-five, a successful author!' If he had thought success at
forty-five was remarkable, he discovered that real success, at fifty, was a
different and altogether headier business.

He was no longer merely a commuter from Blackheath with a pleasing
part-time career as an author (with its pleasing supplement to his
income). He was now a celebrity writer, with large cheques arriving
regularly from his publisher and a large readership pulling him in several
directions at the same time. All this was no doubt exhilarating, but
Smiles had lived every day since his Haddington childhood with the
conviction that poverty lay just a false step away. He frequently deplored
the worship of money. Stephenson, Telford and the others had, he
believed, been moved by a finer impulse. 'I admire commercial enterprise,' he quoted Telford as saying, 'but I hold that the aim and end of
all ought not to be a mere bag of money, but something far higher and
better'. Smiles agreed, but also felt keenly the importance of money as
a safety net above oblivion. For thirty years he had regarded his salary
as providing that net. He dared not let the whim of book buyers replace
it, so he let his two careers grow round him, and in the intoxication of
creative success was unaware that between them he might be crushed.

But in those golden years anything must have seemed possible.
Smiles's granddaughter Aileen pictured him 'on the crest of a wave.[13] The
author of *Self-Help* had suddenly become the fashion and he was deluged
with requests that he should lay foundation stones, sit for his portrait,
present prizes to orphan children, make speeches from platforms.' Even
in Haddington the shopkeeper's son had become someone. He delighted

in boasting gently to Jane Welsh Carlyle after a visit to his home town: 'It was positively the first time that I was ever regarded in the light of a small lion. But a Haddington animal of this sort, even of the very smallest, is such a rarity, that I feel it is possible to be a curiosity, and at the same time a very ordinary creature after all.'[14] For the first time in his life Smiles could, from the crest of his wave, indulge his family. Sarah Anne gave parties, bought new gowns, went to the theatre, attended concerts, and burnished her cultural well-being. The lessons from Miss Martineau's school for girls could now be put to good use. Smiles's delight was obvious. 'Your mother is tremendously taken out this season',[15] he wrote to Janet, at school in Edinburgh.

> In fact she is rapidly to become a star of the first magnitude. She has invitations to a conversazione at the Society of Arts, Kensington Gore – to the Crystal Palace performance of Elijah on Friday (stall ticket) – and to an 'at home' at Mrs S C Halls on the 8th. Last night we met Miss Hayes, Editress of the *English Woman's Journal* and she asked your mother to contribute! Ter-mend-ous! Is it not? She will certainly come out very strong some day, and I think you will give her a lift when you come home laden with accomplishments.

This letter, on first reading, seems a typically patronising view of wife as little woman, harmless in pursuit of her bourgeois diversions. For a mid-Victorian man whose mother was barely literate, who had had to make her own clothes and to work in her shop all day to feed her children, the sight of his wife attending conversaziones in Kensington Gore was a matter of great happiness and pride. He was boasting to Janet; the bantering tone was clumsy modesty. Besides, the final 'ter-mend-ous' referred to Sarah's encounter with 'Miss Hayes', and the invitation to write for the *English Woman's Journal*. The editress was in fact Matilda Hays, the same Matilda Hays Smiles had met almost twenty years earlier, in the Charlotte Cushman-Eliza Cook circle, the Matilda Hays who had translated George Sand's novels and prompted Smiles to write so glowingly of Sand in *Eliza Cook's Journal*. Some years later Smiles's son Willie would marry Lucy Dorling, half-sister of Isabella Beeton. Matilda Hays's *English Woman's Journal* could not have been further from Mrs Beeton's staunchly bourgeois *Book of Household Management*. Hays's

Journal was probably the most radically feminist periodical in London, and Matilda Mary Hays among the capital's leading champions of women's equality and sexual freedom.

Sarah Anne had obviously not lost the open-mindedness that had endeared her to Cushman and Cook and the Howitts, when she had entertained them in Leeds all those years ago. Smiles had remained friends with William Howitt, and although we don't know, it may well have been with the Howitts that the Smiles's met Matilda Hays. Whatever the circumstances, all this suggests that Smiles had not lost his radical sympathies, and that his wife was not for patronising.

Janet was sixteen, the only one of the Smiles children so far sent away to boarding school, when this letter was written. Judging from the number of his letters to Janet, and their tenderness, she seems to have been closest to her father. As with many Victorian men of this generation, he was addicted in his private life to nicknames and schoolboy wordplay ('ter-mend-ous'). Janet was usually Gingers, the three youngest Fuggins, Macduff and Rummy (Edith, Lilian and Sam). Willie, the eldest, remained Willie.

Smiles did not drill his children in the Christian catechism, as his father had drilled him, but used his own text for their moral instruction and admonition. Letters to Janet, with news of Blackheath frolickings, usually first offered a little homily – to 'My dear Gingers':

> You are quite right to be impressed with a sense of responsibility, and of duty, for you have now to depend upon your own judgment and principles against frivolity, temptations, and the vices which flesh is heir to; and though the example you have seen at home will, I hope, always be valuable to you throughout life, you yourself have to act, and think, and work, for your own improvement of mind and heart and character.[16]

Willie, with his own name, kept his own counsel, and in later life found that it did not always agree with his father's.

Smiles in his writing warned young people against depending on patronage, urging them 'to rely on their own efforts in life rather than depend on the help and patronage of others'. Using opportunities was a different matter. He had noted the good fortune of many of his engineers in finding the right patron at the right time – for example Edward Pease and the Stephensons. Now he had no hesitation in using his contacts to help his sons in any way he could. He seemed to think, when Willie reached sixteen, that the tea trade might offer him a good future and approached a City friend of John Murray's, Robert Smith, for help and advice.[17] A year or so later Sam junior's education seemed to need something special. 'Can you recommend me to any good middle class school in Germany to which I might send my second boy', he asked John Murray, 'where I could depend on good discipline & that German and French more particularly will be well taught.'[18]

Smiles had rarely lacked self-belief, though for most of his life he had been on the lower step in any group – a dissenter among the establishment in Haddington, an apprentice among the undergraduates in Edinburgh, a mere journalist dining with the business élite of Leeds, and a servant to railway company directors. Through all this he had held on to a conviction of his own value. He believed in only one aristocracy, the aristocracy of merit. Now he felt ready to be recognised as a member. His wife would go to Kensington Gore and have stall seats for *Elijah*. His children would go to school in Edinburgh or Geneva. A judge and an Archdeacon would propose him for membership of the Athenaeum.[19] And the Smiles's of Blackheath would move to a fine new house specially built for them in one of Blackheath's most beautiful locations. West Bank, complete with billiard room and library, was what agents called 'a gentleman's residence'. It cost, with its fittings, £5,016, including, among much else, £17-17-0 for a French clock, £26-12-3 for library curtains, £13-0-0 for a chandelier from F & C Osler, and £84-4-6 for the billiard table on which Willie and his father would have a game every evening before Smiles settled to work on his book.[20] 'The site was superb', Aileen Smiles said.[21] 'At the back it commanded Lewisham valley, while the front was on the heath itself.'

The house-building project was a demanding task. Officialdom dragged its feet in the 1860s as doggedly as it does today. Among other approvals needed for West Bank was a permit from the Board of Works for a basement, 'and the Board of Works rarely met,' Aileen Smiles said. 'Westbank remained without a basement for what seemed an eternity.'[22] But by the end of 1863 the house was finished and on 26 January 1864, to coincide with Willie's eighteenth birthday, a grand house-warming party celebrated what seemed to be a wonderful moment in the wonderful life of the celebrated author and his family. Many parties followed, many friends called, hospitality abounded. This was not the sophisticated salon life of London hostesses. There Mrs Prinsep had her Sundays at Little Holland House, where Ruskin chatted to Tennyson or Carlyle, and Burne-Jones and Rossetti talked of art with George Frederic Watts, while Kate Lewis at Moray Lodge competed for the leading literary and artistic lions of the day. In West Bank Mrs Smiles competed with her neighbour, the minor novelist Mrs Newton Crosland, for the most popular 'At Home'. Miss Brown came to play the piano for friends; or the dentist, Mr Medwin, called for a game of billiards while his wife took tea and dress advice with Mrs Smiles. Sarah Anne, in Aileen's words, 'practised hospitality in every form' and her husband conscientiously played his part.

Smiles enjoyed this homely social life, but when he climbed the hill from Lewisham station each evening after a stiff day's work in London, his mind was drawn in other directions. His desk was heavy with letters from readers, sometimes with thanks, sometimes with appeals for help and advice. Aspiring writers shared their aspirations, hoping for some of the Smiles stardust. Publishers and translators sought cooperation for foreign editions of *Self-Help*. He had correspondence from people with book ideas, from illustrators, from men looking for jobs, for 'loans', or just for some words from the author of *Self-Help*. Smiles was a natural responder. He wanted to answer them all. He wanted to answer the comments and criticisms of reviewers. He wanted to make progress with his next article for the *Quarterly Review* – but above all, as he reached the handsome front door of West Bank, he wanted to go upstairs, to his real life, to his next book.

Each of the volumes of *Lives of the Engineers* had sold over 6,000 copies, and the *Life of George Stephenson* continued to be in steady demand (Smiles said in his *Autobiography* that it reached 60,000 by 1880). But with 20,000 sales in its first six months, regular reprints of 5,000 copies a time, and overseas editions, pirated or otherwise, appearing all over the world, *Self-Help* operated at a different level. It was undoubtedly a book that had re-invented its genre and elevated Samuel Smiles from respected author to instantly recognised brand. The potential was impossible to ignore, and Smiles agonised. As he had written of Thomas Telford, Smiles 'could not be said to have an indifference for money' and, in the months while West Bank was rising from the ground, he certainly swayed towards the *Self-Help* money-making high road. 'I did at first contemplate a companion book to *Self-Help*', he told John Murray in April 1863, while still at Granville Park Terrace. But he had also been looking at the possibility of a short book on some of the little-known men whose work with iron and tools had made the achievements of his Engineers possible. Perhaps it and the *Self-Help* companion could go ahead at the same time. The iron and tools, however, took over. 'The materials', he told Murray, 'have so grown upon me, as well as the subject, that I find it will be impossible to compress the interesting questions arising out of the investigations I have been making, within so small a compass. The iron and tool makers alone will fill a volume of 400 pages.'[23] And forget about *Self-Help* follow-ups – 'I have materials for a second series comprising the founding of various branches of industry.' His aim was, he said, to do for the mechanical engineers what his previous books had done for civil engineers.

That April 1863 letter to John Murray marks a point of commitment for Smiles. It put aside in a phrase any further question of a companion to *Self-Help*, and surged forward with details, plans, and visions of how the next big engineering book was gathering in his mind:

> the immigrations of the French and Germans and Flemish (opening up a new chapter of English history) ... the branches of industry established by them: this is full of interest ... Dud Dudley, a great forgotten man ... Andrew Yarranton ... after that came the makers of tools in iron and steel ... Joseph Bramah, Joseph Maudsley, Clements, Nasmyth, Murray of London ... the biographies of the tool and machine makers will be found an almost unworked mine ...

Smiles set out to work the mine, convinced that he could repeat the trick of 1856 when he had started the Stephenson biography – the trick of combining business, family life, and intensive writing, by intelligent use of time. He had cited Smeaton, in *Lives of the Engineers*, as 'a great economiser of time ... laid out in such a way as to obtain from its use the greatest possible amount of valuable result.' So Smiles continued to lay out his own time – unable, apparently, to resist any call made on it. Now he was a key member of the South Eastern's management group and took an almost proprietorial interest in its affairs. After the opening of the Charing Cross line he and his colleague Eborall kept pressing their Board to expand the Company's capital and compete for extension of South Eastern's lines through Kent, Surrey and Sussex. They outmanoeuvred their bitter competitors, The Brighton Rail Company, by extension of a line between Lewisham and Tonbridge, via Sevenoaks. Aileen Smiles described her grandfather's attendance at the ceremonial cutting of the first sod – 'the romance for him of that Saturday at Sevenoaks in May 1863, that lovely afternoon when a body of ladies and gentleman, decently crinolined and whiskered, might have been seen marching up and down a grass slope headed by a military band'.[24]

Smiles must have seemed in these years, to people who met him, a man of unshakeable substance, in happy possession of a home of substance, a family of substance, and a career of substance. In his early fifties, fit and smiling, he was a participant in Britain's industrial success, its scribe, and the author of a best-selling manual on how to join in. Samuel Smiles of West Bank, Blackheath, was a gentleman of means well earned but, wondrously, with the touch of literary fame to add a golden glow.

In fact Smiles was haunted by the anxiety of the man on the high wire who can scarcely understand how he got there, but sees very clearly how easily he could fall. Tensions in both the railway industry and in his writing career were ratcheting up. The South Eastern might keep on expanding and the books keep on selling. The iron workers and tool makers celebrated in *Industrial Biography* had marched into place in 1864 behind the giants of *Lives of the Engineers*. Writing the book had been hard work, muscled into the hours he could isolate from his responsibilities to his employer, his family, his publisher and his readers. But the upward trajectory of overall sales of Smiles books had levelled. In August 1865 he wrote to John Murray acknowledging the latest statement of account. He professed satisfaction, though it is 'not so large as in previous years. But we cannot look for a continuous run of luck, and I am content.'[25] And, however exhilarating the expansion of the railway might be, the South Eastern was still poisoned by in-fighting, jealousy and now something approaching paranoia.

The development of the Charing Cross line led to great increases in business but it also involved the frequent raising of loans and calls for extra cash from shareholders. Some of these 'proprietors' became frustrated when the success of the new line did not bring increased dividends. Mr Coles Child, a begrudging director, had lost his seat on the Board in 1862. His supporters put down a motion regretting his loss, and 'that he should have been expelled ... not for any dereliction of duty ... but by an unjust and ungenerous coalition on the part of some of his co-directors'. Though this motion was voted down, Mr Child continued to make a nuisance of himself, but not nearly such a nuisance as one of the bigger shareholders, John H Hamilton. Hamilton's accusations of sharp practice by the Chairman and Secretary, bizarre as they seem, were undoubtedly evidence of a widely held concern about the motives of some railway board members in the hangover that lingered from the days of George Hudson. So obsessed was Hamilton by his perception of a conspiracy at the South Eastern – led, he claimed, by the Chairman abetted by the Secretary – that in 1865 he sent a scurrilous circular to every proprietor, with Smiles as a principal target. 'The Crisis', as Hamilton headed his document, complained of 'insinuations extensively bestowed on the quondam hebdomadal exacerbations of the exemplary Secretary, who, avoiding the Samuel, writes himself Smiles. To be read doubtless Superlative Smiles, for some other reason with which we may some day become acquainted.'[26] He complained that Smiles had refused him access to the Register of Proprietors, had deliberately fed him misleading information, had doctored the Chairman's address and, most seriously, had effectively been involved in share-price rigging and insider trading, and 'that the vital interests of the South Eastern Railway are made subservient to the pecuniary interests of Mr Smiles'.

For a man for whom personal integrity was as precious as life, these accusations, however wild and unsupported, had the capacity to disturb – as had the other, more insidious: that Smiles's writing compromised his work for the Company. Hamilton referred to 'one of our leading officials, absorbed in writing books and editing a Newspaper', and proposed that 'no salaried servant of the company shall be allowed to carry on any occupation, or fill any post, save that of his appointment under the Board'. Smiles should, perhaps, have seen this problem coming;

Robert Stephenson had warned him shortly after his appointment that 'If your Board found that you were not giving your whole time to their business it might cause dissatisfaction.'[27] Now Smiles showed caution. Although a magazine publisher had tempted him with an offer of £700 a year just to lend his name to a proposed new magazine to be called *Self-Help*,[28] Smiles declined, on the sensible grounds that, quite apart from any threat to the value of the Self-Help brand, it might give his employers the wrong impression. A committee of enquiry set up by the South Eastern to investigate all these matters abolished Hamilton's case. Twice Smiles resorted to the courts to demand apology and damages, and twice he succeeded. But while all this was going on he was returning home each evening to try to concentrate on his next book.

Since his early days in Leeds, when he had written with almost visionary fervour of James Watt's work, Watt, even more than George Stephenson, had been his idol. He had contributed an article on Watt to the *Quarterly*, in 1858. Now, as soon as *Industrial Biography* had been handed over to the printer in early 1864, he turned without pause to the big Watt book. Watt had to share the title, as he had shared so much of his career, with his collaborator Matthew Boulton. Boulton and Watt were Smiles's new George and Robert Stephenson.

Smiles wrote as a believer. 'A book containing the life of a true man is full of precious seed,' Smiles had written in *Self-Help*. 'It is a still living voice; it is an intellect.' For him Stephenson and Watt, and the others, were more than biographical subjects, more almost than men. Their lives were manifestations of a profound truth – that humanity's hope lay in progress through mastery of nature by technology. And more than that – happiness could be found only by each man's mastery of himself, through understanding the value of his own character. As one reviewer of *Boulton and Watt* expressed it: 'The story of the chivalry of labour and thought was worthy of a great interpreter ... Where, in the history of the world, shall we look for nobler victories of intellect over mere matter.'

In this missionary frame of mind the success or failure of his books pressed on Smiles even more than on most authors. Small sales would mean a small voice, and with a small voice the message, and not just the income, might be lost.

There had been no pause since finishing the first Stephenson book, no relaxation of the self-imposed pressure. Smiles later made light of the mountain of papers he slogged through for *Boulton and Watt*: 'I had the advantage of consulting the whole of the literature of the firm – in the shape of the immense number of letters in possession of the grandson of Mr Boulton ...'[29] The letters were delivered in great bundles to West Bank, but Smiles didn't spare himself the fieldwork, travelling to Birmingham, Scotland, and Cornwall to be where Boulton and Watt had been.

In fact the letters and papers he uncovered turned the book, and the message, into something different and more nuanced than anything he had done before. What he revealed was that success need not, in every case, depend on the unremitting courage and sense of purpose of one man. Contrary to the original Smiles model, Watt was sickly, irresolute, constantly on the point of giving up – a brilliant, fragile theorist liable to crack in the face of practical difficulty. To those intimidated by the relentless drive and energy of George Stephenson, this may perhaps have come as good news. In happy balance, Boulton, intellectually quite normal, had all the sterling qualities so obviously missing in his partner. As the *Pall Mall Gazette* said in its review, 'Boulton is a really noble character to whom Mr Smiles has done justice, and whose combination with Watt's marvellous ability, but defective practical talents, was of the greatest value to themselves as to the country.'

The book was designed to join the canon of *Lives of the Engineers*, as volume IV, in the same splendid binding, with portraits of both subjects, and seventy other illustrations. Whymper and Leitch again did many of the drawings; Coopers made the engravings. Smiles, on two-thirds of the profits, spared no effort or expense to make sure that the book matched the quality of the earlier volumes. After launch he had high hopes of high sales. Commenting to John Murray on the disappointing results for the previous six months from his other books, he remarked that 'This year I hope to go up to the old figures by the help of Boulton and Watt, which ought to do quite as successfully as "The Engineers"...'[30] The press received the book well, if with a hint of déjà vu. Smiles was now perhaps in danger of being typecast. *The Times* remarked that 'as Mr Smiles has long since conquered the field of industrial biography our

recommendation of this interesting volume is almost needless'.[31] The
new *Pall Mall Gazette*, in more waspish mood, regretted that

> of all the topics of nineteenth century glorification perhaps that of steam
> has become the most threadbare ... we know, or at least we are tired of
> listening about Savery and Newcomen ... all these stories are told, perhaps
> at undue length, by Mr Smiles; we accept them, however, as an inevitable
> necessity.[32]

The *Lives of Boulton and Watt, comprising a History of the Invention and
Introduction of the Steam Engine*, published at twenty-one shillings, was
not the success Smiles had hoped for. *George Stephenson* and the first
volumes of *Lives of the Engineers* had each sold 5,000 copies in their first
year. *Boulton and Watt* struggled to make half that. Smiles's accounts show
that he actually lost £126-8-5 on the book up to 3 December 1865,[33] though
after payment of initial publishing costs it eventually made some contribution to his income. Its relative failure continued to puzzle Smiles, for
he valued the work. Fifteen years later, commenting on the strength of
his back list, he was still showing regret that 'Industrial Biography and
Boulton and Watt, two of the best books I ever wrote, are not nearly so
successful'.[34]

By 1866, though his admiring neighbours in Blackheath would not
have suspected it, the famous author on the hill was feeling the strain of
years of graft. 'When I got home at night, I took a cup of tea to freshen
me up. Then I sat down and used my brain for three or four hours. I
sometimes worked until late. My brain became excited and then I could
not sleep.' But he had to be up in the morning, on to the train, early in
the office, setting an example to those idle clerks. If sleep would not come
to him he would have to reach out and take it.

Drugs in nineteenth-century Britain were easy to get, especially if, like
Smiles, you were a qualified doctor of medicine. He knew the power of
hyosycamus (black henbane) as a 'sedative'. He doubtless understood its
dangers too, but convinced himself that he could control the dosage.
He admitted later that 'the result of taking hyosycamus to provoke sleep
is frightful. It gives one the most depressing views of life; as, in fact, is
the case with most sedatives. But I think hyosycamus is the worst of all
in that respect.' But he used it, and suffered the inevitable breakdown

– the self-helper helpless. In his own words, 'I got hipped, ill, and miserable.'

Whether or not he could have gone on writing in this state is doubtful. He was sure he could not go on steering the business of a strife-ridden railway company. Hipped, ill, and miserable, it was time to go. Smiles, as Secretary, signed the minutes of the sixtieth Half-yearly General meeting of the South Eastern Railway Company held on 30 August 1866, as usual, at the Bridge Hotel, London Bridge. After twenty-one years it was the last act of his railway career. Among the minutes was one recording the motion proposed by Mr William Fenton and seconded by Mr George Gamble (proprietors) and carried unanimously, 'that the best thanks of the meeting be given to Mr Eborall, General Manager, and Mr Smiles, Secretary, and to other officials, for their able and indefatigable services in the interests of the company'.[35] Though the Secretary's departure remained un-minuted, 'a handsome present, including a service of plate', confirmed his employer's esteem for him. They also gave him a pass over the company's lines, with connections to the main continental railways, as long as he lived – perhaps the most valuable present of all, given that he was to spend so much of the rest of his life travelling.

17

The Books Keep Coming

CHARLES GILPIN, liberal MP for Northampton, had been elected to the board of the South Eastern in March 1855, a few months before Smiles joined the company. He would have known Smiles's writings, probably as far back as the *Leeds Times*, for he was a veteran anti-Corn Law campaigner and advocate of universal suffrage, a man who would have been on the same side as Smiles on almost every question of public policy and private principle. The two were natural allies, so when Gilpin, also a director of London's leading life assurance society, the National Provident Institution, discovered Smiles was leaving the railway business, his instinct was not only to help him, but to help the National Provident.

As a proven, highly efficient and conscientious company servant, Smiles would have been valuable to the National Provident. As celebrity author, accomplished speaker, and promoter of the very providence on which the National Provident had built its name, he was a jewel.

> When a man casts his glance forward, he will find that the three chief temporal contingencies for which he has to provide are want of employment, sickness, and death ... It is the duty of the prudent man ... so to arrange that the pressure of suffering, in event of either contingency occurring, shall be mitigated to as great a degree as possible.

Not the snappiest advertising pitch, but these lines from *Self-Help* could have been a manifesto for the National Provident. Their Secretary having just retired, on Gilpin's prompting they hired the author at once. Smiles started work at the Gracechurch Street head office of the National Provident in the autumn of 1866.

As with the South Eastern, not everyone at Gracechurch Street was happy with Smiles's arrival. The trade magazine of the time, the *Post Magazine and Insurance Monitor*, thought the in-house candidate had been cheated. 'In appointing Mr Smiles to this important office,' the magazine scolded, 'the directors of the National Provident have acted most ungenerously towards the gentlemen in the office.'[1]

For Smiles it was the ideal appointment. He was recovering from illness, trying to come to terms with his own fallibility, even questioning his future as a writer. Smiles is generally held up as an unequivocal proponent of sheer hard work as the most valuable of all human qualities. Work was good, work was healthy, work was a moral imperative and a road to happiness. But he was not unequivocal. He had described the damage done to several of his heroes by the pressure of work. Smeaton, 'though naturally possessed of an excellent constitution, taxed his brain too much'. Rennie's 'close and unremitting application early began to tell upon his health'. In the book just finished Smiles had contemplated the weakness of Watt under pressure. Almost thirty years earlier (in his first book, *Physical Education*) Smiles had declared that 'Like labour of the body, labour of the mind is useless unless the object for which it is undertaken presents him with some interest or gratification.' Now, in the change from the bare-knuckle culture of the railway industry to the more benign atmosphere at the National Provident, he might be able to extricate interest and gratification from mere labour of the mind. He gratefully accepted the opportunity to rehabilitate, and a salary equal to his pay at the South Eastern.

Even so, in his *Autobiography* a sense lingers, if not of guilt, then of slight apology that the job lacked challenge: 'My new occupation was of a comparatively easy sort ... I hope that I did the work allotted to me, thoroughly and faithfully. But there is no need to go into any details about it.' His secretarial role was undemanding; his employers valued him as much for his celebrity status. Aileen Smiles rather unkindly described her grandfather at this time as 'a bagman' for his employers, travelling round the country until 'there was scarcely a town in the British Isles unvisited by him'.[2] But Smiles's ambassadorial worth to the National Provident is entirely understandable.

Besides, he had always enjoyed travelling. It gave him time for reflection and opportunity for study. Gradually during those journeys he sloughed off the worst effects of his illness. Of course with such a celebrated name it was inevitable that wherever he went he would be asked to speak. August bodies like the Philosophical Institution in Edinburgh and the Glasgow Athenaeum issued invitations. The old Smiles would have been delighted to accept, but for now he had lost his appetite.

Whatever else had changed, his urge to keep scribbling had not. 'I did not altogether give up the use of my literary faculty. I read a good deal, and made many notes. In course of time I arranged a perfect storehouse of information relative to race and biography.' Race had always intrigued him. Britain's pre-eminence in engineering and industrial progress was one of his favourite themes, and the particular qualities of the national character which he believed had made this true. George Stephenson's life was 'the life of a true man, and presented a striking combination of those sterling qualities which we are proud to regard as essentially English' (again Smiles seemed happy to ignore his own Scottishness). In the opening chapter of *Self-Help* he had noted that 'The spirit of self-help, as exhibited in the energetic action of individuals, has at all times been a marked feature of the English character, and furnishes the true measure of our power as a nation.'[3] But Smiles was not a blinkered patriot. He had read enough and travelled enough to realise that the qualities he admired were at least as apparent in people of other countries. A few pages after highlighting energetic activity as 'a marked feature of the English', he pointed out that 'Foreign, not less than English biography, abounds in illustrations of men who have glorified the lot of poverty by their labours and their genius.'[4]

In this respect no racial group abounded more than the protestant Huguenots of France and the low countries, persecuted by Louis XlV. Their history, their compelling mix of courage, talent, independence, and moral backbone in the face of persecution, appealed intensely to Smiles. Now a people rather than a person would have the Smiles heroic treatment. By the new year he was already deep in research, energy starting to flow again. John Murray, worried about his ailing, itinerant author, suggested several topics to get him writing again. What about something on water supply, possibly the most fundamental of all civil engineering topics. 'I am too busy on the Huguenots,' Smiles responded. 'I am getting some very good materials from the registers of the old French churches at Somerset House, which have never before been ransacked.'[5] While he travelled, and gathered information in the provinces, his research assistant was digging hard in London: 'Martin is doing the work for me and is very competent.'

By May he was so enthused and confident with the subject that, on business in Dublin for the National Provident, he broke his 'no speeches' rule to give a talk to a heavyweight audience at the Ancient Concert Rooms attached to the Christian Young Men's Association. This lecture was little more than a gallop through the histories of some of the French Huguenot families who had fled to England and Ireland after the revocation of the Edict of Nantes. His audience, a slew of Reverends from Dublin's Protestant establishment, no doubt received with enthusiasm his glowing references to the part played by Huguenots in William's victory at the Battle of the Boyne (though in 1843, in *The History of Ireland*, he had rubbished the Orange 'triumph').[6] Smiles also emphasised their role in the creation of Ireland's linen industry. But he had a larger ambition – a book tracing not just the migrations of the Huguenots, but their achievements in their host countries, their contributions there, and, crucially, the qualities that had made all this possible. Huguenot history in Britain was self-help on an ethnic scale.

When Smiles left Dublin he was bristling with ideas for the new project. He devoted his entire spring holiday (three weeks from his new employers compared with only two from the South Eastern) to scouring France for places with Huguenot roots. From the channel to La Rochelle, from Poitiers and Lyons to Grenoble and Briançon, by coach, rail and on foot, he covered many hundreds of kilometres and interviewed dozens of contacts. From Briançon 'the journey was performed principally by walking' he said, 'sometimes at the rate of from twenty-five to thirty miles a day'.

In this macho mood the fifty-five-year-old Smiles, striding through the Hautes Alpes, was keen to show, himself at least, that the books could keep coming. Back at West Bank, after each day at the National Provident's head office in Gracechurch Street, he set himself to rediscover his mastery of time. The intimidating stack of notebooks and papers collected during his travels and in his reading (much of it in French or

German), and gathered by Martin in the historical archives, could and would be turned into a book – within months.

The Huguenots – Their Settlements, Churches and Industries in England and Ireland, was handed over to the printer in October 1867 (Smiles revealed a rare flash of loyalty for his old country when he wrote to Murray: 'Clark of Edinburgh called at the office about our printing there ... It would gratify me much to let him print this book, if you have no objection').[7] Clark duly printed the book and it was offered at Murray's 1867 trade sale and dinner for London booksellers in the Albion Hotel on 11 November. They subscribed for 1,000 copies. No doubt most of these were subsequently bought by root-hunting English and Irish families with French names. In its 530 pages they found good value. The book is rich in genealogical grist, stories of the refugee families, and, as the title promises, of the communities, churches and businesses they founded.

Of course a good story needs villains as well as heroes and the seventeenth-century French Catholic church filled the role beautifully, without turning the book into mere anti-Catholic propaganda. If Smiles had a religious propaganda point to make it was less anti-Catholic than pro-liberty of thought. He condemned Louis's attempts to

> induce men to give up their individuality, to renounce the exercise of their judgment, to cease to think ... But many of the French king's subjects were of another temperament. They would think for themselves in matters of science as well as religion; and the vigorous, the independent, and the self-reliant – Protestant and non-Protestant – revolted against the intellectual tyranny which Louis attempted to establish among them...[8]

Smiles used the Huguenot story to underline one of his favourite themes: the pre-eminence of a working middle class over 'indolent' aristocrats. Inspired no doubt by the French historian Michelet,[9] he links the Revocation of the Edict of Nantes in 1685 to the French Revolution in 1789. On the one hand, he suggests, the flight from France of the protestant working class after 1685 created a fatal vacuum between the peasantry and the aristocrats which made the later revolution inevitable. In 1789,

> there being no element of stability in the state – no class possessing moral weight to stand between the infuriated people at one end of the social scale

and the king and nobles on the other – the imposture erected by the Great Louis was assailed on all sides, and king, church and nobility were at once swept away.[10]

On the other hand, the added value brought by the 'middle-class' refugees of 1685 to their host countries is compared with the apparent uselessness of aristocrats fleeing the guillotine in the 1790s. Smiles was unequivocal: 'there was this difference between the emigrants of 1685 and 1793, that whereas in the former period the people who emigrated consisted almost entirely of the industrious classes, in the latter period they consisted almost entirely of the idle classes'.

'The one emigration,' Smiles adds,

consisted for the most part of nobles and clergy who left no traces of their settlement in the countries which gave them asylum; the other emigrants comprised all the constituent elements of a people – the skilled workmen in all branches, manufacturers, merchants, and professional men; and wherever they settled they founded numerous useful establishments which were a source of prosperity and wealth.[11]

He finished with an extravagant flourish:

Least of all has [England] reason to regret the settlement within her borders of so large a number of industrious, intelligent, and high-minded Frenchmen who have made this country their home since the revocation of the Edict of Nantes, and thereby stimulated, and in a large measure created, British industry; but also influenced, in a remarkable degree, our political and religious history.

In this, Smiles was perhaps issuing an admonition to his countrymen: undervalue your industrious class at your peril, and beware the myth of 'English' genius.

Soon he was on the road again, and now willing to speak in public. Writing *Huguenots* had given him the opportunity to re-examine some of his long-held ideas; in his next public appearance he would reveal subtle but significant shifts. Shortly after finishing the book he accepted an invitation to address the Annual Soirèe of the Huddersfield Mechanics' Institution on 31 October, on the subject of 'Industrial Education'.[12] Back in his beloved West Yorkshire it was a time for some nostalgia as the evening started, with its mix of pomp and homeliness – the distinguished chairman 'coming forth on the platform' accompanied on each side by the other speakers, Auld Lang Syne sung by the Institute singing class, all preceded no doubt by ample tea and ham sandwiches. After the chairman, Earl de Grey & Ripon, had lavished praise on the work of the institution he introduced Mr Smiles, 'author of *Self-Help*'. Over the next forty minutes or so Smiles gave the idea of self-help a considerable tweak.

His theme was, in effect, globalisation, his message a thoroughly modern one: everyone has the technology now, and some of them are getting smarter at using it than we are; if we want to keep our place in the world we are going to need a new attitude to our workpeople and an new attitude to their education.

'Is it really so,' he asked, 'that we who gave the world the steam engine, the locomotive, the spinning jenny, the power loom ... is it possible that we have any grounds for real fear from continental or other rivals?' Then he told them, in terms, that acknowledging such a fear was not only prudent but urgent: 'unless we make haste to educate our population at least up to the continental standard our position as a manufacturing nation must be seriously imperilled'. All the wonderful tools of English origin were now common to the world, and the world was on the point of beating us at our own game. The old bogey of unionisation was invoked: 'while the working-class organisations of this country are enacting regulations for the limitation of skill ... the foreigners are stimulating the skill of their workmen, rewarding those who excel at it, and in all ways promoting the industrial education of their people'. Neither would reliance on native brawn do. Muscle and energy were no longer enough. 'Competition in industry is year by year becoming a competition of intellect, and the nation which most quickly promotes the intellectual development of its artisans must, by inevitable law advance, while the country which neglects its industrial development must inevitably recede.' Smiles was an early herald of the 'knowledge economy'.

And the rewards of the right sort of education, the sort provided by England's rivals, were not just economic, but human, personal, almost spiritual:

Being well educated they are able to live more comfortably and more intelligently, than if they had received a narrow education. The effect of improved culture is not only to render artisans more skilled as workmen, but to raise them in the social scale and to elevate them in the dignity of thinking beings.

As for self-help and the autonomy of the individual, if Smiles had ever meant to imply that a man's best, perhaps his only, chance was to depend on himself, now he issued a clear corrective, both to this and to reliance on the 'George Stephenson' model, the self-taught genius:

> it must be acknowledged that these are exceptional cases ... they went groping after knowledge and conquered success only by dint of valorous self-help ... but with the mass of the people the case is very different indeed. They must be helped to help themselves ... it is the business of society, acting through its organised instrument, the Government, to arrange and settle. And I cannot but regard it as a bounden duty on the part of society, that it should actively endeavour to remove, so far as it can, the obstacles which stand in the way of the social elevation, and in fact the civilisation, of the poorer classes of the community.

Again, as with *Education of the Working Classes* in 1845, Smiles had made a sharp point. For the mass of poor people self-help had a pre-condition: a proper education. It was the government's obligation to provide it. And again, at the behest of the Institution's Committee, Smiles's lecture was reprinted and widely circulated as a pamphlet. The Society of Arts took the point too, and published it verbatim in the December issue of their magazine. Smiles's views on education, so up-to, even ahead of his time, and his willingness to present them publicly with such conviction, suggest that he may have felt momentum re-gathering.

Nevertheless, for his writing his direction over the next few years was less clear than in the past. No longer do we see the tightly focused drive that had produced the *Stephenson* books, the four volumes of *Lives of the Engineers*, *Industrial Biographies*, and, since his illness, *The Huguenots*. Now the impression is of an aging author shuffling through ideas, picking up, putting aside, managing what he has, and wondering if his accustomed surge of purpose is ever likely to return.

Though for the last ten years he had turned with such marked intention to other things, the 'little book' published in 1859 was still seen by the world as Samuel Smiles's defining work. It was natural that the distinguished chairmen in both Dublin and Huddersfield had introduced him as 'the author of *Self-Help*', and that in newspaper reports of his speeches the *Self-Help* label was invariably used. However much he had devoted himself to industrial biography, *Self-Help*, ever since its publication in 1859, had marked Smiles's public identity, dominated his sales, and provided the bulk of his personal income. In the previous five years (1865-1870) his next best-selling book, *Life of George Stephenson*, had sold an average of just over 1,000 copies a year in England. Over the same time *Self-Help's* average was 4,000. However many new titles he produced, *Self-Help* consistently contributed around forty per cent of his income from books. The book was simply too successful to be pushed away.

Publishers from all over the world wanted to bring out *Self-Help* for their own markets, with or without the author's blessing. The Americans had been first off the mark. Within months of British publication Ticknor and Fields in Boston, who had pirated *George Stephenson*, offered £25 for a set of advance sheets of Self-Help. He would do well to accept this, Robert Cooke[13] at Murray's told Smiles: 'generally they offer only £5 or £10 for such a work.'[14] He worked with Ticknor and Fields on the publication, in July 1860, of *Brief Biographies*, a collection of biographical essays, mainly previously published in English periodicals. In the short preface he described the book as being offered to the American public, 'through the medium of Ticknor and Fields, at whose request the collection has been made ...'

Until the 'Chace Act' of 1891 (The International Copyright Act), printers and publishers in the United States could produce and sell the work of authors from any other country in the world without permission, or payment to the author. This made books from the United Kingdom, with no translation cost, particularly attractive booty, and even more so if the American publisher could save himself setting costs by buying plates from his UK counterpart, as happened regularly with Smiles's work. These amounts were better than nothing; one way or another, the pirates would have their book. Dickens, the most eloquent and famous campaigner for an international copyright agreement, saw little for his efforts during his life. The Berne Convention on international copyright was not formalised until 1887 (the United States came to separate arrangements until signing up to the Berne Convention in 1989). Harper Brothers, Smiles's long-term publishers in the United States, treated him comparatively well. In 1894 they agreed, though reluctantly, to publish his book on Josiah Wedgwood. 'Although our reader's advice is not very encouraging, we shall, nevertheless be pleased to publish the work, in view of the fact that we have the honor to be Dr Smiles's American publishers.'[15] They agreed to pay a ten per cent royalty. In the meantime a Dutch translation of *Self-Help* was, according to Smiles, next to appear: 'The first I heard of it was from a Dutch clergyman who was in England attending the marriage of a niece of my friend Mr Eborall.' Soon German and French publishers were knocking on the door. Smiles found negotiations for German rights tiresome and frustrating, but things went much more smoothly in France. 'Some excellent reviews have appeared in the French papers but I have not heard whether the book is selling or not.'[16] In 1864 Smiles suggested to Murray that a French translation might be offered as a reading book for schools. The translation was done by M Fallender, Professor of French at the Royal Military College at Sandhurst. Preparation for publication in India had started. Smiles told Murray that he had had two letters from 'the Madras gentleman to show what is going on in Madras with *Self-Help*. I have declined at present to grant any further permission to reprint the remaining chapters, and also to grant for the present a power of attorney.'[17] It had become obvious that *Self-Help* had worldwide appeal. Eventually it was selling wherever English was spoken, and was translated into at least thirty foreign languages. All this was a considerable distraction, a swallower of time and energy.

At the same time Smiles was increasingly feeling concerned about his family. By the time of the publication of *The Huguenots*, and of the Huddersfield lecture, the three older children were young adults and Sam junior was sixteen and already at work. Smiles, for all his enthusiasm for education, seems to have believed, for his own sons, in the University of Life (a phrase he would surely have loved to have coined himself), and put them straight from school into trade, albeit using his privileged network. Willie had left King's College London at sixteen to join East India

Merchants Harvey, Brand and Co. By 1868, aged twenty-two, he was representing them in Belfast and starting to reveal a strong tendency for independence. Later he was to become the most spectacularly successful member of the family and in effect the founder of his own dynasty. Sam junior, less obviously talented but more obviously loved by his father, had been sent back to West Yorkshire, with A & J Henry & Co in Bradford, also to learn his way in the merchanting business.

Sam, something of a likely lad, was pleased to report to his brother that 'Mr John, who is rather gruff, said to Mrs H that I was an <u>amiable</u> young man ... Our house is the very best for learning the business in Bradford.' Sam was ready to rough it, up to a point. He started in the warehouse, wore an apron and, 'sometimes, work with my coat off'. But there was worse: 'there is one drawback in the warehouse. It is this – all the common men in the warehouse treat the gentlemen, that is educated persons as their equals. I have had to swallow my pride many a time. The men call me Sam, or Smiles.'[18] Ten years earlier his father had written: 'Riches and rank have no necessary connexion with genuine gentlemanly qualities. The poor man may be a true gentleman – in spirit and in life.'[19]

But sixteen-year-old Master Smiles's letter to his brother ended on a sadder note: 'I have not been well lately but you need not tell mother.' The work was heavy and the hours long. 'I look after dyers' carts, hand, mark, lift etc pieces and take them upstairs in the hoist ... I shall go into the makeup room next. It will not be so dirty or such heavy work. My hours will be 8 to 6, pretty long compared to yours!'

That touch of illness, remarked on in the summer, developed by the next winter into something much worse. By the end of 1868 Smiles was writing to John Murray:

> I have just got from my son who has been lately living in Bradford, and find it will be necessary (by recommendation of Dr Peacock) to send him on a long journey. He had a violent attack of pneumonia last year from the effects of which he never fully recovered. We thought of Australia, Rio de Janeiro or Buenos Aires. Do you know anybody in those quarters?[20]

With or without Murray's help, the journey was arranged. Sam left after Christmas, but however indulgent his father was prepared to be, he could not let his son sail off into the blue without a rein on his time. Sam was to take a large notebook, record all that happened, and 'turn his leisure moments to some account'.

In the meantime, dear Gingers, Smiles's adored eldest child Janet, now twenty-three, was living at home, trapped in a web of social trivia. Of course she should have been married, or at the very least betrothed, but had dismissed all the suitors her mother had put in her way. Aileen Smiles described her as 'an earnest conscientious girl made even more so by her father'.[21] She had been sent to Bradford to take care of Sam during his illness, her father's surrogate. 'My impression,' he wrote to her in a typical letter, 'is that Sam should have iron as well as quinine, the best preparation being citrate of iron. Suggest this also.'

Home again at the start of 1868, while Sam was on his way to the far side of the world, Janet was able to join the family holiday party to Switzerland – mother, father, fourteen-year-old sister Lilian and, as a companion of her own age a shy, scholarly young neighbour, John Hartree. The Smiles and Hartree parents knew each other, but were not close friends. Mrs Hartree's father was John Penn, a hugely wealthy iron master. Her sons had been to Cambridge (John took a first in Natural Sciences at Trinity College in 1865) and she apparently regarded the Smiles's, with sons in trade, as of a lesser class. John, on his twenty-first birthday, had become heir to a fortune. When, inevitably, the Swiss holiday produced love and a proposed engagement between John and Janet, his mother outraged the Smiles's by implying fortune-hunting (a bizarre echo of Smiles's own experience when he was courting Sarah Anne). But love, of course, triumphed and however chilly the atmosphere between the two families, the Rev. Hon. Henry Legge consecrated the marriage between John and Janet in the Parish Church Lewsiham on 2 April 1868.

Smiles never forgave the Hartree parents, describing them to Willie as 'musty, fusty, crooked-tempered folk'.[22] But the marriage was a great success. Janet remained close to her father, and John Hartree (usually Jack) became a third son, with whom Smiles eventually found more in common than he had with either of his own.

In this fallow period, Smiles turned his mind to goings-on in his old battle-ground of the railway companies. The travelling public's hot-and-cold relationship with the railways was going through a noticeably chilly phase, most visible in an outcry against increased fares, and the usual accusations of waste and directorial skulduggery. Smiles, from his disinterested perch in West Bank, decided to offer the world his opinion. 'Dr Smith has put my article in the place of honour in the Quarterly,' (the *Quarterly Review*, October 1868) he told Janet, 'heading it with the alarming title of "The Great Railway Monopoly." Perhaps it will attract a little interest.' Of course it did, not least because, in this salvo against his old employers, Samuel Smiles, the great advocate of free enterprise, proposed the nationalisation of the railways. In this, as in his plea for more government involvement in education, Smiles showed himself to be the concerned pragmatist rather than the laissez-faire ideologue of later perception.

'There can be no doubt', he pronounced,

> that the idea on which Parliament originally set out, of allowing private individuals to project, construct, and retain as their absolute property the national highways, and the right of working them for their sole profit, was short-sighted and foolish; and that the theory entertained of applying the principles of free trade to railways was absurd in the highest degree.

On the current issue of fares, he accused the companies (without naming the South Eastern, though it had been the main object of public criticism) of being 'too prone to fall back on the stupid and indolent policy of raising fares wholesale in the hope of thereby increasing dividends, though the more usual result has been the increase of irritation and discontent among their customers.' He believed that it was time for the state to take responsibility, deeming it 'expedient, in the interests of society, that the State – which is but Society organised – shall resume possession, and become the owners and controllers as in former times, of the great highways of the kingdom.' It was an acerbic goodbye. 'It will probably be', he told Janet, 'my last railway production.'[23]

For now, his garden was his interest. It was October, but in Blackheath 'the roses are still flowering – gloire de Dijon, and Britovia has at last come out in his vestments.' Still no book seemed to be in hand. Hints appeared from time to time that something may have been started. In March 1869 he mentioned another biography to Robert Cooke, without being specific. Uncharacteristic pessimism marked his tone: 'I have been working at the 'Biography' of late but my spare bits of time are so few that I have almost given up hope of being ready with anything this year.'[24] A few weeks later he wrote to John Murray,[25] this time referring to another project, 'The Characteristics of Biography', which did not re-emerge until years later, in a different form. A book on 'Great English-men' is mentioned in the same letter, and although 'I hope to be able to begin on it in good earnest', it failed to resurface.

More significantly, the first signs appear at this time of Smiles's subsequent love affair with Italy. While expressing himself scarcely able to 'help envying you your stay in Rome', he thanked John Murray for sending him a copy of *Volere è Potere* (roughly, 'Where there's a Will there's a Way'). This strange Italian cousin of *Self-Help*, by an Italian scientist-turned-journalist, Michele Lessona, had apparently prompted Italy's new Premier and Foreign Minister, General Menabrea, to identify Smiles's book as a model for inspiring the Italian people. The General sent a remarkable circular letter to Italian Consuls throughout the world advising them that

> Mr Samuel Smiles has published a book which has obtained great popu-larity in England, in which is narrated the lives of those men who, though born in poverty and growing up amongst hardships and obstacles of every kind, succeeded in overcoming the latter by the energy of their will, and raising themselves to conspicuous social positions for their own benefit and that of their fellows.

Menabrea clearly believed in the propaganda potential of such a book – if a patriotically Italian version could be produced. 'It is proposed,' he announced, 'to bring out a similar book in Italy, drawing the examples exclusively from the lives of Italian citizens.' His proposal to the no doubt startled Consuls was that between them they should create a sort of global database of Italian rags-to-riches stories as ingredients for the book,

> for if it were once circulated among the masses it could not fail to excite their emulation, and encourage them to follow the examples therein set forth ... I trust you will contribute your contingent to a publication which in the course of time may exercise a powerful influence on the increased greatness of our country.

This was another brilliant publishing idea that bit the dust, but the General was right in spotting *Self-Help*'s appeal to Italian readers. The Italian translation, *Chi si aiuta Dio l'aiuta* ('Who helps himself God helps') became one of Smiles's greatest successes.

More spectacularly, in every sense, *Self-Help* was about to become a best-seller in Japan. Since the accession of their new Emperor Meiji in 1867, Japan's leaders had determined to take their country from its feudal, agricultural, and deeply traditional past, into the modern world of economic and industrial progress, and where better to look than Victorian Britain? Among the Japanese intellectuals who went out across the world in search of understanding to aid this cause, was the scholar and translator Nakamura Keiū, who spent some time in England. Nakamura knew that the critical factor in his country's transition would be an understanding of the real value of its people – *all* its people, and the fostering of a bond between national and personal ambition. On his long voyage back to Japan Nakamura read Samuel Smiles's *Self-Help*, and believed that in its pages lay an important message for the new Japan.

Nakamura's translation, its title based not on the main title, 'Self-Help', but on the sub-title: 'with illustrations of conduct and perseverance', emerged as *Saikoku risshi hen*, approximately translated as *Admirable Ambitions in Western Countries*.[26] The impossibilies of exact translation are demonstrated by the alternative, *European Decision of Character Book,* quoted by Smiles in his *Autobiography*. For the book, its translator's admirable ambitions were met. After publication in Tokyo in 1871 Japan's literate classes, at every level, received *Saikoku risshi hen* with enthusiasm. Members of the samauri, especially Government officials and educators, were lining up – even camping overnight – to buy the book.[27] Smiles was delighted to learn that his little book had become, in Japanese, a volume of 2,000 pages, printed on paper like silk, and that the Emperor had been presented with six specially bound volumes.

His writing interest in the meantime turned to Sam, now back from his travels, complete with diary. Smiles loved his younger son and always found reasons to praise him. He wanted the world to share his pride. Later, when Sam returned to trade, his father took huge pleasure in describing his achievements to the rest of the family. Now he was determined that the travel diary, and the letters Sam had sent home describing his adventures, should be put together as a book. Of course, as he had done with his brother Robert's articles twenty years earlier, Smiles felt the need to 'look over' his son's work before offering it to Murray's. The fact that it took almost a year to bring it to publication standard suggests that the over-looking was substantial, perhaps frustrating.

As he approached his sixtieth birthday, Smiles found himself at that dangerous age when the music of life starts to sound different – its pace, its rhythm and its tone unfamiliar. His children had grown up. All but one had left home. For his insurance work, and increasingly by choice, he spent large parts of the year travelling. The house so proudly built at West Bank was an empty theatre. Six years earlier it had cost him just over £5,000. At the beginning of 1870 he sold it for £3,750 with fixtures, including the Osler chandelier and the library curtains, at valuation.[28] The fate of the billiard table is unknown.

The reduced family – Smiles, Sarah Anne and Lilian – moved just down the hill to a leased house, Oakfield, in Eliot Park. There he tried to recover something of the dynamism of earlier years, of thorough involvement with his 'business' during the day in London, and with his literary work in the evenings at home. Inevitably the conditions were more cramped than he had become used to. Inevitably, almost four years after his last book, the writing did not come so easily.

As well as the editorial chore of young Sam's book he had taken up work on a theme which he had been pondering for some time, prompted by the final chapter of *Self-Help*. 'The crown and glory of life' he had stated there, 'is Character.' Now he wanted to develop that thought – to expound on the full meaning of 'character', and on its unique moral potency – using the *Self-Help* model of short biographical examples. Smiles later implied that, like *Self-Help* in the 1850s, a draft for *Character* had been lying around for years. 'I had written it out many years before, and stored it away in my literary cupboard.'[29] In a masterpiece of self-deception, given his history, he claimed that 'It was, like my other books, the result of my evenings' leisure.'

So, no pressure. Smiles was writing again, but again a crash was imminent.

18

The Vale of Years

'LEISURE' for Smiles had its own meaning. It was not a clear space in which mind and body could rest. When Smiles saw a space his first instinct was to fill it. Over in Belfast, as his relaxation after work, Willie was taking up golf. His father had a different interpretation of leisure, and if he needed fresh air and exercise he could find them by travelling about the continent collecting material for his writing. Otherwise he could exercise his pen. By the end of August 1870 he had turned the first half of young Sam's travel diary into a decent manuscript and handed it over to Murray's, with the agreed title: *A Boy's Voyage Round the World*. His other work-in-progress, *Character*, was almost finished: 'I hope to have it set up after the month of August, against my return from my trip to Denmark.'[1]

The 'trip to Denmark' was another of Smiles's fact-gathering tours, like his journey round France for *The Huguenots*. This time, aligning himself with the English, his aim was to find evidence for his theories about the origins of the English character. 'Where did we get our perseverance, our industry, our inventiveness, our constructiveness, our supremacy in commerce, our love of home, and yet our love of the sea, and of wandering over the face of the earth?'[2] This modest list of attributes came mainly, he suggested, from a link with the people of the north Frisian Islands. He spent those late summer weeks travelling on the north coast of Denmark and through the offshore islands. He liked the people there, 'All freeholders, tilling the land. The whole country seemed full of well-being ... you see the same thatch-roofed farm-steadings, spreading far away to the north, as far as the eye can reach.'[3] This evocation of a northern pastoral is a hint that Smiles was modifying his adulation of industrial progress. He certainly chose less iron-clad subjects for biographies in the years ahead. The signs had been coming. The previous year, writing to John Murray about possible reprints of Stephenson, he had remarked that 'I have come to the conclusion that my 'industrial biography' literature has come to be regarded, as very much a drag.'[4]

Back in England he exchanged the gentle steamboat journeys through the Frisian islands for daily commuting between Eliot Park and the National Provident office in Gracechurch Street. He spent the evenings of that winter writing and editing, to complete the manuscripts of *Boy's Voyage* and of *Character*. By the turn of the year he had at last finished 'writing out' both books, and early in 1871 he handed the manuscripts to Murray's. He turned to his notes on Frisia, considering how best to use the material, but soon piles of proof sheets of the other two books had taken over his desk. Smiles found this part of the book production process a chore: 'Correcting printed sheets is always more fatiguing than writing them in manuscript. It requires closer attention to minute points, such as commas and semicolons and full stops, while there is not the interest of writing out fresh thoughts.'[5]

All summer he devoted himself to the commas and semicolons, and at last, by the beginning of October, the job was done: 'I have now finished my corrections of "Character" and the Boy's book is all set up and will be ready for printing in about a week. 5000 may be printed of the former, 1500 of the latter.'[6] *Boy's Voyage* was, he knew, a self-indulgence. He wanted Sam to show up well. Earlier he had tried to reassure Robert Cooke: 'the little book will be unique. The picture is really vivid, of Australian life. There will be a very good bit about the United States. Harper are to reprint both books.'[7]

With the books in his publisher's hands and a trade launch imminent, Smiles decided it was time for a break. This year he would head for the clear air of Yorkshire. But even then he was not prepared to let go of work. He would be away, but not absent:

I leave tomorrow for about ten days – Prospect Hotel Harrogate. When does your sale come off? ... will you do whatever you may think desirable in making allowance to the trade, in order to ensure a good subscription. I have not troubled them with a book for four years, and this time I hope they will give me a bumper. PS I will send you lists of papers to which the books are to go. You will find that I have presented pretty liberally. But it will come to a good heavy knock when we are about it.[8]

He wanted the heavy knock mainly for his son's sake, though credits for *Boy's Voyage* are equivocal. The title page simply states: 'Edited by Samuel Smiles, Author of Self-Help etc', with no mention of Sam junior. Smiles's preface claims the book as 'the work of my youngest son ... the Editor's work having consisted mainly in arranging the materials, leaving the writer to tell his own story as much as possible in his own words.' That 'as much as possible' may be the best clue to the father-son balance in the work. The book is generally included in any list of 'the works of Samuel Smiles'. If Sam junior wrote *A Boy's Voyage Around The World*, it was his first book, and his last.

Character, the book published at the same time, was unequivocally from the pen and mind of Samuel Smiles. Soon he had reason to wonder if it would be his last. In view of what would happen, the closing lines of *Character* seem laden with premonition:

> And when we have done our work on earth – of necessity, of labour, of love, or of duty, – like the silkworm that spins its little cocoon and dies, we too depart. But short though our stay in life may be, it is the appointed sphere in which each has to work out the great aim and end of his being to the best of his power; and when that is done the accidents of the flesh will affect but little the immortality we shall at last put on.

In an almost exact rerun of his breakdown five years earlier, his obsessive approach to work and 'leisure' was wrecking Smiles's health. He describes snatched lunches during the day, dinner missed in the evening, a few cups of tea before sitting down to work at night. 'The brain weakens under protracted labour, especially at night. After writing for some hours, my brain got excited, and refused to lay aside its capacity for thinking. I ceased to sleep, and in sleep only does the brain get perfect rest.' This time there was no henbane, but 'I knew that something must be going wrong; for I was subject to palpitations, and had frequent flushings of the face ...'

Sitting in his room at home one evening checking proofs of the next edition of *Character* (the first run of 5,000 had sold within weeks), he felt a humming in his head and a tingling at the points of his fingers. He got up, walked about the room, sat down and tried to work again, but the sensations returned.

> I turned down the gas, resolved to cease working for the night. On trying to turn the handle of the door with my right hand, I found that it was powerless ... Everything passed away from my recollection; and the next sensation I had was of being carried from the chair which I occupied towards the sofa. In short I had experienced a sharp attack of paralysis.[9]

The stroke which Smiles suffered was severe. At first he could neither move nor speak. For some time muscle and mind seemed strangers to each other, but gradually feeling, like a distant memory, crept back. To move his fingers, to hold a pen and, most wonderful of all, to draw the trembling line that made his name – he won all these early victories – but nothing beyond his name. Samuel Smiles, to whom command of words meant as much as command of breath, now found words beyond his control. His stroke had brought aphasia, the brain's inability to create language. He spent weeks either in bed or in an armchair by the fire. Because he could follow speech but not read, Sarah Anne often read to him, though anything that stimulated thought made his head ache. Despair must have been very close.

But at his lowest, in his own words, 'I determined to 'pull up'. If I recovered I might spend a few more years on earth.' Self-help, in ruthless purity, became the key to life. He accepted the discipline of what he called 'long and perfect rest', and then, through his sixtieth birthday, through Christmas and the turning of the year, working on whatever would work, he applied himself to clearing the mist. By the end of February he was answering letters again, though with a wistful air. To his old friend William Lovett he apologised for not answering earlier:

> my illness has prevented my acknowledging until now. I have been laid up for about three months ... I have many pleasant memories of the times we used to work together for the Howitt's Journal ... With kindest wishes to yourself, and hopes that you are comfortably going along the vale of years like myself.[10]

9 William Lovett: 'I have many
pleasant memories of the times
we used to work together for the
Howitt's Journal'.
(The Mary Evans Picture Library)

'Comfortably going along the vale of years' hardly suggests thrusting ambition. Smiles may at the time have felt empty, yet in the life he rebuilt after this illness he achieved more than most people manage in a whole career.

One of Smiles's first actions when he realised the severity of his stroke had been to resign from the National Provident. Charles Gilpin tried hard to dissuade him, offering extended leave, time for recovery, then possibly a different, less demanding role, but Smiles refused. Another old acquaintance, Sir Edward Watkin, probably the most dynamic railway developer of his time, made him what Smiles called 'a handsome proposal'. Frustratingly, we are given nothing more specific, but Smiles declined the handsome proposal too.

The attitude to Smiles of these two highly successful and influential men is intriguing. Gilpin and Watkin had much in common with each other, and with Smiles. In their earlier years all had been active in radical causes – the Anti-Corn Law League, universal suffrage, secular education. The three were cut from the same ideological cloth. Watkin had started a radical newspaper, the *Manchester Examiner*, in 1845, when Smiles was at the *Leeds Times*, campaigning for all the same causes. Gilpin and Watkin both became Liberal MPs, on the 'left' of the party. Smiles was a member of the Greenwich Advanced Liberal Association.[II] (Gladstone represented the constituency, and a few months earlier Smiles had opposed an address from the Association congratulating the Prime Minister on his policies, on the ground that he had failed to keep his promises to the working classes.) Both Gilpin and Watkin were railway men, who had sat together on the board of the South Eastern when Smiles was Secretary. But clearly they saw their ex-employee as much more than that. They shared his values, admired his achievements, and no doubt valued his voice. Their eagerness to go on supporting him, even in his sixties and in apparently fragile health, throws an interesting light on the continuity between the older Smiles and the world of his radical past.

Despite their overtures, however, his stroke had convinced him that his twin-track career had finally reached its end. *A Boy's Voyage* and *Character* had been launched during his illness. Both quickly went into second editions. By June 1872 *Boy's Voyage* had sold almost 4,000 copies and *Character* 9,500.[12] Smiles was hugely gratified by the reception of his son's book, and to the end of his life insisted that he had been merely its editor. Reviewers were generally complicit in this version. 'The book abounds in agreeable and instructive matter,' said the *Morning Post*, 'and Mr Smiles jun. may be honestly congratulated in making so promising a literary début.'[13] For the next few years *Boy's Voyage* continued to sell in pleasing numbers, certainly covering its production costs.[14]

Without his National Provident salary (which he described as 'handsome') Smiles was now, for the first time in his life, dependent entirely on writing for his income. Literature, which he had always vowed would never be his 'crutch', now became just that, though rather more a platform than a crutch. In the fifteen years since the publication of the *Life of George Stephenson* he had built up an extremely healthy backlist. With the help of their energetic author, Murray's had managed the Smiles brand brilliantly, with revised and repackaged editions of the books regularly refreshing sales. Between 1861 and 1865 Smiles's annual book income had averaged £1,800, or almost twice his salary.[15] But in the years between his first illness and his most recent – 1866 to 1872 – this had dropped to £640. Of course he had savings, and no doubt pension income from both his previous employers. At the time of his resignation he was perhaps contemplating a total income of about £1,000 a year. This would still have allowed him a life of considerable prosperity (Mrs Beeton had declared that £1,000 a year at that time was enough to afford a cook, upper housemaid, nursemaid, under-housemaid, and man-servant)[16] – but on an income of no more than half what he had been used to. The success of *Character* was very welcome.

Reviewers' attitudes to *Self-Help*, not so much to the book as to its perceived readers, had been patronising. It was spoken of in terms of what 'they' might learn from it, how 'they' might benefit by reading it. *Character* was immediately seen as son-of-*Self-Help* – certainly much of it reads as though assembled from offcuts of the earlier book – and it received much of the same response. 'By writing another book in the class to which *Self-Help* belongs, Mr Smiles has hit upon a good subject in 'Character'. He has selected examples from among the great men to illustrate the different forms of character,' wrote the critic in the *London Daily News*, and then proceeded to categorise it as a book for others. You and I, the critic seems to suggest, have nothing to learn from such simple messages, but others will do well to attend, particularly the young: 'The boy who reads this volume can hardly fail to benefit by it, and to learn some things which may contribute to his own improvement.'

All of this did no harm at all. Not only did *Character* sell handsomely (10,000 copies in its first year), but it gave *Self-Help* a new lease of life, increasing its visibility and introducing it to a new generation. This became something of a pattern, each new Smiles title drawing in its wake fresh interest in the former ones – especially *Self-Help*. Samuel Smiles, as he recovered from his illness, found that his voice was still welcomed. With Britain's prosperity now reaching its peak, vast numbers of citizens were learning to be middle class – learning not just how to get there, but how to behave once they had arrived.

Character offered a guided tour of the moral landscape. *Self-Help* showed men achieving greatness through mental fortitude; *Character* showed them achieving grace through the moral equivalent. *Self-Help* lauded perseverance, application, self-education. *Character* extols (as listed in Smiles's preface to the 1878 edition) 'truthfulness, chasteness, mercifulness, integrity, courage, virtue, and goodness in all its phases'. But though it often reads like it, *Character* is not all Sunday-school slogans and moral abstractions. For Smiles, good and evil are strictly practical matters: good means work, evil means idleness. Chapter Four is one of the most often quoted passages from *Character*. 'Work' Smiles declares, 'is the law of our being – the living principle that carries men and nations onward ... It is idleness that is the curse of man – not labour.'

Smiles had gone in his youth from rural East Lothian, where tradi-tional patterns of employment in either local trade or agriculture were still in place, to the manufacturing town of Leeds in the throes of industrialisation. In observing the contrast he had seen at first hand the nineteenth-century labour revolution in practice – at its worst the creation of the 'wage slave', the de-humanisation of work, and the de-personalisation of employment; at its best the possibility of increased earnings, social flexibility, and national economic progress – the dream of a prosperous people in a prosperous state. It was a revolution which caused extended national soul-searching on the meaning and purpose of work, and by corollary on the virtues and vices of idleness. It was the most troubling philosophical issue of the time, inescapable at every level of society. Every serious-minded commentator, from Carlyle, Ruskin or John Stuart Mill to Dickens, Elizabeth Gaskell or George Eliot, had views on the subject, often extravagantly expressed. On one point consensus had been reached: work was virtuous, and no longer incon-sistent with gentlemanliness. Work had come to be seen as not just acceptable at every social level; work had become a matter of conscience. As Smiles bluntly put it, 'Life must needs be disgusting alike to the idle rich man as to the idle poor man ...' Without work life was worse than nasty and brutish; it was empty. Thomas Carlyle famously said 'Labour is Life.'[17]

In his other books Smiles had exalted hard work as a means to practical achievement. In *Character* he extols it for its own sake, stepping right over any debate about whether or not work is a good thing. 'Work', he roundly declares 'is the law of our being'. He goes on to quote Lord Stanley: 'As work is our life, show me what you can do, and I will show you what you are.' Again and again Smiles insists on the psychological value of work, generally by pointing out the psychological cost of the alternative. Work's value is its power to cure the pain of idleness. He quotes at length from *Anatomy of Melancholy*, in which Robert Burton warns that however rich or well-placed anyone may be – 'so long as he, or she, or they, are idle, they shall never be pleased, never well in body or mind, but weary still, sickly still, vexed still, loathing still, weeping, sighing, grieving, suspecting, offended with the world ...'[18] Work, on the other hand, is the path to happiness. 'True happiness',[19] Smiles says 'is never found in torpor of the faculties, but in their action and useful employment.'

Many of Smiles's views on work echo the earlier writings of Carlyle, who had praised the 'perennial nobleness, and even sacredness, in Work', and he acknowledged Carlyle's influence. But Smiles was explicit in describing the fundamental difference between himself and his great contemporary: 'He is emphatically a puller-down, not a builder-up', he wrote in his essay on Carlyle in *Brief Biographies,* published in 1860. 'He has no sympathy for such notions of making men better ...' And by placing his emphasis on the link between work and 'happiness' Smiles marks another sharp difference. 'Blessed is he who has found his work, let him ask no other blessedness', Carlyle wrote, but he derided 'the Greatest Happiness principle'. Smiles had always been a Benthamite utilitarian, believing that the purpose of society, indeed the purpose of life, was the greatest happiness of the greatest number.

And of course the greatest number includes women. 'The habit of constant useful occupation,' Smiles advised, 'is as essential for the happiness and well-being of woman as of man.'[20]

Smiles's attitude to the nineteenth-century 'woman question' is on display in *Character* more than in any of his other books. Despite his engagement with Eliza Cook and with unconventional women like Matilda Hays and Charlotte Cushman, his views on women's work were conservative. He firmly endorsed the nineteenth-century notion of men's and women's separate spheres. Women, he says in his chapter on 'Home Power', 'accomplish their best work in the quiet seclusion of the home and the family, by sustained effort and patient perseverance in the path of duty'. He explained to his readers that 'Man is the brain, but woman is the heart of humanity; he its judgment, she its feeling; he its strength, she its grace, ornament and solace.'

As *Character* was flooding the English bookshops Smiles's eldest son Willie was marrying Isabella Beeton's half-sister, Lucy Dorling (15 April 1872). Though by then poor Mrs Beeton, almost twenty-five years younger than Smiles, was dead, in *Character* Smiles speaks with a Beetonian voice. 'Habits of business do not relate to trade merely' he wrote, 'but apply to all the practical affairs of life – to everything that has to be arranged, to be organised, to be provided for, to be done ... It requires method, accuracy, organisation, industry, economy, discipline, tact, knowledge, and capacity for adapting means to ends.' Even Isabella might not have demanded such a galaxy of accomplishments from her followers, but she would surely have agreed with Smiles that there was 'one special department of woman's work demanding the earnest attention of all true female reformers ... We mean the better economizing and preparation of human food, the waste of which at present, for want of the most ordinary culinary knowledge, is little short of scandalous.'[21] In the Smiles view the 'home power' of women need have no limit, but the thought of giving them political power made him nervous. There was no reason, he said,

> ... to believe that the elevation and improvement of women are to be secured by investing them with political power. There are, however, in these days, many who anticipate some definite good from the 'enfranchisement' of women. It is not necessary here to enter upon the discussion of this question.

Much better, he implied, to concentrate on the economising and preparation of human food.

Smiles's success as a writer was founded on conviction. His readers believed what he told them because he believed it himself – in individual responsibility, self-help, useful occupation, 'happiness and well-being' as a moral construct. In recovering from his illness he instinctively turned to these principles. For the first time in thirty-five years he had no obligation to leave his house each morning, no employer except himself. His one determination was that for the rest of his life he would never be without employment.

It is easy to imagine him, still in his armchair, *Character* open on his knees, nodding in agreement with the lines near the end of Chapter IV: 'It is not work, but overwork that is hurtful; and it is not hard work that is injurious so much as monotonous work, fagging work, hopeless work. All hopeful work is healthful; and to be usefully and hopefully employed is one of the great secrets of happiness.'

At first his useful employment was confined to managing his own recovery. His constitution had been badly damaged. He had lost several stone in weight, and much of his mobility; control of speech and language returned only gradually. Friends who remembered him as 'a handsome middle-aged man' noticed his sunken face and muddied complexion, and heard the slur in his voice. 'His tongue tripped and faltered.'[22] The vigorous, prolific author had surely gone.

Slowly, by disciplined rest, exercise and sensible diet, he regained enough strength to contemplate travelling. His first urge, as soon as he was able, was to visit his eighty-four-year-old mother in Haddington. Sam was in Dublin, still trying his luck in the tea trade. Janet and John Hartree had moved to Belfast, where Willie had made his first entrepreneurial move. With Sarah Anne, Smiles visited them all. By the time he returned to Eliot Park he was back almost to normal, not quite confident enough to start writing, but determined to work on his other talent, for drawing and painting.

Smiles was already a highly competent draughtsman; surviving sketches and watercolours, made all through his career, show considerably more talent than the average recreational Victorian painter.[23] The attraction of art, sparked when he was a boy by his cousin Yellowlees, had never gone away. He signed on as a student at the National Art College in South Kensington (now the Royal College of Art). In his lessons there, and visits to the College's Bethnal Green branch for copying, the 'mature student' rediscovered his creative enthusiasm.

> Tuesday I went over to Bethnal Green', he wrote to Sam 'and finished my picture. I am next going to do ... either a copy from George or from Cuyp – either will be good, only I must do them in watercolour – perhaps afterwards copying them in oil. But the one I have done after Guardi is almost as good (in water) as the original.[24]

He wrote that letter on 3 July 1873, just over six months after his stroke. Its sense of returning energy indicates that he was ready to go back to writing.

At first he worked only on existing material. A pile of unused notes on the Huguenots, covering their earlier history, became *The Huguenots in France After the Edict of Nantes*, published in October 1873. The next year he worked with Murray's on another profitable recycling project. This entailed, by judicious revision, adaptation and addition, a five-volume edition of *Lives of the Engineers*. Smiles became thoroughly involved, though he knew he must be cautious. 'I think I could do the revision of the other volume' he wrote to Robert Cooke in March 1874.[25] 'But I will be able to speak with more certainty when I have revised the lives of Smeaton and Rennie ... I need scarcely inform you that I must still take the greatest care of myself as I don't like to see a "softening of the brain".' He suggested to Cooke that he might prepare the first four volumes that year and add the fifth in the year following. In the event the splendid five-volume set appeared in time for Christmas 1874, at 7/6 a volume surely a generous gift for any gentleman though, as the advertisement was careful to point out, 'Each volume is complete in itself and may be had separately'. The Smiles brand was being kept alive. As with the publication of *Character*, the success of the five-volume *Lives* helped all the other Smiles titles. In 1874 his income from books was £1,534, not far from its 1860s peak. It was, however, a sad year.

First it was wonderful. April brought two weddings – Sam's to an Australian girl he'd met on his travels, Sally Peddington, on the 8th in Belfast, then Willie's to Lucy Dorling on the 28th in Pimlico. Smiles could not miss Sam's wedding, and made the trip to Northern Ireland, where the partying was lively. The Pimlico wedding was a good deal quieter and the groom's weary father stayed at home, to welcome the guests at the reception. Over the next few weeks, against a background of general socialising, visitors, parties, and dances, he tried to concentrate on his work. News from Haddington, however, intervened. His mother's health had deteriorated and on 19 June she died. He travelled north again, for the funeral, gratified no doubt that in the years since his father's death the Smiles family had moved into the mainstream of Haddington society. 'All the principal people of the town attended the funeral, including the Provost and the Minister of the Established Church.'[26]

In the months following, Smiles worked to pick up the threads of his dealings with Murray's, corresponding regularly, on the progress of the new *Lives*, on pricing policy for *Self-Help*, on reprints of *Character*. He told Murray how pleased he was at the way sales were going: 'Sales of my books are very satisfactory. I hope we may be equally successful in the reissue of 'Engineers' which is about to take place.'[27] But, in the Victorian fashion, after his mother's death the letter was on paper edged in black. Soon the blackness thickened.

Edith was the quietest, certainly the least remarked on, of the Smiles children. A few years earlier she had been married in Lewisham Parish Church to a young local man, Herbert Jones, notable, apparently, for no more than his fine baritone voice. They were happy, and soon their son was christened, Bertram Edward, in the same church. Edith and little Bertie, living locally, gave the Smiles grandparents great joy. But very soon Lewisham Parish Church had to open its doors to the Smiles family again, this time for the funeral service of Edith. When she died of appendicitis on 10 November 1874 she was just past her twenty-seventh birthday. Bertie was two.

For a time the older Smiles's were at a loss. Only Lilian was now at home, when she was not visiting one of her siblings in Belfast (she had a beau there, who when he jilted her caused her father much agitation). West Bank had gone. Even Oakfield had become too big. A generation had moved on and the Blackheath house, with its unused rooms, seemed grey and empty.

Samuel and Sarah Anne moved out and for six months shuffled between Belfast, Scotland and the south coast. With Willie, Sam, and Janet, and their growing families all settled in Belfast, and Lillian being courted by a County Down man, the centre of gravity of the family seemed to have moved to Northern Ireland. For a time, but not for long, the older Smiles thought of moving there. 'I tried Ireland for a month and detested it,' he told Cooke. 'I shall only return to it again on a brief visit.' Perhaps too, he dare not contemplate anything that might feel like withdrawal.

19

New Direction

THE ANSWER to everything, even to his child's death, was work. As a new base in 1875, Smiles chose St Leonard's-on-Sea in Sussex. There, in Pevensey Road, in a bright house with tall windows, he was able to turn his mind away from loss. Later he made it sound simple. 'In the meantime,' he wrote in his *Autobiography*, 'my writing faculty returned.' The clear sea air of St Leonard's suited his mood. By the end of May he was confident enough to promise Murray's another book. 'If my health keeps good, as it is at present, I shall be ready with my book ... I have still two months to devote to it, and shall not be ready to put up the manuscript to the printers until about the end of July.'

The old Smiles seemed to be back, restless to be involved with the business of his books – with the price of the five-volume Lives: 'I had some thoughts about bringing out a cheaper edition of the Stephenson volume ... I would also give the woodcut frontispiece, but none of the illustrations' – with competitive print quotes: 'Cheapness of getting up, you will readily understand, is a considerable point with me' – with the structure of the new book: 'It will be about the same size as 'Character', but without notes.'[1] Even the combative, slightly arrogant tone of former years is apparent. Young Sam, who in general could do no wrong, had decided to question the copyright arrangements for *Boy's Voyage*. 'I do not know what my son intends to do about the book', Smiles wrote to Robert Cooke. 'He thinks I rather mismanaged it before, and thinks he can do better. I am annoyed about this, as it never would have been a book but for me. However he must now take his own course.' There were, however, no tears. The copyright was transferred for £50 from father to son. 'I am glad to say' he was able to tell Cooke, 'that my young son is perfectly happy with what I have done.'[2]

The sense of peace at St Leonard's, the light on the sea, the crisp air, helped Smiles to settle again to a routine of write, exercise, relax, write again. He would like to have stayed at St Leonard's. 'I feel that this place does me good' he told Cooke, 'and I would love to live here, because the sea air, especially in the heights above the town, is refreshing. But alas! My wife dislikes the place because she has no friends here, and it is exceedingly probable that before the end of the year we shall be located somewhere about Hampstead.'[3] The book was not finished by the end of July. In fact by then he was on the move again, and nowhere near Hampstead.

After the St Leonard's idyll Smiles was restless, but surprisingly full of ideas and projects. The editor of *Good Words* wanted articles from him, but Smiles reassured Murray's that they would always get his books. He had, he told Cooke, three or four on hand, 'and I wish I may live to write them. One is 'Characteristics of Biography',[4] for which I am collecting information. The others are Ships and Shipbuilders, Men of Business (Captains of Industry), and 'Thrift'. The last I think might prove most useful, and would go with Character and Self-Help.' But *Thrift* would not be ready just then, as originally suggested. 'I cannot write so well or long as I once could, and therefore must proceed slowly. I am obliged to attend to my health, and not overwork my brain, which is rather rickety at present.'

With his rickety brain he moved on to Haddington in July, where he was able to continue working on *Thrift*. It was a book written on the move, which may account for its patchy nature – more a collection of essays than a sustained exposition. After a few weeks he left Haddington's smiling country to travel to Banff, two hundred miles north on the flat grey coast of Aberdeenshire. He spent a week there, exploring the atmosphere of the old fishing town, enjoying walks by the bright August sea, and talking to Thomas Edward, local shoemaker turned naturalist, whose story he had touched on in *Self-Help*. Another book was taking shape.

Back in Haddington he produced a few more chapters of *Thrift*, but in September he was off again, to Newcastle-upon-Tyne and then to Darlington, invited as an honoured guest at the fiftieth anniversary celebration of the opening of the Stockton and Darlington railway.

> I am going in spite of fate. Aged [his pet name for Sarah Anne] is also going, not to appear in the procession, but to look down on the railway magnates from the Ladies gallery ... a Mr Hodgkin (I suppose he must be a Director) has invited us to stay with him during the celebration. His carriage will be waiting for us at Darlington station.[5]

Smiles enjoyed his status as celebrity railway historian. He was sharp too, in defence of the accuracy of his work. When Miss Gurney wrote to *The Times* a few months later claiming the invention of the steam blast for her father, Smiles was quick to reply.[6] 'Miss Gurney is of opinion that I was mistaken in giving Stephenson credit for this invention.' Shocked, he quoted his sources: 'I think these passages, without citing any more, should be sufficient to establish the fact communicated by the late Robert Stephenson, and which I inserted in my life of his father.'

Thrift had still to be finished, and a settled home created. It would, it seemed, have to be in London, so as a base for their search the Smiles's took lodgings in Guilford Street, beside Russell Square. There the book was completed, proofs corrected, the index prepared by Jack Hartree, and everything sent with a note of urgency to Messrs Watson & Hazell in Aylesbury. Smiles apologised to Jack for the rush (increasingly his son-in-law became a sort of honorary editor of Smiles's books, invited to 'look over the points and phraseology and correct where necessary') – 'I wrote the book very hastily, at St Leonard's, Haddington and Banff, and without any access to books, & therefore it may have many errors worthy of correction.'[7]

As the book was finished, so was the wandering. They found a house, at 4 Pembroke Gardens in Kensington, which had everything the elderly Smiles wanted. It was near the park, so that he could walk; near the South Kensington Museum and School, so that he could visit exhibitions and go on painting; and central enough to be easy for his family to visit. While he waited impatiently to move – 'We cannot get into our house until 15th inst. The paperers and painters are at work' – he had the satisfaction of reporting to Jack Hartree on a bumper sale for *Thrift*.

'Murray sold 10,000 copies of 'Thrift' last night. The index did it. A large sale. 3,200 'Self-helps' & 1,500 'Characters' were also sold ... – Tell Willie about the sale of 'scraps".[8] (Willie had once dismissed his father's most famous book as 'no more than a collection of scraps'.)

The success of *Thrift – A Book of Domestic Counsel*, surprised Smiles. He had agreed a first printing of just 5,000 copies. When he wrote *Self-Help* he had not intended to become a 'self-help' author. His ambition was as biographer of the men who made the modern world, and historian of technical and industrial progress. But *Self-Help* had resonated too strongly for Smiles's name ever again to be used without the accompanying title. 'By the author of *Self-Help*' became an essential qualifier for all his other books. It would have been unnatural if he had not at some point in his career revisited the genre which had made him rich and famous. So *Character* had been offered overtly as an extension of *Self-Help*. Its preface described it as 'in some respects a supplement to 'Self-Help'. The power and influence of character are summarised in that book, but much more remains to be said.'

The popularity of *Character* showed that an enormous public was ready to listen. Now, four years later, *Thrift* came forth as the next member of a dynasty. 'This book' Smiles announced in the preface, 'is intended as a sequel to 'Self-Help' and 'Character'.' That may have been what he intended. It is hardly what he delivered.

No doubt Smiles went back to his notes for *Self-Help* while he was writing *Thrift*. In the new book, Chapter V has strong echoes of the original. Its teaching-by-example technique is identical. It extols individual effort, quoting Goethe: 'What is the best government? That which teaches us to govern ourselves.' It uses old Smiles favourites, like George Stephenson and James Watt, to show thrift hand-in-hand with perseverance leading to success. But in its fundamental argument, and the manner of making it, *Thrift* is a very different book, with a different attitude.

Self-Help, though it may have preached, preached *to* its subjects; it was on their side. In large part *Thrift* preaches *about* its subjects, the 'improvident' working classes; it is on their critics' side. In its most vibrant passages *Thrift* reads less like a sequel to *Self-Help* then an extension of that bitter pamphlet of 1861, *Workmen's Earnings, Strikes and Savings*, where Smiles had put the blame for poverty firmly on the shoulders of the poor. 'Poverty', he had declared then 'is to be secured not so much by conferring greater rights, as by implying better habits.' In *Thrift* the tone became even more outraged: 'The intense selfishness, thriftlessness and folly of these highly-paid operatives is scarcely credible. Exceptions are frequently taken to calling the working classes 'the lower orders', but 'the lower orders' they will always be, so long as they indicate such sensual indulgence and improvidence.' In paragraph after paragraph the tone of shocked disapproval is sustained. Those who cry for help should use 'a little self-denial, sobriety and thrift'. The thousands who complain of poverty 'have wasted what they have'. And so the finger goes on wagging. It wags at the East End of London, subject of so much horrified comment at the time, noting that there 'They abandon themselves to their sensual appetites; and make no provision whatsoever for the future.'[9]

'Sensual appetites' for Smiles meant habitual drunkenness. This was the real target of his wrath, the pit into which the 'high wages' were tossed. He expressed his thesis bluntly: 'Increased wages, instead of being saved, are for the most part spent in drink.'[10]

Smiles was not alone in his profound concern about the problems of alcohol in Victorian England. The temperance movement was born and flourished then. Though this was mainly a middle-class campaign, many working-class people saw how drunkenness damaged their cause; there had been Chartist Temperance Associations at the height of the suffrage campaign. The beer-soaked husband, spending his wages in the public house while his wife and children starve in their hovel, is an abiding image of the time. So bad did the authorities judge the situation to be that a Parliamentary Committee was set up in 1872 to look at the causes and possible remedies. In *Thrift* Smiles offered his own advice: 'look around and see how much is spent and how little saved; what a large proportion of earnings goes to the beer-shop and how little to the savings bank or benefit society'. His time with the National Provident must surely have been a factor in the writing of *Thrift*.

In his cry against what he saw as the working class's tragic tendency to self-destruct, Smiles wrote almost in desperation. Everything that he had spent so many years campaigning for had been realised, and seemed to have achieved nothing. 'We have had household suffrage and vote by ballot ... relief of taxes on corn, cattle, coffee, sugar, and provisions generally ... Yet these measures have produced but little improvement in the condition of the working people.'[11] Was reform really pointless? Was self-help a hollow dream? The penniless young men gathered in the hut in Leeds, determined on self-improvement, had disappeared into mythology, and been replaced by a new image of over-paid drunken louts on the streets of London, bent on self-destruction.

Yet Smiles was not ready to give up hope. His most cherished instrument for the improvement of humanity – education – was more available than ever. W E Forster's 1870 Elementary Education Act had delivered much of the educational progress that Smiles had so long campaigned for.

> The large earnings of the working classes is an important point to start with. The gradual diffusion of education will help them to use, not abuse, their means for comfortable living ... Surely it need not be so difficult to put an end to the Satanic influences of thriftlessness, drunkenness, and improvidence![12]

This section of *Thrift,* with its strident polemic, seems today to be the most highly charged part of the book. Contemporary critics largely ignored it, choosing bland praise for the bland remainder. 'With its stores of biographical anecdote it mingles instruction of a sound and homely kind' (*Daily News*, 28 Dec 1875). 'Altogether, in fact, as complete and interesting a little treatise on a somewhat homely subject as can be imagined' (*The Graphic*, 5 Feb 1876). 'It contains most valuable advice, and it is pleasant to see that Mr Smiles insists upon the value of taste as a promoter of economy' (*Morning Post*, 2 Dec 1875). Even the papers which mentioned more contentious issues either endorsed or excused them. The *Pall Mall Gazette* looked down its nose at the book's 'several repetitions and a good many, perhaps inevitable, commonplaces' but gave the author a pat on the back for complaining, 'as well he may, of the monstrous folly of highly paid artisans who spend half their wages in selfish pleasure ... the higher the wages, the larger is the consumption of beer and spirits' (25 Jan 1876). *Reynold's Newspaper* worried that 'the large number of oft-repeated and frequently incorrect matters that it comprises will seriously militate against its prosperity', but was relieved that 'Mr Smiles gives many and very pleasing instances of how men were weaned from habits of drinking and extravagance by the example and persuasion of wives and other kindred means.'

Both in its commonplaces and in its condemnations *Thrift* reflected the mainstream attitudes of its time. Over the next two years it sold 20,000 copies and for more than a decade was one of Smiles's best-selling titles.

Comfortable in his new home in Kensington, he was eager now, not so much to resume his career, as to follow its new direction. For over twenty years he had studied and written about the heavyweights who had made Britain's industrial miracle possible. The men who had done it had excited him – the Stephensons, Rennie, Telford, Watt and the others. The landscape had been tamed, transport and production revolutionised, and the material prosperity of the people transformed. Machinery was the voice of the future. But after 1875, after his stroke, the deaths of his mother and of Edith, after the St Leonard's sabbatical, and the rootlessness, one can almost hear the clamour die.

For the rest of his life Smiles's writing took on an altogether quieter tone. In the ten books he produced after his mid-sixties, eight had nothing to do with engineering. Of the other two, *Men of Industry* was prompted by his personal interest in Ireland and particularly in Belfast's shipping industry, with which Willie was associated. The other was a co-authored memoir of a still living engineer, James Nasmyth, who was a friend. In fact from now on personal engagement played a much bigger role in Smiles's work than it had ever previously done.

In *Self-Help*, among 'the common class of day labourers', he had noted that 'a profound naturalist has been discovered in the person of a shoe-maker at Banff, named Thomas Edward, who while maintaining himself by his trade, had devoted his leisure to the study of natural science in all its branches'. This was the man Smiles had travelled in August to meet, in the company of the Aberdeen artist and Scottish Academician, George Reid. The thirty-three-year-old artist was so enthusiastic about the subject, and so keen to enjoy the expedition to Banff and the surrounding coast, that he volunteered to illustrate the planned book, a life of Thomas Edward, naturalist. Reid's portrait of Edward became a star feature of the finished volume. As a result of their cooperation on the book, the young artist and the elderly author became lifelong friends. Smiles's relationship with Thomas Edward also lasted beyond the publication of the book, though in a more problematical way.

Edward intrigued Smiles because he truly was a self-made man; that is, someone who had turned himself from an illiterate, penniless child with no formal education into a natural scientist of real significance, simply by the bloody-minded pursuit of his curiosity. He had done this from a position of isolation, without the support of any scientific community, or seat of learning, or even access to a proper library. He was the ultimate outsider, who had achieved no material gain from his work, and precious little recognition. He had been made an Associate Member of the Linnean Society, but only an Associate, and had been marginalised by the scientific establishment. He had struggled all his life to keep himself and his wife by working as a cobbler. When Smiles went to see him in the summer of 1875, when Edward had the demeanour of an old man (he was two years younger than Smiles), he was still working as a cobbler. Had he been serene in this simple life, fulfilled by his scientific discoveries, and indifferent to the world's applause, he would have been a perfect model for self-help. The trouble was that he had a powerful sense of resentment, a huge chunk of Aberdeen granite on his shoulder.

Smiles tried hard in his book to play down the 'old man's' bitterness, but he was too honest a writer to hide it, even though Reid said Smiles had 'cast a halo about him', and Smiles later admitted to Janet that he had 'idealised him a bit'.[13] Against his inclinations Smiles quotes Edward complaining: 'I know what I could have done ... had I got but a little help ... say if I can be blamed because I occasionally grieve that I had no help.' The triumph of self-help seems far from this man, who proclaimed 'For these reasons I sometimes consider my life to have been a blasted one, like a diamond taken from the mine, and, instead of being polished, crushed to the earth in a thousand fragments.' There is a suspicion here of Smiles being perhaps carried away on his own rhetoric. In the end, of course, in the interests of the pursuit-of-happiness message, he had to set aside the grumpy cobbler's self-pity. 'Edward must,' the biographer insisted,

> to a great extent, have enjoyed a happy life. He was hopeful and cheerful. He had always some object to pursue, with a purpose. That constitutes one of the secrets of happiness. He had an interesting hobby: that is

another secret ... He had the adventure, the chase, the capture, and often the triumph of discovery.

Smiles had some genuine liking for the man he called 'the Shrymper'. He enjoyed his time in his company, among the beaches and rocks, watching the herring boats coming into Banff harbour in the evening with their 'shining cargo', and the herring gutters on the quay. Back in London he settled to writing again, rebuilding his necessary routine. 'I spend my forenoons in writing – the afternoons in walking – & the evenings in reading something or other.' For a 'literary' man he had constrained literary tastes. He was happy with Thomas Hardy, he told Janet, but though 'we are taking "Daniel Deronda"...[14] I really do not think much of it – no more than I did of "Middlemarch". Of course this is very bad taste. Novels are written to amuse people. If they do not amuse me they are failures.' But he was clearly enjoying his own work.

> I have got a beautiful engraving of the Shrymper from Reid ... Reid took a sketch of him in October. I am nearly halfway through the memoir of the Shrymper ... I hope to get pretty well through it by the time you come. I wish the proofs to be got ready for George Reid, who has volunteered to illustrate the book. If the other illustrations are as good as the portrait they will be very fine.[15]

As with his views on *Middlemarch*, Smiles was resolutely unintellectual. He certainly affected discomfort in the presence of anyone he deemed elitist. 'On Sunday we were at Mrs Harty's. Those present included Browning the poet, Harrison the Comptist ... and other bigwigs. There was a Miss Sitwell. Who is she? She seemed to have been drawn through a mangle. I suppose she must be a philosopher.'[16] In truth Smiles was happier away from these London gatherings, going north. In July, still preoccupied with the Scotch Naturalist, he headed to Aberdeen by boat, and on to Thurso and Cape Wrath – 'I expect to see the Shrymper on my way.' They had corresponded regularly but Edward was a prickly character who, now that he found himself the object of a famous author's interest, was not afraid to be assertive. He had been Smiles's first living biographical subject and the author was keen to avoid any friction.

In going to Thurso, almost as far north as John O' Groats, he was on the research path again, this time for information about another artisan scientist, Robert Dick, who had spent his life as a humble baker in the town while at the same time doing for botany and geology what Thomas Edward had done for zoology. No doubt Smiles chose to write about both these men because he was fascinated by their lives, and by how they had managed to learn so much from such unpromising beginnings. But he was also aware that natural science had become a national hobby. The thrill of discovery was not on a distant continent. It was at everyone's feet, if they chose to look. Darwin had questioned the very meaning of life by his discoveries, and turned Britain into a nation of bug collectors. Smiles described Edward, proudly, as his 'man in the street'. Books about man-in-the-street scientists would surely sell.

Of course Smiles had an eye on the market, and was often shrewd, or lucky, in his choice of subjects. But he also believed that what he wrote could do some good. *Life of a Scotch Naturalist: Thomas Edward*, published in November 1876, achieved almost everything he had hoped for it. It sold well – the usual 5,000 copies of the first edition was taken up by the trade on the day of launch. It shone a bright light on distant Banff, and gave Thomas Edward some of the public recognition he had always craved. He was the subject of a 4,000-word article in *The Times*, praising his achievements and noting that 'All readers are bound to be grateful to Mr Smiles for having, in a beautifully illustrated volume, rescued the fame and character of Thomas Edward as a most accomplished naturalist.' But the book did even more, because Smiles was able to use it to campaign for a Royal pension for Edward.

He had known Theodore Martin, Parliamentary Solicitor, and himself a biographer (his *Life of the Prince Consort* appeared in 1874), for some years. With Martin's guidance Smiles first contrived to get enough of the right sort of signatures for a memorial, and then managed the protocol that governs such matters, to bring the book to the notice of the Queen. It was hard work. 'Tam Edward has given me a good deal of trouble over the last few days,' he told Jack Hartree.[17]

I have been running about obtaining signatures for a memorial to the Queen to place him on the Civil List for £50 a year. If I succeed it will be one of my few good deeds upon earth. I sent the Queen a copy of the book through Theodore Martin ... I have reason to believe that the memorial will be successful. I got it signed by Dr Allman, President of the Linnean

Society, Dr Hooker president of the Royal Society, Professor Owen and Charles Darwin. I found them all most cordial. Professor Owen (whom I found in his den in the British Museum) forced upon me a donation for the subscription list getting up at Aberdeen on behalf of Edward.

Smiles particularly relished his visit to Darwin, deep in the Kent countryside. 'He almost embraced me. I stayed to lunch with him and his family.'[18] The two elderly men (Darwin was sixty-seven at the time, Smiles sixty-four) had much in common. Both had been medical students in Edinburgh. Both had had their most famous books published in the same week in 1859 by John Murray. And both talked a lot. 'He was full of talk – and he, as well as myself, could scarcely eat for speaking [the letter has a note here, in Sarah Anne's hand: '*I believe this*'].The tongue cannot be used both ways. He went over no end of things. He seems to have an insight into everything.'

The public announcement that Her Majesty had been graciously pleased to grant Thomas Edward a Pension of £50 a year came barely a month after the publication of *The Scotch Naturalist*. Smiles, perhaps inwardly delighted by the thought of Victoria poring over his book, gave the credit to the Queen. 'Edward has got his pension,' he told Janet. 'The suggestion originated with the Queen herself, and she sent me a message through Theodore Martin "thanking me very much for the book".'[19]

The only sour note was the reaction to the limelight of Edward himself. He was carping and ungrateful to Smiles, and seems to have been, at best, tactless in his efforts to exploit his new found fame. George Reid was the main force behind 'the subscription getting up in Aberdeen' to help Edward, but soon he became annoyed with the cobbler's antics with the local people. 'As for Edward,' he told Smiles 'two or three repetitions of the Aberdeen business would dispel the halo you have cast about him.'[20] When Edward suggested that he should have some share of the proceeds of the biography, and demanded that his papers be returned, Smiles was philosophical and refused to take offence The next year, when he found out that Edward was planning some sort of follow-up, he simply remarked that 'He (Edward) is about to publish a continuation of the book. I have no doubt some publisher has induced him to do so. But I fear he will cut the gilt off. I idealised him a bit and that worked the miracle.'[21]

By that time Smiles's mind was filled by other projects. In February and March his articles were to appear in *Good Words*, the high-minded, high circulation monthly magazine edited by Donald Macleod. In April he left on a trip to Holland, where nostalgia took a hand. 'I remember the last time I was in Utrecht',[22] he wrote to Sarah Anne.

> It was in 1838. I had been staying at Leyden for a few weeks to get a degree, and then started on foot with a knapsack on my back. I remember looking out for the humblest sort of lodgings. Nevertheless I saw the place – the cathedral, the grand town, the beautiful promenades round the old fortifications. Now it is different.

So was Smiles. No more humble lodgings, no more unqualified admiration for the sedate Dutch. He described his hotel, the Pays Bas, as 'a good hotel though a little behind the age. I fancy that it is the character of the Dutchman. He is like Athelstan the Unready, a little slow and wants spurring a bit.'

Smiles spurred himself. Besides the series of articles for *Good Words*, he had started work on the life of Robert Dick, the geological baker from the far north. Dick, unlike Edward, was dead, which had the advantage that, unlike Edward, he would stay quiet, but the disadvantage that his story would have to be compiled from letters and the memories of others. Smiles was, of course, well used to this process and set about his research thoroughly; (he was also used to the fact that the death of the subject did not protect him from the wrath of his descendants, which, in the case of Dick, happened). When he got back from Holland he headed north again, to John O'Groats, and some gentle socialising with the Earl of Caithness (Samuel Smiles's celebrity was such by this time that the Earl had learned of his visit from an announcement in an Aberdeen paper). From there he drove round the coast and across the sands to Thurso, where he spent several weeks following the trail of Robert Dick and, most satisfying, making sketches of the coastal scenery as illustrations for the book. Another attractive volume would arise, this time without the need for a Scottish Academician. Smiles expected, when he got back to London with notebooks and sketchbooks stuffed full, to settle down to drafting the book. But a quite different challenge awaited him.

20

The Publishers Believe in Me

AGNES MOORE, second wife and recent widow of the enormously wealthy lace manufacturer and philanthropist George Moore, wanted to commission Smiles to write her husband's biography. His first reaction was to decline. Moore had been notoriously pious, and, as Smiles said to John Murray, 'It would have to be a religious biography and should be written by a clergyman to give it the proper tone. Not that any of my books are of a different character, but they are not written in religious phraseology.'[1] The request did not go away, but he greeted the widow's next attempt with derision.

> I have received Mrs Moore's 'liberal' proposal. She proposes that I should pay her £150 for the materials for the life of her husband, give her a number of copies of the book, and proceed at once so that it may come out before December ... Of course I have refused the 'liberal' offer. Mrs Moore must have a strange notion of biographers and their work.[2]

Money, however, and Smiles's regard for Moore's single-minded commitment to good causes, settled the argument. For an agreed fee of £500 and a flexible deadline, he settled down at the end of May to write the book. He was out of sympathy with the character and found writing about him laborious and unsatisfying. More interesting subjects nagged at his mind. While he slogged on at Moore's pale history he was aware of his pages of sketches, and fat notebooks on Dick, waiting in the wings. It became an unhappy summer; the family found him cantankerous, and complaining. They were selfish he said, ignoring their parents.

'Are you and Jack really so much involved on business,' he asked Janet,
'– are you both working so hard – working between life and death, that
you can, neither of you, spare a few minutes to tell us how our grandchildren are? Oh selfish generation! But you are all alike. All wrapped
up in yourselves.'[3] He was being pestered, not just by Mrs Moore, but by
a league of other Mrs Moores, believing that Samuel Smiles must be
waiting, pen poised, to immortalise their loved ones in a handsome biography. 'I seem to be regarded as a "biographer general"',[4] he wrote to John
Murray. Aileen Smiles listed the families of Thomas Wright, Sopwith,
George Parker Bidder, and Thomas Brassey, among the supplicants.
In August he was attacked by another such intrusion, this time a more
serious one. The sisters of Dr Livingstone, of 'I presume' fame, had
decided their brother should have a Samuel Smiles biography. Between
the Miss Livingstones's neighbour, Thomas Annan, and John Murray
(who could see the sales potential), Smiles came under sustained
pressure. But, ensnared by Moore, Smiles had no interest in another
missionary, even in such a public hero as Livingstone, or even in the large
profits which might flow from such a book. It was the baker from Thurso
who occupied his head. In August he took a break from Moore to go
north again, taking the opportunity on the way back to spend a few
nights at Haddington. He reported from there to Murray, in suppressed
excitement, 'I have been very successful in picking up information as to
Robert Dick, the Scotch geologist. I think I may be able to make a good
book out of the materials I have collected.'[5]

Over the next few months he strove conscientiously on the *Life Of
George Moore*, but he must have taken days off, like a truant, to spend time
working on Robert Dick. As he said in his preface to Moore, 'I was far
advanced with another book ... which I was unwilling to postpone.' Nevertheless, he was diligent in showing chapters to Mrs Moore as they were
written, and although he was able to tell Janet that 'she says she is delighted',
he also commented that 'The book has been a great burden, involving a
great amount of labour. Whether it will be generally liked I cannot tell.'[6]
But at last, almost a year after Mrs Moore's first approach, he was able to
place in her hands a 150,000-word memorial of her late husband.

She was delighted, and so were her nominated publishers (not John
Murray, but the *Self-Help* rejectors, George Routledge). To Smiles's

10 Dunbeath, on the east coast of Caithness (one of Samuel Smiles's drawings from *Robert Dick, Geologist and Botanist*): 'The landscapes will be pretty fair...'
(*Robert Dick, Baker of Thurso*, John Murray, 1878, p.193, courtesy The London Library)

surprise the book was a considerable success. *George Moore, Merchant and Philanthropist*, gave a boost to Smiles's bank account, and to his determination never again to take on anything he had not chosen himself. When the 'Smiles for Livingstone' campaign reappeared that summer his refusal to Murray came with triple underlining.

> Thank you for your proposal as to the life of Dr Livingstone. But I cannot undertake to write it. First I have no time. I want a holiday without a book on my back. Second, because I have rather a dislike (if you will excuse me) to African travel ... Third, because I am getting old, and do not intend to write any more books unless I am involved with the subject.[7]

Robert Dick did involve him. While Moore was still at press Smiles was writing to Janet, full of enthusiasm for the next book, and especially for his new role as artist. 'I am busily engaged drawing the illustrations for Robert Dick. Though I have no George Reid this time,

11 The Dick monument (drawn by
Samuel Smiles, engraved by R Leitch,
from *Robert Dick, Geologist and Botanist*):
'It will end the book [it didn't]. I have
now done the last drawing.'
(*Robert Dick, Baker of Thurso*, John Murray, 1878,
p.416, courtesy The London Library)

the landscapes will be pretty fair. They will be for the most part the rocky coast of Caithness.' By September he was able to write to Jack, with a mix of excitement and trepidation.

I have finished the book ... and hope you will think well of the finish ... I have now done the last drawing – Dick Monument. It will end the book. Harper Bros [in New York] have accepted my offer of £200 for the electroplates. This will diminish the cost of the illustrations which will amount, I think, to £400. 5000 are to be printed – an awful lot I think, and then I don't think the book will be found nearly as interesting as the Scotch Naturalist. I shall indeed be pleased if it pays its expenses.[8]

Smiles was uncharacteristically tense in the lead up to the trade sale of *Robert Dick, Baker of Thurso, Geologist and Botanist*. The evening before the sale, Cooke asked him to come in to the office to talk about the price of the book. He revealed that at the planned price of 10/6, on a sale of 5,000, it would not cover its expenses. They discussed a price of fifteen shillings but, as he told Jack, later that night Cooke

called on Mr Miles, of Simkin Marshall [wholesale booksellers], and said he was going to offer at 12/6. Miles said it was worth the money. 'I'll take 2000!' That fixed the price. I went to Murray's dinner at the Albion and saw the proceedings. 'Dick' was offered first. Simkin took 2000, Mudie (next to whom I sat at dinner) took 1250, Hamilton Adams 500, and so on, until the subscription rose to 6000 Thus the whole of the first edition is sold, and we go to press at once for a further 5000. I think that a great success. The booksellers must have great faith in me![9]

Nevertheless, just as Dick and Edwards had died penniless, and Moore enormously wealthy, so the life of Robert Dick, baker, eventually sold less well than the life of George Moore, millionaire. Smiles was surprised and disappointed. He saw something romantic about hidden heroes like Edward and Dick, who renounced the world to follow their passions. But 'the multitude evidently like successful men. Perhaps if I had written about millionaires, I might have been more successful myself ... The best course is to write full-hearted, and make the most you can of your subject.'[10]

He had managed to show how Edward and Dick had finally found some recognition in places where quality of mind took precedence over size of bank balance. That year he had also been gratified to find himself honoured in the way which he valued most. Early in the previous year George Reid had mentioned to him that 'I wish Edinburgh University would make you an LLD.' Within a few months Reid was writing again, confirming that 'I have put in a word for your LLD with Professor McKay.' The award came a year later, just as Smiles was finishing *Moore*, in April 1878.

By the end of that year he had completed two books, escaped from the biographical traffic jam, and settled into a comfortable home. With a handsome income assured by decades of 'turning his leisure moments to some account', and honoured by his home university for a lifetime's contribution to literature, the sixty-six-year-old author could surely stop climbing, and for his remaining years sit back to enjoy the view. For a time it seemed so. Even his railway career was becoming part of history. In the new year Sir James Byng, his old chairman at the South Eastern wrote to him: 'I may think my railway career is over. The prosperity of the South Eastern of late years was entirely owing to you and a few others originating the Charing Cross Railway and me being chairman at the time.'[11] It all seemed a long time ago.

A few weeks later Smiles set off with Sarah Anne, making good use of the South Eastern's free pass, to travel to Italy, not for research, but for the warmth of the climate, and of the applause he suspected might be waiting. He had always been a convinced northerner, an admirer of people hardened by cold winds, bred in cultures of tough protestant self-reliance – sense more apparent than sensibility. Yet the exuberant Italians loved him, and he them. He spent three months among them that year, delighted by the unfamiliar openness of their admiration. He and Sarah Anne stayed at the Hotel Quirinale in Rome. One of their first hosts was the sculptor, Antonio Rossetti, who specialised in lush figurative statuary. This remarkable Smiles fan had produced the ultimate tribute – he had 'executed a very fine statue of "Self-Help" – a girl plaiting her hair, and with the book upon her knee, reading it while she does her dressing, & thus making the most of her time'.[12] There it was, time as capital, even in Rome – though of course in white marble. Professor Rossetti, as Smiles styled him, also insisted on making a bust of the author.

England's governing élite paid little attention to Smiles. The Queen had been gracious in the matter of Edward's pension, as protocol required. Gladstone had accepted copies of the books and was said to be an admirer. He even praised the author and his ideas in public, when the occasion was right. Smiles was worldly enough to accept the flattery for what it was worth. 'I see Gladstone has been puffing me a bit in his speech at Buckley on Monday,'[13] he wrote to John Murray. 'Will you please send him a copy of "Dick". He is as good as a walking advertisement.' Some years later Smiles declined an invitation from Gladstone's cousin, Anne Bennett, to write a biography of his father, Sir John Gladstone.[14]

In Italy Smiles found himself lionised. Both the ex-Prime Minister, General Menabrea, and the current leader, Benedetto Cairoli, enter-tained him while he was there. Cairoli's wife had translated *Character* into Italian. 'The Signora', Smiles recorded,

> speaks English very well and was able to interpret my conversation. She was pleased to say that I was the only living writer who devoted his time to elevating the people by pressing upon their consideration moral and social subjects and that my books have been about the best read and most valued in Italy.[15]

Signora Cairoli promised to present copies of Smiles's latest books to the Italian Queen.

Queen Margherita subsequently made it known that she was 'desirous of an interview with me, being an admirer of my works'. Smiles was obviously entranced by the young Queen. 'Queen Margherita is charming not only as a Queen but as a woman ... I found her simple, gracious, dignified and yet thoroughly simpatica.' With great tact Her Majesty expressed the view that she found German novels flat, French naughty, and English novels, of all others, her favourites. Happily neither George Eliot nor Disraeli seem to have been mentioned. Smiles would have been pleased by the Queen's good opinion of Scott and Hardy. After an hour he left the palace, 'delighted with my interview, not less pleased with the Queen's high-bred tact and graciousness of manner, than with her goodness, sweetness, and intelligent conversation'.[16] As a young newspaper editor Smiles had been scathing about royalty and everything it stood for. Queen Margherita may have helped to change his mind. His own Queen never gave him the opportunity, though he came to admire her as a woman.

12 Queen Margherita of Italy: 'She looks as pretty as ever. She is the most popular person in Rome.'
(www.gogmsite.net)

He was received by Garibaldi in Rome. A newspaper reporter offered a delightful picture of the meeting. 'I think I told you that Samuel Smiles was here', he wrote.

> The papers are just with him as they were with Garibaldi during the first days of his visit. He is here with his wife and is profiting by his visit, taking notes for his new work, which is to be called *Duty* ... he is a fine-looking old man, with silvery whiskers encircling a kind and genial face ... Garibaldi, as [one] witness of the interview told me, was quite expansive

and seemed quite electrified when he heard Smiles's name ... Even those who did not understand English, caught the impression ... that an extra-ordinary conversation was being carried on by these two men. Smiles will never forget Garibaldi.[17]

The Smiles's moved on from Rome to Florence, and then to Bologna. Everywhere Samuel Smiles went he was greeted with the same enthusiasm and respect. Before he left Italy, a presentation was made, of a fine album bound in beautiful Florentine decoration. It carried the inscription 'Al Dottore Samuele Smiles – Alcuni tra I molti che in Italia sentono la gratitudine pel bene fatto dai suoi libri. Firenze, 28 Aprile 1879' ['To Dr Samuel Smiles – with gratitude from some of the many who have benefitted from your books'], and was signed by twenty-one leading Italian scientists and writers. It is hardly surprising that Smiles, after twelve weeks' immersion in such rapturous attention, may have felt under-appreciated at home. Nevertheless, in view of Edinburgh's generosity, his later comment that 'It seemed as if I must cross the Alps and come a long way from home, to have my small services to literature recognised',[18] sounds a little churlish.

After three months being treated more as writer emeritus than as someone in mid-career, there is a sense that 'the fine old man with silvery whiskers' was becoming more concerned with his legacy than with his future. On his return home he brought his name again to the notice of the Italian royal family, through General Menabria (by then ambassador in London), asking him to offer a copy of the *Life of George Stephenson* to King Umberto. 'It occurred to me that His Majesty, who is renowned for his patronage of the arts of industry, might desire to know something of the inventor.'[19] Smiles also approached the Secretary of the Académie Française, submitting several of his books for consideration for a Montyon Prize. 'These books,' he wrote, 'have been translated into most European languages, and some of them have been instrumental in doing much good. I shall feel it an honour to be recognized by the French Academy.'[20] His nomination was not successful (the Prize was endowed by Baron de Montyon as an award for, among other things, 'the book which during the year rendered the greatest service to humanity').

In the autumn of 1879 he left London with Sarah Anne for another tour of his beloved northern coasts of Scotland, ending, again with a hint of retrospection, at Haddington. He told George Reid that he might settle there. The artist wrote back strongly discouraging the idea. 'I think you'll find it very dull living at Haddington.'[21] He returned to London, to the familiar world of work, of publishing and bookselling.

Smiles equated work with happiness. Besides, he was a writer. The itch that he had felt when, as a twenty-year-old, he sent 'pieces of intelligence' to the *Edinburgh Chronicle*, had not gone away. So when John Murray approached him with a writing project that Smiles must have known would be demanding, he allowed himself to be drawn in. He had, after all, planted the idea himself. 'It is some months since I heard the expression drop from your lips,' Murray wrote to him.

> You said you would like to write the life of my Father. If I am not mistaken in this, and you really continue of the same mind, I should be very glad indeed to confer with you at your convenience. My Father, I venture to think, deserves a Biographer. I know not where we would find so good and appreciative a one as you.[22]

Smiles should have been on his guard, against the man who 'deserves a Biographer'. And doubly so when it became apparent that something much more than a straightforward 'life' would be involved. 'The materials are copious and interesting', Murray warned,

> the subject is a wide one, involving the literary history of this country for some forty years [in fact more than sixty], and the labour of selecting and arranging the material will be great ... those who knew him are reduced to very few and my own scanty recollections may quickly pass away, unless something be done soon to record them. Will you do me the honour to consider this?

Smiles could not resist the appeal. It came, after all, from the man who had made his writing career possible.

But first there was another 'little book' to be drawn up from the *Self-Help* well. Smiles probably had it in mind during his fallow period earlier in the year. The Italian journalist who had reported the Garibaldi meeting certainly knew about 'his next work, to be called "Duty"'. Before the year ended, and he was able to settle into the necessary routine to produce the book, there came the final Italian accolade. At the beginning

of January the King of Italy conferred on Samuel Smiles the rank of
Chevalier of the Order of Saints Maurice and Lazarus – 'as a token of His
Majesty's appreciation of my very valuable works.'[23]

For the spring of 1880 the Smiles family took a furnished house at St
Andrews in Scotland , with a view over the golf links and within easy reach
of the beach. These were joyful months. Sarah Anne was happy. The big
holiday house had space to entertain family visitors, and she found her
Scottish neighbours more amenable than the housewives of St Leonard's.
Smiles could make progress on *Duty*, and find time to relax with their
friends. The 'writing up' of the book went well, and it was ready in good
time for the printer to produce copies for the Murray trade dinner in
November. Smiles was, however, strangely dissatisfied with *Duty*. He may
have felt that he rushed it. The big Murray life was a lurking shadow, and
he had also agreed with his friend James Nasmyth, already featured in
Industrial Biography, to help him with his autobiography. When he wrote
to Jack Hartree about the index for *Duty* he insisted that 'This is the <u>last</u>
book in the series, though I have another written out for ten years which
I intended to call "Characteristics of Biography". I am sorry that "Duty"
is not better done.'[24]

The Smiles name, however, was enough to keep the booksellers satisfied.
'I write to say that 15,000 of "Duty" were sold last night by Murray,' he wrote
two weeks later. 'All the other books as usual. The publishers evidently
<u>believe</u> in me. Whether the customers do or not remains to be seen.'[25]

The customers were happy, though after the previous books the shelf
of potted sermons presented in *Duty* seems crushingly familiar. In this
view, *Duty* is little more than a commercial exercise in re-packaging old
material under a new title. But at another level the book is interesting as
a development of Smiles's reflections on the theme of happiness. *Self-
Help* had set the scene by proposing the possibility of each individual
deciding his own fate by his own hard work and perseverance. *Character*
carried the idea forward by considering the capacity of work to create
happiness, in contrast to the pain of idleness. *Thrift* embraced the joys
of prudence and self-control.

Compared with those practical manuals, *Duty* is the most spiritual
of Smiles's books. In it he digs deeper, in search of the impulse that
motivates these other behaviours, and he finds it in 'conscience' – he calls

it 'the innate monitor'. Duty then becomes more than an opportunistic one-word book title to match three others. Duty is conscience in action.

> It is conscience alone which sets a man on his feet, frees him from the dominions of his own passions and propensities. It places him in relation to the best interests of his kind. The finest source of enjoyment is found in the paths of duty alone ... At its fullest growth, conscience bids men do whatever makes them happy in the highest sense, and forbear whatever makes them unhappy.[26]

With its reflections on the nature of good and evil – on the nature of life itself – *Duty* suggests a man looking towards an end. The final chapter of the book is entitled simply 'The Last', and its closing paragraph underlines the notion – 'To everything under the sun there is a last. The last line of a book, the last sermon, the last speech, the last act of life, the last words at death.'[27] If, as he wrote them, Smiles thought that these rather morbid truisms were relevant to himself at the time, he soon changed his mood. Before the Albion dinner at which *Duty* enjoyed its successful launch, he had already turned to the next book – in fact, to the next two books.

21

In the Company of Homer

BEFORE the publication of *Duty* Smiles had written to Jack Hartree (22 October 1880): 'I saw Nasmyth a few evenings ago. He read me some of his autobiography – the matter is first-rate. I will write it out again. But it will be as good as Edward.'[1] The comparison was a strange one for Smiles to make, for he had much more in common with James Nasmyth than with the prickly, demanding naturalist. The *Life of a Scotch Naturalist* had, however, sold well; at this stage Smiles was optimistic about the prospects for Nasmyth. The Murray memoir was still in hand, but Smiles was excited by the idea of working with the old engineer. They had met almost twenty years earlier, when Smiles was working on *Industrial Biography*, and wanted to include Nasmyth and his steam hammer – 'the Vulcan of the nineteenth century' he had called him.[2] Nasmyth's mighty hammer was just the sort of power-harnessing creation to fascinate Smiles –

> one of those gigantic engineering works which are among the marvels of the age we live in. It possesses so much precision and delicacy that it will chip the end off an egg resting in a glass on the anvil without breaking it, while it delivers a blow of ten tons with such a force as to be felt shaking the parish.

Smiles was also drawn to the man. Nasmyth came from a family of artists. His father, Alexander Nasmyth, was one of Scotland's most admired landscape painters. His eldest brother Patrick was a professional painter who had exhibited at the Royal Academy in London, and both his sisters were artists. Smiles could see in Nasmyth's engineering drawings clear evidence of an exceptionally talented draughtsman at work. All the illustrations for the book would be by Alexander Nasmyth or by the engineer himself. The appeal to the artist in Smiles was immediate. This, and a sense of shared values, overcame any doubts he may have had about repeating the joint authorship experiment of *Boy's Voyage*. The book would be *The Autobiography of James Nasmyth*, Edited by Samuel Smiles.

Besides, any friction with his other writing partner had been long forgotten. Sam junior remained the adored younger son who, in his father's eyes could do no wrong. As Smiles grew older his adult children, and their spouses, became an increasing source of pleasure and comfort to him. He criticised them less often and boasted about them more openly. And, joy of joys, young Sam and his family were about to leave Ireland and return to set up home near London again – in fact in original Smiles territory, in Granville Park, Blackheath. 'My son and his belongings are about to leave Belfast and come to London to settle', he wrote to a friend. 'He has done wonderfully well since he began business, and is likely to be rewarded according to his desserts. My other son has laid the foundations of a large and prosperous business and I trust he also will be rewarded.'[3]

His other son, Willie's, 'large and prosperous business' was well on its way to becoming, not just one of Belfast's, but one of Britain's largest industrial enterprises. Ten years earlier Willie had left his employers to set up a wholesale business in partnership with William Lowson, a more experienced Belfast businessman. A year later they bought a half-share in a small rope-making concern but soon quarrelled. Lowson went on his way and twenty-six-year-old William Smiles set about expanding the business, aware that, on the riverside nearby, Gustav Wolff and his partners were creating a vast shipbuilding industry, and an insatiable appetite for ropes. The history of the Belfast Ropeworks is well documented. By the end of the nineteenth century it had become the largest rope-making business in the world. Under Willie's leadership its workforce grew from 25 to over 3,000, and its works from a shed to a manufacturing plant spread over forty acres. Perhaps Smiles felt that Willie's astonishing achievement was so self-evident as to need no more

13 William Holmes Smiles – Willie –
on his way to rivalling any
success story in *Self-Help*.
(With kind permission, the Deputy Keeper
of Records, Public Record Office of
Northern Ireland (D3437/B/3B))

than faint praise from him. Or perhaps somewhere a tinge of jealousy lurked, that the son who had so often ignored his (unsolicited) advice, and dismissed his father's most famous book as a 'collection of scraps', was on his way to rivalling any success story in *Self-Help*. At any rate, Smiles senior was keen, even at this stage, to claim some credit. 'It is pleasant to think, in our declining years, that our children will not be worse off from our example and that they proceed humbly in the way of Self-Help.'[4]

The heat had certainly not gone out of *Self-Help*. 'The sale of Murrays was indeed very good,' he wrote with delight to Janet in November 1881.[5] 'It indeed amazes me how books sell. Self-Help for instance, published twenty-two years ago, sells better now than it did from ten to fifteen years since.'

In the meantime Nasmyth, two years older than Smiles, continued working at his home in Kent, his manuscript accumulating while his 'editor' in London groused gently about old age. 'Nasmyth is writing his autobiography, which I am to edit', he wrote to Janet. 'After that I shall take things very quietly. I shall have completed my 68th year on the 23rd of December next ... after that a man has not much work left in him.'[6] Smiles was determined, of course, that there should be a great deal of work left in him, but he had reached that time in life when age can be used to manage expectations. He was inclined to flourish his years, like an old soldier proud of his wounds.

The pattern of work imposed by both the Nasmyth and the Murray books, though pitted with frustrations, turned out to suit the life-style Smiles now adopted. From this time he spent almost as much of each year away from home as he did at Pembroke Gardens. His diary must have been the sort any prosperous pensioner would dream of – a few weeks in Switzerland in the spring, summer in Scotland or on the south coast, a quick trip to Paris, a month in Italy ... all interspersed with times at home in London, dining with friends, entertaining children and grandchildren, visiting the opera or art gallery. The discipline of previous books, of regular hours devoted each day to writing, no longer applied, nor could it, for now Smiles was in a co-operative. Without the next instalment of raw material from James Nasmyth, or the answers to his questions, he could not proceed with the autobiography Without the next consignment of papers from one of the Murrays he could not advance the plan for the Murray memoir. So he switched between the two, working on whatever came to hand, and travelling while he worked.

Of course wherever Smiles went the notebooks went too, and the latest batch of papers from one or other of his collaborators. If these trips were not working holidays, they were not holidays free from work. The Nasmyth autobiography turned out to be more troublesome than Smiles had anticipated. The subject himself did all that he had promised, providing a comprehensive story and all the back-up detail Smiles needed. The papers continued to arrive, Nasmyth's writing often testing Smiles's eyesight – 'A good deal of it was written out in almost micro-scopic handwriting. If anyone were to see the original book they would recognise the labour I had in bringing the recollections and the narrative into shape.'[7] His subject's growing timidity created the main frustration. After Smiles had put in more than a year's work, and brought the manuscript to the point when it might have been prepared for the printers, Nasmyth had second thoughts about publication. Early in 1882 Smiles wrote to Janet in a tone of resigned disappointment. 'I may tell you that Nasmyth is not to come out this year. The old man is getting nervous about the book appearing in his lifetime. So I have agreed to lock it up in a box.'[8] But he could not bring himself to criticise the man he so much admired. 'Nasmyth has behaved quite handsomely in the matter.'

Murray had stalled at much the same time. At Albemarle Street the stacked shelves and file-boxes of letters, documents, and manuscripts –

covering most of the century, hundreds of authors, and thousands of books – had never been professionally archived. The younger John Murray ('John Murray IV') and his brother Hallam, were finding it increasingly difficult to keep up with Smiles's needs. Unconcerned for the time being, his mind stayed busy on other schemes. Donald Macleod, editor of *Good Words*, had asked him to write a series of articles on 'Bolton Abbey in the Olden Times' (the Olden Times were still a great attraction for Victorian sightseers). 'But I have said no. I have a considerable quantity of MS on the subject, written some 40 years ago and if I can get George Reid to illustrate the book, I think I will publish it some day.'[9] He had even joked about a book on his son's friend and Belfast shipping magnate Gustav Wolff. 'Wolff wants me to write his life (with his amours!) but the latter would be a sorry subject. I will tell him to go to Ouida! He might make her happy.'[10]

Gustav Wolff was part of a group – which included Willie Smiles – of highly successful Belfast businessmen leading the great industrial development of Belfast at the time. Smiles later described Belfast as 'one of the most enterprising towns in the British Islands'.[11] Ireland then was, of course, part of the United Kingdom, with no distinction made between northern Ireland and the rest of the country. Willie, and Smiles's grandchildren, were becoming Irish. But Irish in a particular sense, for around Belfast a second, invisible, pale was being erected. The surging economic success of the region, led mainly by protestant incomers, was drawing Ireland's north-eastern counties, emotionally, culturally, and politically, further and further away from the rest of the island.

In July that year, 1882, Smiles left the mounting pile of Murray documents at home to have a holiday in Ireland – 'off to "the land of the blest", but I certainly wish the Erinites would not rip up the cattle and cut off their tails'.[12] This tone of black humour revealed his equivocal affection for the Irish. He had written with great sympathy for the Irish people in his 1844 book, blaming most of their problems on English mismanagement. What he saw during this holiday nearly forty years later, when he toured from the west coast to Belfast, prompted inevitable heart-searching. Confronted by the contrast between industrial and economic triumph in the north-east (in which his own son was playing a significant role), and an apparent slide into stagnation in the rest of the country, his instinct was to attribute Belfast's prosperity to the innate qualities of its people – 'we are now among a new race' he wrote as he travelled towards Belfast – 'where industry, self-reliance, and energy are regarded as among the essential elements of manhood'. By corollary, according to this reading, the plight of the rest of Ireland must be due to the absence of those same characteristics. A few years later, in *Men of Invention and Industry*, he attempted a fuller examination of this argument.

In the meantime James Nasmyth had had a change of heart. The book could press ahead. It accompanied Smiles to Scotland, where Sarah Anne's rheumatic gout caused them both to spend some time in a hydropathic spa (Smiles much entertained by the school-like discipline – 'all the 'musts', and fines for being late – late at breakfast! late at dinner! late at prayers!')[13] But Edinburgh, where they also spent a few days at the Royal Hotel, sent him into raptures. 'This city is looking as beautiful as ever. I have really seen nothing like it in all my travels.' On the way home they rested at the Drummond Arms in Crieff before heading back to London. In the calm of Pembroke Gardens the manuscript for Nasmyth's autobiography was finally concluded. Though its joint authors were not able to finalise the proofs in time for publication ahead of Murray's November sale that year, in the first week of the new year, 1883, Smiles could write, with his usual hint of pre-launch nerves, to Janet: 'I have printed 5000. Rather bold you will say, but I think my name will carry the book a certain way.'[14]

In fact *James Nasmyth Engineer – an Autobiography* was one of Smiles's less popular books. Reviewers were again polite, but perhaps by the late nineteenth century readers had lost interest in steam hammers. Smiles was disappointed, not for financial reasons, but because he valued the book, and the man, and had expected the public to share his enthusiasm (which was not for money). He had sent Janet a cheque for £500 a few days earlier, remarking that 'It is not necessary for me to have any more money. I have more than is needful ...' Now wearing the grand mantle of seventy years, Smiles increasingly showed his conservative side. He did not approve of women's rights. Janet was asked to hand the money over to Jack, 'for the common good. I do not like the new law [the 1882 Married Women's Property Act] which was smuggled through Parliament by

Jacob Bright. It may be useful for husbands who are cruel and selfish, but not where the married people are happy, as you are.'[15] Did Smiles really not consider that the existence of 'husbands who are cruel and selfish' might be precisely the reason for the Act?

With *Nasmyth* in print, Smiles was happy now to feel in control of his own work schedule. When Leslie Stephen asked him to contribute to the new 'British Biographical Dictionary' (to become, in 1885, the *Dictionary of National Biography*), he declined, saying he was too busy.[16] His plan at the time was to proceed sedately with the Murray book. Occasional interruptions in the supply of information at this stage did not alarm him. There was plenty of time. His aim was to complete it over the next three years, for publication in November 1886. That, at any rate, was what he believed he had agreed with John Murray.[17] Things turned out rather differently.

In the meantime, though now a fully-fledged septuagenarian, he always had another book to work on. This time it was to be a collection of biographical essays on 'Men of Industry', presented, for obvious marketing reasons, as a continuation of *Lives of the Engineers*, *Industrial Biography*, and *Self-Help*. Smiles's real interest, however, was in creating a vehicle for an account of the shipbuilding industry, prompted by his connections with Belfast. 'My next book may be about ships,'[18] he remarked to Janet as early as March 1883, though the book did not come out until November the following year. While he was working on it he had another health scare, with frightening echoes of this problems in 1871. One morning in March, while hanging a picture at Pembroke Gardens, his mouth suddenly filled with blood. 'What? Was this the foreshadowing of the end?'[19] Apparently not, for he was soon passing it off light-heartedly in a letter to Janet. 'Dr Parr stopped my port and whisky. Is life tolerable on these terms?'[20] A month later he was in Belfast, meeting Willie's shipping friends, and in particular spending time with E J Harland, whose personal contribution was to form the final section of the new book.

Men of Industry and Invention, for eleven of its twelve chapters, is very much what its preface promises – more of the same industrial biography, this time with an emphasis on shipbuilding, and particularly Belfast shipbuilding. But Ireland puzzled and worried Smiles. His visits there, and the cruel contrasts he saw, provoked a mix of admiration and frustration. In this book he felt compelled to offer his own analysis of the problem. He did not discuss the situation in political or religious, but in economic terms (though the shadow of agrarian violence and the role of the Catholic Church lies across much of his commentary. Violence frightens away investment, he pointed out, and Church expenditure on its own buildings is not economically productive.)

The chapter in which he discusses the condition of Ireland is headed 'Industry in Ireland'. This might more pertinently have been 'Why Isn't There More Industry in Ireland?' His answer was the one he had used so often before, at different times, for different situations, using 'industry' in both its senses. Industry, which would provide employment and prosperity for the people, and lead to progress for the whole of society, depended on the individual industry (industriousness) of the people themselves. 'A country may be levelled down by idleness and ignorance; it can only be levelled up by industry and intelligence.' He cited the inertia of the Irish fishing industry as an example, suggesting that by indolence the Irish had failed to harvest the riches round their coasts, instead allowing the Scots to sail across and take away their treasure. 'The people round about, many of whom were short of food, were expecting providence to supply their wants. Providence, however, always likes to be helped.' This generalised call for entrepreneurial energy, and silence about the historical causes of so much of the country's decay, would hardly have struck many cords with an evicted tenant in the west of Ireland; and the vision of Belfast shipping magnates and rope-making millionaires, new arrivals from across the sea, as their country's saviours would have been equally jarring. The idea of Ireland 'levelled down by ignorance and idleness' was certainly a popular prejudice in England at the time, but Smiles was not anti-Irish. If he had been, he would not have been so convinced that Ireland could find its own salvation. In the introduction to this part of the book he quoted the great Irish patriot, Daniel O'Connell: 'Ireland may become a nation once again, if we all sacrifice our parricidal passions, prejudices and resentments on the altar of our country. Then shall our manufactures flourish, and Ireland be free.' Smiles offered the same dream, pointing out that

to found industries that give employment to large numbers of persons ...
is a most honourable and important source of influence, and was thus
worthy of every encouragement ... God endowed men [in Ireland] as
elsewhere, with reason, will and physical power; and it is by patient
industry only that they can open up the pathway to the enduring prosperity of the country.[21]

Compared with Smiles's earlier works, *Men of Industry and Invention*
stirred scant interest in the English press. Even the Irish newspapers paid
little attention, though his other books were proudly shelved in the country's new Free Libraries.[22] The *Saturday Review* produced what Smiles
described as 'a shabby notice'.[23] But then, as he remarked, 'they gave the
"Huguenots" an even worse review', and that had sold satisfactorily.
In fact *Men of Industry and Invention* did well. 'I am of course exceedingly
pleased at the 10,000 being largely exhausted,' he told Robert Cooke.
'I did not expect this, as many of the chapters were old articles and old
accumulations.'[24]

Now it was time to turn with full commitment to the book which had
been a recurring presence for the last four years – the Murray memoir
first mooted in 1879. With cooperation from the younger Murray partners,
John IV and Hallam, he could surely meet the target date of 1886. Through
1885 and most of 1886 things moved forward without undue strain.
The work was of course demanding, and the co-operative set-up delicate.
In effect, Smiles's clients, and publishers, were also his research assis-
tants. He depended on John and Hallam Murray, both less than half his
age, for finding, selecting, and ordering the papers he needed, and, as he
read through the material, for answering his questions and filling the
gaps.

He was able to write to their father, John Murray III, in July 1885,
thanking him for the accounts for the previous twelve months, 'which
are perfectly satisfactory. Everything I have known of you, during the
quarter of a century that we have had business transactions, has been
most kind and honourable and I shall never forget it.' The following
month he left with Sarah Anne for a holiday in Germany and Switzerland. Naturally his work went too, and caused him some alarm. From
Homburg, near Frankfurt, he wrote to Murray:

14 Samuel Smiles, sketch of Bass Rock: 'I am going to North Berwick
next week, and for a time will cease my fuming.'
(With kind permission, the Deputy Keeper of Records, Public Record Office
of Northern Ireland (D3437/A/2/8))

We arrived here on Saturday last but without our luggage. The two
baggages seem to have gone wandering along the line for about a week ...
One was found and arrived on Thursday; the other only this morning
... One of the trunks contained the early chapters, with many notes,
connected with the life of John Murray – had they been lost I doubt if
I could have raised the courage to begin again. I think Carlyle's rewriting
of the first volume of the French Revolution ... was a truly heroic work.
But Carlyle was a comparatively young man at that time [he was about
forty] and youth is always a great help. Now I have got the MS safe and
will keep my eye on it until I return. Of course the work proves much more
formidable than I ever expected it to be.[25]

Back at home, as Smiles struggled to build a narrative from the
disordered, and sometimes interrupted, stream of papers arriving at his
door, he fired off question after question to his young collaborators in
Albemarle Street.

On what day were Byron's memoirs burned? Moore says it was on 27th
May 1824, but in another account I find the 17th of May mentioned. – I find
that Wordsworth offered his collected poems in December 1826. Were
these published by Mr Murray? If not, why not? – Did Mr Murray publish
Thackeray's history of the Earl of Chatham? – What was the reason for
the estrangement between Murray and Byron from 23rd October 1822 to
25th February 1824? ...[26]

The questions kept coming, and a hint of frustration started to show,
a mixture of impatience and guilt. '... you will excuse my asking all these
questions. You are my principal helper, and you know I cannot make
bricks without straw ... I am going to North Berwick next week, and for
a time will "cease my fuming".' North Berwick, on the coast barely ten
miles from Haddington, had always been one of Smiles's favourite
haunts. In his youth he had made pencil and watercolour sketches of the
Bass Rock, a great knuckle of chalk rising from the sea beyond North
Berwick harbour.[27] He painted it again in April 1885, a scene of grey-blue
calm, the perfect antidote to stress. Although he made many visits abroad
during these years, to quiet his fuming he seemed to find his best answer
in the familiar Scottish seascape.

After the fusillade of letters in the first half of 1886 some hiatus
occurred in the Murray project. Smiles revealed as much in later correspondence, when he suggested that the launch of the new *Murray Magazine* was diverting effort in Albemarle Street from his book.

If Smiles was in a very slight sulk with the Murray brothers at the end
of 1886 he revived his spirits in the new year. In December he had entered
his seventy-fifth year, in a mild glow of sentimentality. 'About my birthday', he wrote to Janet '... Aged and I married 43 years ago and she still
buys every year a quantity of bridal cake to remind her of it.'[28] After
enjoying the Royal Academy Exhibition in London in January, he set off
with Sarah Anne for the country where he knew he was loved without
reservation. In February he wrote from the Hotel Quirinale in Rome to
John Murray, describing the Carnival, the strings of carriages along the
Via Nazionale, and his friend the Queen,

going here and there, backwards and forwards. She looks as pretty as ever.
She is the most popular person in Rome. I think of staying here for another

fortnight ... I don't know that you have praised the Quirinale enough [in the Murray Guide]. It is the best, cleanest, healthiest hotel in Rome.[29]

A few weeks later he was reporting with glee to Robert Cooke that 'Many people come to look me up. Indeed I seem to be even better known in Italy than in England. "Self-Help" continues to have a very large sale.' But charmed as he was, Smiles was becoming weary of Rome's distractions, and happy to take refuge in his writing. 'I have written a chapter of my next book,' he told Janet, 'and will go on with the next tomorrow. It is quite a pleasure to me to do this, as sight-seeing has become rather tiresome.'[30]

He had put the frustration of the Murray book behind him and was eager to talk about the 'other work'. 'I have finished, while here, another volume of the Self-Help series. I wrote it some fifteen years ago, and Harper made me an offer for it. I will show you his letter when I return. I have nearly copied it out, and finished it with some new illustrations.' Apparently inexhaustible, the elderly Smiles couple continued their journey around Italy, Sarah Anne rhapsodising about the scenery as they travelled. 'We had a very interesting though long journey, from 10.30 to 3.30. There were so many picturesque old towns to travel through ... the place is wonderful for situation – a blend of plains and mountains, finishing in snow ranges, a very beautiful view'[31] – though sometimes Smiles felt the 'very trying climate ... latterly your father could not walk much and admitted it hot today'. They spent several demanding weeks, seeing sights, and being seen, in the Hotel Bonificia in Perugia (Smiles's letters to Janet studded with gems of English and Italian society in the hotel – Lady Mary Wortley Montagu, Contezza Maria Salvadigo, M. and Madame Villari ...).

From Perugia they moved to Florence and finally, at the beginning of May, back to London where Smiles, at his desk in Pembroke Gardens, could settle again to the task of bringing a book to publication. Murray's, he assumed, would share his enthusiasm. 'I enclose a listing of the proposed chapters in the forthcoming book', he told Cooke.

> I wrote the greater part of it more than eighteen years ago, with many other chapters, but I have rewritten and revised those and now propose to publish ... The title I fixed upon many years ago was "Characteristics of

Biography", but I have not been satisfied with this title. If you can help me to another and better I shall be very glad ... Mr Murray with his large experience may be able to think of something better.[32]

Most of Smiles's recent dealings with the House of Murray had been with Cooke or, more problematically, with John IV and Hallam, both still in their thirties. At times the difference in generational perspective had shown. But on the evening of 18 June he was able to sit at the Lord Mayor's Mansion House Banquet in the company of seventy-nine-year-old John Murray III, with whom he had shared most of his writing life. His loyalty to his publishers could never be less than total. Nor, after all his youthful criticism of the monarchy, could his loyalty to the queen. She and her late husband had, after all, overseen the age of technical and industrial progress of which Smiles had been such a passionate advocate. The queen had presented Prince Louis of Hesse with a copy of *Lives of the Engineers*. Smiles, from his place in Westminster Abbey at the Memorial Service two days later, was able to observe 'All honour to that thoroughly good, humane, and noble woman, the best of wives and the best of mothers ... the best and wisest Queen that has ever sat upon the throne.'[33] Like a character from *Self-Help*, Victoria was someone to be admired, not for her majesty, but for her humanity; not for what she was, but for who she was.

Through that Jubilee summer Smiles worked happily on the new book. For diversion he was able, for a moment, to feel again the warmth of praise from across the world, this time from Argentina. There a colourful and gifted soldier of fortune, Edelmiro Mayer, had become involved in a movement (in an interesting parallel with the Japanese situation in 1871), to modernise Argentina's economy. Mayer, an ex-soldier who had been a close supporter of Lincoln's in the American Civil War, was now a literary figure in his native country. He had translated into Spanish the works of Edgar Allen Poe, and now, the improving works of Samuel Smiles. He sent the author presentation copies, described, in Smiles's words, as 'four octavo volumes beautifully bound in Russian morocco, gilt-edged, printed in fine type, and contained in a case, over which was inscribed, *El Evangelino Social*: The Social Gospel'. The 'Gospel' consisted of Spanish language versions of *Character*, *Duty*, *Self-Help*, and *Thrift*. In his *Autobiography* Smiles, by now surely permitted the gentle boastfulness of an old man, protests that 'It is not possible to cite the testimonies of the Buenos Aires press. They would bring a blush to the author's and even the translator's cheeks', and then does just that, including, from *Deutsche La Plata Zeitung*, the pronouncement that 'Alexander the Great slept with Homer, Demosthenes, and Thucydides; and every noble man of the times should have at hand a copy of the Social Gospel.'

So, happy in the company of Homer and his peers, Smiles visited the William Smiles's and the Hartrees in Belfast, wondered again at the marvels there of shipbuilding and rope-making, and spent restful weeks in Harrogate, passing through Leeds on the way, feeding his mood of nostalgia. 'We started for Harrogate', he wrote to Janet in August, 'through Leeds and its murky atmosphere. It was the place, however, where I was married, and you were born. Good luck to the place!' That year, 1887, came to be for Smiles an emotional high water mark, a point from which the tides that had carried forward so much of his life started to recede.

22

'Are we all to be dead...?'

WRITING TO Janet at the end of August 1887 Smiles appeared buoyant. 'My 'wee bookie' is nearly corrected' he reported.[1] But next day the wee bookie seems to have lost some of its shine. Never, since 1856, when John Murray III had so eagerly accepted the *Life of George Stephenson*, had a Smiles submission been met in Albemarle Street with anything less than enthusiasm. Now, for the first time, doubt appeared. 'Murray and the printer,' Smiles admitted to Janet, 'think my new book will be a failure – too much repetition, but my brains are going.'[2] The new book, now with the title *Life and Labour or Characteristics of Men of Industry, Culture and Genius,* was very much the formula as before.[3] Smiles at seventy-five was happy to revisit old ground, though in Albemarle Street the new generation were disappointed.

But the writer was still a battler for his work. When Murray's raised objections Smiles pointed out that

> the book in question was for the great part written 17 years ago, before I had my paralytic stroke. Towards the end of last year, having nothing else to do [perhaps a dig at delay in help with the Murray memoir?] I brought the manuscript from its rest and rewrote it. I referred to old notes, and perhaps I have repeated myself in certain cases. But I think you and the printer have made rather too much of it ... I will, however, go over the proofs, and make alterations where necessary. Many names are repeated, but these cannot, under the different chapters, very well be avoided.[4]

To a degree Smiles won the argument, but felt obliged, in print, to acknowledge the problem. 'It has been objected by some who have read the proofs', he wrote in the Preface to the published book, 'that certain names have been too much repeated and reintroduced ... But this has been found necessary in order to force home the lessons which they are intended to teach.' (No subtlety here about the author's didactic aim.)

Murray's reservations are understandable. The ghost of the cob-webbed manuscript of seventeen years earlier haunts the book. *Life and Labour* often reads like a tired work by a tired author. By now, however, Samuel Smiles had achieved the status of 'national treasure', and contemporary critics treated him accordingly. The *Pall Mall Gazette* struck the appropriate note:

> he enforces his old lesson, in the old way, by illustrations from the lives of men ... The good Doctor often ambles along a very turnpike of common-places, macadamized with stock stories familiar to us all since we learned to read ... It is a kind of general residual deposit of material not otherwise disposed of, and covers the most various of subjects.[5]

And yet, true to the indefinable edge that made Smiles different from the legion of moralisers around him, the book provides its nugget of sur-prise.

The Smiles gospel of work has a revised version. 'Overwork has unfortunately become one of the vices of our age, especially in the cities. In business, in learning, in law, in politics, in literature, the pace is sometimes tremendous, and the tear and wear on life becomes excessive.' But more dramatically, 'Idleness is not all idleness.'[6] At least not for the brain-worker – and here Smiles is most obviously speaking with the memory of his own experience.

> In the case of the brain-worker, it is his only remedy for sleepless nights, excited nerves, fluttering heart, irritability of temper and difficulty of digestion ... the gospel of leisure and recreation is but the correlation of the gospel of work, and the one is as necessary for the highest happiness and well-being as the other.[7]

There are, in this version, two sorts of idleness. 'There is a sort of idleness which may be called a waste of existence, and there is another which may be called an enjoyment of existence. Leisure is always valuable to those who can find a change of occupation in the spare time at their disposal.' In insisting on a change, and not an absence, of occupation, Smiles is ensuring no renunciation of his old faith.

Life and Labour is not as macadamized a road as the *Pall Mall Gazette* suggested. It reveals new views, and an ageing man adjusting his perspective. 'And for what is literary instruction desired?' Smiles asks himself.

> Glory and fame? A slight noise in a little corner of the earth ... Sensitive minds cannot help reflecting on the fleetingness of all human enjoyments. There is an intellectual sadness which overcasts the best and the brightest – the thought of man's utter insignificance in the immensity of the creation in which he lives.[8]

Smiles's career had been based on suggesting the very opposite of man's utter insignificance. 'What is the great idea that has seized the mind of this age?' he had asked in 1845.[9] 'It is the grand idea of *man* – of the importance of man as man; that every human being has a great mission to perform, – has noble faculties to cultivate, great rights to assert, a vast destiny to accomplish.'

Man's ability to shape his own life by his own efforts was at the heart of Smiles's appeal. And man's power to reshape the physical world for his own ends, to command nature and realise 'progress' – this was his proof of man's significance. Stephenson, Watt, Rennie, Telford and the others had not shrunk before the immensity of creation. Thirty years earlier, on the publication of his *Life of George Stephenson*, Smiles had proclaimed himself 'A success at last!' Now, in elegiac mood, he confronted his own triviality, and the prospect of his work as a slight noise in a little corner of the earth.

But the self-help impulse was too strong to be dismissed. However much he might reflect on the fleetingness of all human enjoyments, his first conviction was his strongest – 'that men must necessarily be the active agents of their own well-being and well-doing'. He had another book to complete.

The story of the House of Murray should have been topped out in 1886, but now, at the start of 1888, it was still no more than an untidy pile of building materials. Smiles longed to see it rise, as a tribute to the firm's founders, and as possibly his last major biography. Besides, he hated unfinished business; at seventy-five it might hint at waning powers. With *Life and Labour* behind him, and no other book simmering, he had to establish the Murrays' real level of interest in the project. In January he offered to send back all the papers he held. 'I am about to leave home for several months, for my wife's health as well as for my own', he wrote to John Murray III on 23 January. ' I think it better for safety's sake that I should return the remaining papers and volumes connected with the proposed life of the late John Murray.'[10] He made clear the amount of time he had already spent, and the hard work he had put in.

> I commenced this life, at your request, and though I have, in the mean-while prepared Nasmyth's autobiography, I have worked at your volumes for three or four years, examining innumerable letters and volumes, copying, annotating, and making a file draft of the subject. I intended to have finished this work (as stated to Mr John Murray jun), by the end of 1886; but when I asked for the remainder of the correspondence, extending for about eighteen years, I was told that you were so busy (probably arising from the preparation of the new magazine) that I could not at that time have any more ...'

It was an ultimatum, which almost backfired. Murray responded, some-what tartly, asserting that it had been Smiles's own wish to write his father's biography,

> repeated by yourself in Robert Cooke's office ... My son John has devoted no inconsiderable amount of time in selecting letters out of a very large correspondence and in docketing them with the object of saving you trouble ... and if he has relaxed at all of late it has been less because he has been extra busy than because we thought you were also relaxing, which from your advanced time of life and frequent indispositions did not surprise us ...[11]

Murray put it plainly: he thought Smiles 'would not regret to be relieved from the heavy task of the life of my father', and invited him to return the manuscript as far as it had gone.

It was not the answer Smiles expected, or wanted. He replied at once, denying that he had ever expressed the wish to drop the work. 'The only thing I said in 1886 was whether you <u>wished</u> me to drop the work ... Send

me the whole of the remaining correspondence and I am ready to proceed at once.'[12] Within days both sides were happy to revert to business
as usual. Soon the stream of documents resumed. 'It matters not', Smiles
wrote to Murray junior at the beginning of February, 'to refer to the
past. Now, it appears from your letter that I can go on to the end. The
accumulation of MS I have written already is something enormous, and
I shall of course be glad to see the whole of it in your father's hands.'[13]
He told Jack, with relief, that things were back on track. 'Murray has
promised the rest of the correspondence, so I hope to finish soon.'[14]

No doubt the Murray family shared his hope, but they had a growing
business to attend to, many other authors to deal with, and still, at that
time, a preoccupation with their new pet project, the *Murray Magazine,*
the cause of the 1886 problem. They made sure that the touchy old author
was kept supplied with papers, but were often unable to 'docket' them
in the way he wanted, or to answer his questions as quickly as he
expected. These logistical problems, and the sheer volume of documents,
meant that it took years rather than months to haul the book to the
finishing line, and that in those years there would be, between a young,
ambitious publishing team and their elderly author, recurring tensions.

As early as March 1888 Smiles was beginning to show the strain.
Reporting on what he had managed so far, he warned that, 'I will then
ask for the remainder – some twelve years' of correspondence. Indeed it
is getting to be a terrible affair. However, I hope to be able to finish it. At
the same time, I should like not to have any more of the correspondence
I have already examined.'[15] For some months, from his lair in Torquay,
Smiles worked on, checking on detail – 'J S Mill offered his MS on logic
(Feb 1842). I am under the impression that it was published by Parker,
Strand – did Mr Murray publish the "Found in Attica" for C Wordsworth,
then of Harrow? – What was the book published by Lord Caernarvon in
1836?' – and so on: a fascinating glimpse into early nineteenth-century
literature, but for the author, a chore. 'I will go over the whole batch of
letters I have in hand and then will bring them, like Oliver Twist, and
"ask for more". I will then have an interview with your father on the
various aspects of the work.'[16] Even poor, rheumaticky Sarah Anne was
not spared. 'I shall have to look over the 1837 letters. My wife will leave
the 1835 & 6 at Albemarle Street on Monday.'

In July Sarah Anne was advised by her doctor to spend some time in the spa waters at Royat, in the Auvergne. Smiles told Murray that he would accompany her – 'Of course I will take my work with me, and proceed as if I were at home.'[17] But at the French spa he did not simply settle in a deck-chair by the baths. 'As it was somewhat tedious waiting at Royat after the examination of this correspondence had been completed, I resolved to make a short tour round the south of France.'[18] His main destination on this tour was Agen, for many years home of the local poet Jacques Jasmin. Smiles had written a magazine article about Jasmin thirty years earlier and had ever since been an admirer of the 'barber poet' who had become a national hero in France. He took a room in the modest Hôtel de Petit St Jean in Agen town centre, opposite the statue erected in the square by the townspeople in honour of Jasmin, and near the small shop on the Gravier where the poet had carried on his barber's trade. Smiles, on his own, was in research mode again – hunting for the places and the people to help him bring his man alive, as he had done with George Stephenson thirty-five years ago on Tyneside, but now in the warm July sun by the Garonne. By the time he left to rejoin his wife at Royat for the journey home, his notebooks were full.

Back in England he reverted to 'Murray', and for a moment to the tetchy mood that had threatened the project almost from the start. The old squabble reignited, about supply of documents, and who had tried to drop whom in the 1886 fracas. After a frosty exchange of letters, Smiles sued for peace. 'Send me the whole of the remaining correspondence and I am ready to proceed at once.'[19] Sarah Anne's continuing poor health did not make things easier. Young Murray should know how conscientious his author was being. 'Our doctor recommended us to go to the Riviera, or Torquay. Now that I have this important work to finish, I shall go to Torquay. Will you be kind enough to send me the first three years of the correspondence (which I have not yet had) that I may begin on them.'[20]

At Torquay, at Hastings, at his home in Kensington – even during trips to Monte Carlo and Rome – for almost another two years the Murray monolith followed Smiles wherever he went. Even when he had given Murray the completed first draft – 2,000 handwritten pages of it – in January 1889, his task was far from over.[21] 'You complained yesterday', he wrote on 18 January,

about the information introduced into the memoir respecting Captain Hay
... It was very difficult to know what to do with the materials relating
to Lord Byron ... I have only endeavoured to do my best in a long and
intricate correspondence, and I think what I have done will on the whole
be found very interesting. Of course it might have been done very much
better but I think few people would have had the time or the courage
to go through the correspondence of nearly three quarters of a century
examining every letter from beginning to end.

Quick to mollify, Murray replied at once. 'My dear Smiles, I pray you
must dismiss from your mind the idea that I complain of anything in
your memoir of my father. I am delighted with the work as a whole.'[22]
But, inevitably, more work was needed. 'No doubt certain alterations will
be required before the book sees the light, as you yourself have generally
and liberally proposed.'

The main narrative was now, however, finished, and Smiles's respect
and affection for the Murray family, and for Robert Cooke and the people
at Albemarle Street, was too strong to let grudges linger. By the middle
of 1889, while still keeping in contact with the work, even while on
holiday, his tone had become noticeably warmer. He told John Murray
about the weather in Monte Carlo – bright, fair, blue sky, blue sea – about
the gamblers – 'Lord R Churchill threw away a lot of money the other
day as quickly as he threw away the Chancellorship of the Exchequer'[23]
– about his impeccable fellow guests – 'the residents in this house (Hôtel
des Anglais) are intensely respectable; for the most part, I should think,
retired soapboilers and soapboileresses.' But of course the business of
the book must be kept in view. 'My object in writing to you is to tell you
this address, and if you have anything to say to me about the progress of
the work I shall be pleased to have a line from you. Please give my kindest
regards to your father, Mr Cooke, and Hallam.' In this benign mood he
arrived a week later in Rome; if the Murray book had given him any self-
doubts, in Rome they fled.

Smiles was to write of the man who was perhaps his favourite
biographical subject (and who was much in his mind at this time),
Jacques Jasmin, that he had one fault, 'which he himself confessed. He
was vain and loved applause, nor did he conceal his love.'[24] And nor, a
thousand miles from home, glowing in Italian plaudits, did Samuel

Smiles. 'I cannot tell you how much I have been made of at Rome', he told John Murray.

> The literary and scientific people entertained me to a splendid reception, with all manner of people, from Princes to Artists. And I have been asked to sit for my portrait by the President of the Academy. It seems I must go abroad to ascertain that my small literary labours have been of some use. No one honoured me like the Queen. No one talked to me like the King. No one entertained me like the Association de la Stampa. In fact, I was like the fatted frog. I must burst with vanity.[25]

Of course he tried to hide behind Anglo-Saxon faux modesty, and the Smiles theory of the common denominator of effort. 'I know that my powers are small, only I have made the best use of them. I suppose that the reason for my éclat here is that my books (very well translated) have sold in unusual numbers – some 100,000 of "Self-Help", and "Character" runs it very hard.' The elite of Naples, it seemed, wanted to shower their own honours on the British author, 'but I wish to avoid excitement, and these things excite me too much. I hope to return home alive and in my usual health.'

At home, though his mind was full of plans for his book on Jasmin, he had still much to do in correcting and filling the gaps in the Murray volumes. But at last an end seemed near. 'I take my work with me,'[26] he wrote to John Murray from Hastings just before Christmas 1889.

> The last chapter [of the memoir] will be very good. I expect the next time I write to you to send the remainder. I now see the end very clearly before me; and I shall be glad when it is finished, as it has cost me more trouble, in searching and investigation, than any other work that I have ever had to do with. Therefore I shall set up a loud hurrah when it is over.

Smiles wrote that on 29 December 1889, but halfway into the following year he was still asking about the last chapter. Where was it? What was the delay? 'I should like to see the conclusion before I go abroad', he told John Murray on the 7 June 1890. 'My wife is affected with neuralgia and I think it possible we may go to Royat as before.' He stayed at home for a few more weeks, fretting, until John Murray issued a plea from Albemarle Street, bidding for time.

The Memoir and Correspondence of my Father [always with a capital] is
a work so momentous in its bearing for us at no. 50 – so many questions
of verification of fact, testing of results, have started up that my son has
been obliged to devote a great deal of time to the revision as well as to
include my own suggestions and recollections.[27]

So, Smiles need expect no swift conclusion, but at least the slowdown
had been acknowledged, and some compensation offered. Murray
accepted that the delay was 'hardly fair' to Smiles, as 'you have placed
the ms in our hands now many months ago – and that you ought no
longer to be left waiting for at least part of the honorarium agreed on for
the copyright. I have therefore the pleasure to enclose my check for £500
as an instalment.

Smiles had little choice but to respond with grace. 'I was beginning to
think from the long halt that had taken place that the memoir was all
but condemned and was not about to appear … your faithful son has
been the greatest possible use in revising and adding to the memoir.'[28]
But he knew that the book had fallen victim to serial editing.

In August he took Sarah Anne to Royat for her neuralgia, and the
Jasmin manuscript for his own diversion. He claimed, in a letter to
Murray junior from the Grand Hotel, that he was relaxing. 'I am loafing
at present. It is too hot to work. I have, however, brought the last chapter
of Jasmin to write.' Back in England in October, he continued to chafe.
An attack on publishers in *The Times*, by Archdeacon Farrar, gave him
an excuse to prod Murray again. 'Don't you think the time is ripe to issue
"The Life of a Publisher" – one of the greatest? I think it would excite a
great deal of interest.'[29] By the beginning of November his tone had
sharpened. 'I wonder how it is the Life and Correspondence of the Great
Publisher is so long appearing. Are we all to be dead before it comes
out?'[30]

But at last proofs started coming through, and by the year's end Smiles
had corrected and returned everything. Yet in March 1891 he was still
pleading: 'When is the Publisher and his Friends to come out? I am
looking anxiously for its appearance.' Then there it was, announced in
the pages of the *Pall Mall Gazette* on the 11 March, the two portly volumes
publicly introduced, and their author named alongside the greatest
biographer of all: 'What Boswell did for Dr Johnson and the literature of

the eighteenth century,' the correspondent announced, 'Dr Smiles, the author, of "A Publisher and his Friends" hopes to do for the literature of the first half of the present.'[31] The magazine's reporter went on to note the immensity of the task:

> Look here' said Mr Murray to the present writer in the course of a recent interview. 'Those parcels cover only two or three years.' Twenty or thirty large brown paper parcels lay piled upon the shelves at my side. Seeing that a period of eighty years is covered by Dr Smiles in his book, it will be easy to form some notion of the magnitude of his task.

The Times covered the publication at length, and confidently predicted that 'These volumes will perpetuate his [John Murray's] memory, for they may be placed side by side with "The Life of Scott" as books that will bear perpetual dipping into, and we could hardly bestow higher praise.'

23
Yesterday Afternoon

THIS HAD BEEN a Herculean exercise in perseverance under difficulty, but now Smiles, approaching his eightieth birthday, at last showed signs of slowing. An interview he gave to *Pall Mall Gazette* a few weeks later,[1] though suspiciously like a contrived publicity exercise for *A Publisher and His Friends*, probably gives a fair picture of Smiles in these years – gently boastful, content to play the part of cheery, slightly bufferish old author – but still an author. 'I am an old man, more than seventy-eight years of age,' he chuntered, though, according to the interviewer 'there is no sign of old age about him, other than the white hair and beard which tell the visitor he has passed the usual limit assigned to frail humanity'. But he was hard at work, 'the sort of man who dies in harness.' The pictures over the mantelpiece tell a story – images of George Stephenson, Darwin, Newman, James Martineau, J S Mill, Victor Hugo – 'you see I am very Catholic and broad-minded in my tastes.' The interviewer passes on the message. 'They are all there, for are they not splendid instances of resolution, indomitable perseverance and self-help?' Smiles explained with pride how he always visited the places with which his subjects had been connected, and how he made notes and sketches everywhere – and the old hankering to be an artist shows again – 'Oh yes! I sketch a good deal. Come into the drawing-room and I will show you some of my work.' The domesticated Smiles is presented too. Aged makes her appearance – 'a singularly handsome old lady', who cut short the interview. 'Get on your boots and go out for your usual walk before luncheon,' she commanded her husband.

Smiles was happy with the impression, and amused by the Aged's portrayal. 'You will see in Pall Mall gazette', he told Jack, 'I am sat upon at home.'[2] But he was more interested in the reception given to the book. '"Murray' seems to be a success. Gladstone is to review it in Murray's magazine.'

The work over which the *Pall Mall Gazette* had found Smiles's head bent was *Jasmin – Poet, Barber, Philanthropist*. It was published a few months after *Murray*, in November 1891. Even more than Edward or Dick, the French poet seemed an unlikely hero for the biographer of all those mighty engineers. Yet after the host of lives he had studied, and the examples

15 Samuel Smiles in late life: 'there is no sign of age about him, other than the white hair and beard.'
(*The Autobiography of Samuel Smiles*, ed. Thomas Mackay, John Murray, 1905)

16 Sarah Anne Smiles in late life: 'a singularly handsome old lady'.
(www.geni.com)

he had offered, Smiles showed more empathy with the obscure Gascon writer than with any of the great men. Jasmin had invented nothing, built nothing, and discovered nothing – except the joy of offering his poetry to the rapturous crowds of common people who shared his language, and of giving to charity the great sums of money (about half-a-million francs according to Smiles) subscribed by his followers. 'No poet had so many opportunities of making money and of enriching himself by the contributions of the rich as well as the poor. But such an idea never entered his mind.'

Observing Jasmin, Smiles, the prophet of manufacturing, spoke more like a disciple of Ruskin. 'The art which produces verses one by one depends upon inspiration, not upon manufacture.' Inspiration alone was not, of course, enough. Jasmin was yet another bearer of the Smiles message, that 'it is possible for a poet to become all this voluntarily by dint of patient toil and conscientious labour.' He was a self-helper, but not for himself. 'He worked solely for the benefit of those who could not help themselves'. *Jasmin* was, in its way, a perfect rebuttal to the misled, who years ago had judged *Self-Help* 'merely by its title, to suppose that it consists of a eulogy of selfishness'.[3] Jacques Jasmin, more than George Stephenson, or Watt, or any of the others, was Smiles's ideal – 'Loyal, single-minded, self-reliant, patient, temperate, and utterly unselfish.'[4] How different from the jaded aristocracy. The papers in London were full of the notorious 'Bacarrat Trial' at about this time. The spectacle of the Prince of Wales and a slew of his aristocratic playmates, caught squandering money on illegal gambling in a country house, brought out all Smiles's old contempt for their class. 'This is our aristocracy,' he snorted. 'These are our leaders. Jasmin is worth the whole bundle of them.'[5]

Jasmin was a work of love – of affection for the man, and love for (or perhaps addiction to) the activity of writing. Smiles did not need to write for money. 'I do not expect much success,' he wrote to John Murray. 'It has been a fad of mine for some time to write the book.'[6] Even copyright theft hardly bothered him.[7] He had provided for his family – a provision seen as a man's moral obligation. 'I don't need more money', he told Janet. 'I am going to divide the Murray pay among the babbies', and joked that he didn't 'want to leave the Aged a rich widow, otherwise she'll be pestered'.[8]

He seemed for the next half-dozen years to settle into a stereotypically serene old age, grousing occasionally about the state of the world, worrying about his health, and finding joy in his love for his grandchildren. Willie's eldest daughter Lily was given the role Janet had filled thirty-five years ago, of confidante and protégé. She became 'My Magniloquent and Superb Grandaughter', repository for his advice, complaints and prejudices. 'Never mind hockey. Improve your mind, and attend diligently to your lessons.'[9] She was offered the mantle of successor. 'I look upon you as the coming literary lady of the family,' he wrote to her at school in Brighton. 'I feel myself growing old and stupid, and can scarcely write as much in a day as you can in an hour.' When she told him about a school debate – 'Is England going down hill?' he was quick to answer. 'I must express my feelings strongly on the subject. My impression is that the country is <u>not</u> going down hill, but is surely and properly in the ascendant ... It is by her inventive power that England has made her enormous progress within the last century.'[10]

Even though the old Smiles's social life had slowed – they had given up going to weddings, dinners and funerals – he often revealed to Lily that he was still writing. His device of self-deprecation persisted (now perhaps with justification). Apologising for delay in answering a letter, he explained, 'I ought to have answered it sooner, but I had a lot to write – mostly rubbish. You know that I am growing dreadfully old.'[11] A few weeks later all was revealed. 'I was finishing a book which I left with the publisher yesterday, and which will now be in the hands of the printer.'[12]

It was the middle of 1894 and Smiles was almost eighty-two. The book was *Josiah Wedgwood FRS – his Personal History*, which, Smiles was proud to explain in his Preface, had been largely based on hitherto unseen Wedgwood family papers, lent to him by a Mr C T Gatty. Unfortunately Mr Gatty had failed to tell the Wedgwoods what he had done, thus moving Godfrey Wedgwood to write to *The Academy* to deny 'that the Wedgwood family have voluntarily contributed to a life of their ancestor, exhibiting extraordinary want of knowledge of the special field of his activity. The evidence of this ignorance is strewn throughout its pages.'[13]

Wedgwood was published by Murray in November 1894. It was Smiles's last book, though only weeks later her father told Janet that he was thinking of writing another.[14] His decline after this was gradual but obvious. For some years he remained active, walking each day, even in the hard winter of 1895:

Here we are suffering from intense frost. We are without water – except what we buy in the street. Altogether things are miserable. Nobody calls on us and old friends are departing ... but I am going to take a short walk. All the lakes and ponds are full of skaters. At night they skate by torch-light.[15]

He clung to the old determination to enjoy the small things of life. His 'Dear Lady Grandaughter' was told after Christmas that 'our plumcake is dismissed, our port wine is drunk, our crackers cracked and we are about to settle down in our role of Darby and Joan.'

Though Sarah Anne's rheumatism was getting worse, they managed to take holidays in Torquay with the help of a companion. Smiles's spark still showed. He enthused about the beauty of the coast and loved sharing with Lily his discovery that their companion, Mrs Plummer, had married a descendant of a surviving 'Babe in the Wood', immortalised in pantomime. The hotel, he told Lily, was 'full of old fogies besides ourselves, including a lady from Armagh – she has a husband, and from what your grandmother thinks – she sits on him!'[16] The old Smiles fogies still showed great love for each other. When Sarah Anne went on her own for a short stay with Sam junior's family at Beckenham, he wrote to 'My Dearest and most perpendicular aged' to reassure her that 'the great cook' had put her best foot forward and sent him up a dinner he could eat, and that his manservant Wright 'has been most attentive ... This day is fine & we shall take a little drive together & come home by Palace Gardens. I have no doubt you are properly worshipped ... ever your affectionate & perpendicular Tyrant.'

A flash of old glory appeared the following spring, when the King of Serbia, 'having read with admiration your books, desires to give you a mark of his high appreciation by appointing you Knight Commander of the Cross of his Royal Order of Sava'.[17] But by then Smiles was probably slipping into the early stages of the memory loss and confusion which grew in severity over the final years of his life. John Murray, kind and sensitive, trod gently when confronted in June 1897 with a Smiles manuscript for an unpublishable book. 'I have found it – like all your biographies – very interesting and instructive, but it is perhaps inevitable that in dealing with such a subject you should travel over some of the same ground in which you have already attained such remarkable success.'[18]

A 'misunderstanding' about what they had agreed on issuing cheap editions of the popular titles almost led to the old man going off in a huff. But diplomacy saved the situation, and from that time Sam junior effectively assumed power of attorney in dealing with Murray's. 'His memory is very bad, & in future it would be well to have all in writing. My family and myself are quite aware you and Mr Hallam are quite incapable of doing anything disreputable', he wrote to John Murray in October 1897. They would, Sam hoped, be able to avoid any more embarrassment. 'I am glad also to have the opportunity of thanking you for your note respecting the "Conduct" ms. for I should much regret the publication of anything. It is far too late.'[19]

It would be comforting to think that it was too late for Smiles to understand much of what happened in the few years he had left. In spite of Sam's efforts his father resubmitted 'Conduct' a year after its first rejection, and forced another feat of diplomacy from John Murray. 'The book market is in a very depressed and unsatisfactory state ... I am afraid I cannot recommend you to launch your new book this year.'[20] *Jasmin* and *Wedgwood* had subsided. When Murray published the three-and-sixpenny editions of the other books, Hallam wrote in September 1898 to explain the fall in payments – 'we had to recall, and give allowance for, a large number of copies (especially of Jasmin and Wedgwood).'[21] But Smiles was no longer concerned.

Just after Christmas he suffered what was probably a severe stroke, and for several days his family feared he might not survive. He did, for another six years, but they were years in which the fabric of his life fell away. When Janet died in February 1900, then the adored Aged just weeks later, Sam junior and his family moved into 8 Pembroke Gardens to look after the old man. But as though by a malevolent family curse, 'young' Sam survived for only another few months and Willie, dynamic rope-making tycoon in Belfast, and mustard-keen golfer, was left to manage his father's affairs. The books were still selling well enough to produce significant cheques for the Smiles account, and a big deal was afoot for a low-price volume for Indian schools – 10,000 copies for the first run. 'I hope your dear old father is well,' Hallam Murray wrote to Willie in 1902. 'He is often in my thoughts and I seem to see his kindly face and his cheery voice as I write.'[22]

It would, in a way, be right to leave Samuel Smiles here, for the image of a smiling face and cheery voice, brightening the rooms at Albemarle Street, tells a truth about his life. But so does the vision of a gaunt figure stretching perseverance to its limit in a grim game of survival. Not until Willie had gone, struck down by a heart attack at his golf club in County Down, did Samuel Smiles agree to leave. Willie died on 7 February 1904. His father followed on 16 April.

To whom, in a family so broken by recent deaths, could John Murray address his letter of condolence? He wrote to 'Samuel Smiles Esq' (the third Samuel Smiles, son of Sam junior) at 8 Pembroke Gardens:

> The first tidings I had of Dr Smiles's death was a very brief paragraph in the Observer yesterday. I was not sure who to write to, or I would have written yesterday afternoon to tell you and the other members of your family how sincerely my brother and I regret the loss of our dear old friend.[23]

In new-born Edwardian England Samuel Smiles was already yesterday afternoon's man, an outsider at his death as he had been in his youth. 'It has always been a source of regret to us', Murray wrote to Lucy Smiles,

> that successive governments have taken so little notice of the extraordinary influence for good which Dr Smiles exercised through his works. My father did bring the matter before a now deceased prime minister, and he took it up warmly, but owing to some extraordinary blunder on the part of the statesman, it came to naught.

Another version appeared in the *Daily Telegraph*'s obituary of Smiles: 'The late Queen wished him to accept a title in appreciation of his services to the country and mankind, but this he respectfully declined.'[24] Sir Samuel Smiles? No, probably not. He knew how human value was truly marked. 'The elements of nobility are in him', he had told the working people of Leeds sixty years earlier – 'far above the titled nobility of man's creation'.

AFTERWORD

SAMUEL SMILES was buried on 19 April 1904 in a grave in the north-east corner of Brompton Cemetery, the same grave where Sarah Anne had been buried four years earlier. His estate was valued at £79,964-10-11 (£74,420-7-4 net)[1] – a substantial legacy, worth in today's terms several million pounds, divided equally between his four nearest surviving family members – a tidy, well-ordered arrangement. But what of Smiles's other legacy, the legacy of his work? That is a good deal less tidy, and altogether more difficult to value, though this has not discouraged plenty of people from trying. For such an optimist (the *Athenaeum* once said 'he was all his own surname'), Smiles might have been saddened by some of the results. Peter Sinnema called his reputation 'tenacious and unfortunate'.[2] Samuel Smiles, and *Self-Help*, have been burdened with a reputation unfortunate both for the alleged propagation of a doctrinaire political stance, and for the inspiration of an exploitative and fantasy-inducing genre of 'self-help' literature.

Though he wrote so much else, the idea of self-help, and those words packed with implication, have come to be seen as Smiles's legacy. But a word's assumed meaning is not necessarily the one its user had in mind. More often others impose on it what they choose. Immediately after the publication of the first edition of *Self-Help*, Smiles recognised the problem. 'In one respect the title of the book, which it is now too late to alter, has proved unfortunate', he wrote in the Preface to the second edition, 'as it has led some, who have judged it merely by its title, to suppose that it consists of a eulogy to selfishness: the very opposite of what it really is, or at least of what its author intends it to be.' With such a slippery word, playing the legacy game becomes a matter of confrontation among a host of commentators, each with their view of the 'real meaning' of self-help.

This enticing scope for interpretation has bred quite an industry of essays and articles on Smiles himself, and in references to him and his work in books about 'the Victorians'. For a long time much of this discussion had a political or ideological context, initially from a left-wing perspective, attacking self-help as a creed of laissez-faire capitalism and individual self-interest. Even some of Smiles's obituarists assumed an apologetic tone: 'Since Dr Smiles gave Self-Help to the world, the point of view has changed somewhat', said the *Daily Chronicle* days after Smiles's death, in an obituary otherwise blandly sympathetic.[3] Socialists spoke of him as 'an arch philistine', and of his books as 'the apotheosis of respectability, gigmanity and selfish grab',[4] (though Robert Blatchford, himself a leading socialist and Fabian journalist, who expressed these views, described Smiles as 'a most charming and honest writer'). Edwardian attitudes were so dismissive that H G C Matthew later described them as representing Smiles as 'an almost burlesque figure in the early twentieth-century reaction against Victorianism'.[5] Robert Tressell, in *The Ragged-Trousered Philanthropists* (1906), mocked *Self-Help* as a book aimed at 'ignorant, shallow-pated dolts ... suitable for perusal by persons suffering almost complete obliteration of the mental faculties'.[6] In 1914 John Murray IV (by then Sir John Murray), was provoked to defence by an article in the *Saturday Review*,[7] which had merely suggested 'that the simple philosophy of "Self-Help" has lost much of its appeal to young Englishmen must be attributed to the other undoubted fact that the self-made man is no longer the hero he once was'. Sir John thundered in return:

> of course I am well aware that the doctrine of 'Self-help' [*sic*] is out of fashion with the modern school of radicals, who teach a man that if he is 'down in the world' it is the fault of someone else, or of 'Society', and that if he is to succeed he must do so by Act of Parliament, at the expense of someone else, aided by the Radical party.

As late as 1970 Smiles was being described in the *Observer* as 'probably the most despised of the great Victorians'.[8] The writer quoted David Thomson, Master of Sidney Sussex College Cambridge, and a contributing author in *The Penguin History of England*, who had mocked *Self-Help* as 'sunny lay sermons ... connecting always the practice of such virtue with the reward of material prosperity ... the shoddiest mentality of the time'. Cyril Connolly, writing in *The Sunday Times* in 1958, declared that, in politics, 'Samuel Smiles was a Tory individualist'.[9]

But, most markedly in the 1980s, right-wing advocates had tried to turn that image to their advantage, to co-opt the message of *Self-Help* as one of virtue expressed in hard work and self-reliance – the core value of the honest, hard-working individual not depending on state handouts. Sir Keith Joseph, Margaret Thatcher's Minister of Education, in an introduction to an abridged edition of *Self-Help* published in the Penguin Business Library in 1986, avoided any mention of Smiles's view that 'the duty of helping oneself in the highest sense involves the helping of one's neighbours'. Matthew dismissed the abridged version with the comment that 'A Bowdlerized edition of *Self-Help* ... with an introduction by Sir Keith Joseph, did him little service.' In fact the 'Business version' has been accused of removing passages 'which run counter to the rampant individualism suggested in Sir Keith Joseph's Introduction and advocated widely by more like-minded politicians'.[10] *Self-Help*, Sir Keith Joseph wrote, is 'a book for *our* times: the purveyor of a message that we, government and governed, employer and employee, in work and out of work, need to take to heart and keep in mind'. For a time, Smiles became something of a darling of right-leaning groups such as the Institute of Economic Affairs, and inevitably this tended to reinvigorate his left-wing critics.

But over the last half-century partisanship has been much less evident. Scholars have taken over the forum, devoting their interest to Smiles's historical significance, without being drawn into overt political points-scoring.

And then there is the third combatant in the battle for the soul of self-help, most easily denoted by the term 'self-help guru'. In this arena, as in the political, there are two sides. On one stand the believers, who find 'self-help' a useful label for whatever advice, practical or otherwise, they want to offer. Organisations of impeccable integrity, like Britain's National Health Service and the Royal College of Psychiatrists, offer 'self-help' advice. While on the other hand a chorus of derision rises from those who see the self-help 'movement' as at best flaky and delusional, at worst cynical and exploitative. In this essentially commercial argument, the word self-help has usually become completely detached from any reference to Samuel Smiles's book, and his name is rarely used. But when in 2009, to mark the 150th anniversary of the publication of

Self-Help, the BBC broadcast a programme on Radio Four, they chose to call it 'Samuel Smiles, the grandfather of self-help'. The linking of the man and the genre was obvious, and is always tempting.

Nevertheless, to type 'Samuel Smiles' in the search box on any relevant academic or historical website is to reveal the amount of serious commentary devoted to his work. The tendency of such commentary is generally to be restorative, to be in one way or another helping to rescue Smiles from ideological stereotyping. Inevitably all this becomes a matter of selective quotation-swapping, so that in the game of proving what Smiles 'really means', no one ever wins. As in any holy writ, in Smiles's unholy writ, for every quotation supporting one view, another can be found to prove the opposite. Smiles is not to be pinned down.

Is it the biographer's role to attempt the pinning-down – to offer the subject, fixed, like a perfectly preserved specimen, perfectly labelled, perfectly defined? That would be arrogant, and boring. Biographers, rather than pinning down, try to bring alive, to set free their subject. Samuel Smiles used biography to set free a host of ideas, often qualifying each other, often throwing light from different directions. What he really believed he hardly knew himself – 'you see, I am very Catholic and broad-minded in my tastes'. Smiles was not a one-idea man. His writing, always opinionated, ranged over so many topics and ideas, and his career covered so many generations, that by careful selection he can be represented as advocate for hugely diverse, often quite contradictory, points of view.

In emphasis and perspective his argument could zig-zag alarmingly, but in his underlying conviction Samuel Smiles never wavered: life means the right to some expectation of happiness, and whatever the circumstances, the happiness that gives life its reason flourishes in occupation and energy of mind. In apathy it withers.

ACKNOWLEDGEMENTS

THOUGH an author's name appears on its spine, no book can be, I suspect, the fruit of one person's work. Certainly self-help alone would not have produced this one. I have many people to thank.

Without the skilled guidance of the staff at the West Yorkshire Records Office, first in Leeds then in Morley, I wouldn't have been able to navigate the vast Smiles collection they hold. In Belfast the archivists at the Public Records Office of Northern Ireland have been immensely helpful, both during my visits and in correspondence.

David McClay, curator of the John Murray Archive at the National Library of Scotland, was one of the first to share his special knowledge of Samuel Smiles and the collection in the Murray Archive, and to encourage me in my work on this book. To him and his staff in Edinburgh I am immensely grateful.

I should also like to thank Jonathan Wilkinson, who helped so much with papers from the National Railway Museum in York, Eva Bradford at the Thoresby Society, and Sheila Millar and her colleagues at the East Lothian History Centre, whose expertise, so generously shared, has been invaluable. Marianne Smith at the Royal College of Surgeons in Edinburgh provided essential information. The wonderful staff at the London Library have been unfailingly helpful, as have the staff in the manuscripts room at the British Library, and in the National Archive in Kew. I thank them all. I wish to acknowledge with gratitude the help of archival and library staff at Manchester Central Library, the London School of Economics, the Athenaeum, the London Metropolitan Archive, and the West Sussex County Record Office.

For sharing their special knowledge or special skills I want to record my gratitude to Robert Thorne, David Williams, Richard Holmes, Charles Hunter, Jocasta Shakespeare, Richard Simms, Alexandra Hayward, and the Scotts – of both Broad Hoath and Paciano. I owe a special debt to Mark Hammer for his work on the cover design. Catherine Pope's intimidating knowledge of all things Victorian, and her editorial acuity were, quite simply, priceless. I want also to thank David Gillott at Birkbeck, who read an earlier version of the manuscript and offered invaluable suggestions, though of course, as always, any errors are entirely the author's responsibility. Under the 'without whom' heading must come Anthony Werner, my estimable publisher, whose wisdom, experience and patience made the book a reality, and Jean Maughan of Alacrity, for whom the word meticulous is too faint praise. And finally and always, I want to thank Janet, as wise as she is generous, for a hundred technical rescue missions, but most of all for sharing her home with a man in a bubble.

BIBLIOGRAPHY

BOOKS BY SAMUEL SMILES

Physical Education, or the Nurture and Management of Children, founded on the study of their nature and constitution, Edinburgh, 1838.

History of Ireland and the Irish People under the Government of England, Leeds, 1843.

Railway Property: its condition and prospects, London and Leeds, 1849.

The Life of George Stephenson, John Murray, 1857 (abridged version, 1859).

Self-Help, with illustrations of Character, Conduct, and Perseverance, John Murray, 1859.

Brief Biographies, Ticknor & Fields, Boston, 1860.

Workmen's Earnings, Strikes, and Savings (pamphlet), John Murray, 1861.

Lives of the Engineers (3 volumes), John Murray, 1861-2.

Industrial Biography, John Murray, 1863.

The Lives of Boulton and Watt, comprising a history of the invention and introduction of the steam engine, John Murray, 1865.

The Huguenots, their Settlements, Churches, and Industries in England and Ireland, John Murray, 1867.

A Boy's Voyage Round the World, ed. Samuel Smiles, John Murray, 1871.

Character, John Murray, 1871.

The Huguenots in France after the Revocation of the Edict of Nantes, John Murray, 1873.

Thrift, John Murray, 1875.

Life of a Scotch Naturalist Thomas Edward, John Murray, 1876.

George Moore, Merchant and Philanthropist, George Routledge, 1878.

Robert Dick, Baker, of Thurso, Geologist and Botanist, John Murray, 1878.

Duty, John Murray, 1880.

Men of Invention and Industry, John Murray, 1884.

James Nasmyth Engineer, an Autobiography, ed. Samuel Smiles John Murray, 1883.

Life and Labour or Characteristics of Men of Industry, Culture, and Genius, John Murray, 1887.

A Publisher and his Friends: Memoir and Correspondence of the late John Murray, John Murray, 1891.

Jasmin, Barber, Poet, Philanthropist, John Murray, 1891.

Josiah Wedgwood FRS – his personal history, John Murray, 1894.

The Autobiography of Samuel Smiles, ed. Thomas Mackay, John Murray, 1905.

For a comprehensive bibliography, including articles and pamphlets, see A E Jarvis, 'An attempt at a bibliography of Samuel Smiles', in *Industrial Archaeology Review*, Vol. 13, No. 2, Spring 1991.

BOOKS ABOUT SAMUEL SMILES

Adrian Jarvis, *Samuel Smiles and the Construction of Victorian Values*, Sutton Publishing, 1997.

T H E Travers, *Samuel Smiles and the Victorian Work Ethic*, Garland Publishing, 1987.

Aileeen Smiles, *Samuel Smiles and his Surroundings*, Robert Hale, 1956.

Karen Boiko (PhD thesis), *Samuel Smiles, Radical: a critical biography*, New York University, 2002.

T B Green, *Life and Works of Samuel Smiles*, with Preface by Mrs Alec Tweedie, 1904.

SELECT BIBLIOGRAPHY

A J King and J Plunkett, *Victorian Print Media*, Oxford University Press, 2005.

Alexis Weedon, *Victorian Publishing: the economics of book production, 1836-1916*, Ashgate, 2003.

David Finkelstein, *The House of Blackwood: author-publisher relations in the Victorian era*, Pennsylvania State University Press, 2002.

Humphrey Carpenter, *The Seven Lives of John Murray*, ed. Candida Brazil, with additional material by James Hamilton, John Murray, 2008.

George Paston, *At John Murray's: records of a Literary Circle 1843-1892*, John Murray, 1932.

Asa Briggs, *Victorian People*, Odhams Press, 1954.

Asa Briggs, *Victorian Cities*, Odhams Press, 1963.

Lynda Nead, *Victorian Babylon: people, streets and images in nineteenth-century London*, Yale University Press, 2000.

Herbert Sussman, *The Victorians and the Machine*, Harvard University Press, 1968.

T Tholfsen, *Working Class Radicalism in mid-Victorian England*, Croom Helm,1976.

W E Houghton, *The Victorian Frame of Mind*, Yale University Press, 1957.

Belinda Norman Butler, *Victorian Aspirations*, Allen & Unwin, 1972.

D J Bradshaw and S Ozment (eds), *The Voice of Toil: 19th-century writings about work*, Ohio University Press, 2001.

Thomas Carlyle, *Past and Present*, Chapman & Hall, 1843.

Joseph Marie, Baron de Gérando, *Self-Education*, trans. Elizabeth Peabody, 1830.

Louis Aimé-Martin, *Education des Meres de Famille*, 1834.

Matthew Arnold, *Culture and Anarchy: an essay in political and social criticism*, Smith Elder, 1869.

Fredrerich Engels, *The Condition of the Working Class in England*, with preface written in 1892 (trans. F K Wischnewetzky), Allen, 1920.

H Mayhew, *London Labour and the London Poor, 1849-1850*, selected and introduced by Victor Neuburg, Penguin, 1985.

F Gray and J H Jamieson, *A Short History of Haddington*, Spa Books, 1944.

John Martine, *Reminiscences of the Royal Borough of Haddington*, 1883.

Black's *Guide Through Edinburgh*, A & C Black, 1851.

I G Lindsay, *Georgian Edinburgh*, Scottish Academic Press, 1973.

M Joyce, *Edinburgh, the Golden Age 1769-1832*, Longman's Green, 1951.

M Cosh, *Edinburgh, the Golden Age*, John Donald, 2003.

M Fry, *Edinburgh, a history of the city.* Macmillan, 2009.

L M Rosner, *Medical Education in the Age of Improvement, Edinburgh Apprentices 1760-1826*, Edinburgh University Press, 1991.

Helen Dingwall, *A Famous and Flourishing Society: The history of The Royal College of Surgeons, Edinburgh 1505-2005*, Edinburgh University Press, 2005.

R Gordon, *Great Medical Disasters*, Hutchison, 1983.

W White, *Dictionary and Topography of the Borough of Leeds*, 1842.

James Wardell, *The Municipal Borough of Leeds*, 1846.

J Marshall, *The Annals of York, Bradford, Leeds and Halifax*, 1860.

M Beresford, *East End, West End: the face of Leeds during urbanisation 1684-1842*, The Thoresby Society, 1985-1986.

R J Morris, *Sect and Party: the making of the middle classes, Leeds 1820-1850*, Manchester University Press, 1990.

R J Morris, *Men, Women and Property in England 1780-1870: a social and economic history of family strategy amongst the Leeds middle classes*, Cambridge University Press, 2002.

W G Rimmer, *Marshall's of Leeds, flax spinners 1788-1886*, Cambridge University Press, 1960.

Mrs B Bosanquet (ed.), *Social Conditions in Provincial Towns*, Macmillan, 1912.

J F C Harrison, *Social Reform in Leeds, the work of James Hole 1820-1895*, The Thoresby Society, 1954.

J F C Harrison, *Robert Owen and the Owenites*, Routledge Revivals.

Alex Tyrell and Paul Pickering, *The People's Bread: a history of the Anti-Corn Law League*, Leicester University Press, 2000.

E Baines, *The Life of Edward Baines, late MP for Leeds*, Longman, Brown, Green and Longmans, 1851.

E Hopkins, *Working Class Self-help in Nineteenth-Century England*, University College London Press, 1995.

Jonathan Rose, *The Intellectual Life of the British Working-class*, Yale University Press, 2001.

A Burns and J Innes, *Rethinking the Age of Reform in Britain 1780-1856*, Cambridge University Press, 2003.

R E Leader (ed.), *Life and Letters of John Arthur Roebuck*, Edward Arnold, 1897.

A M Lee, *Laurels and Rosemary: the life of William and Mary Howitt*, Oxford University Press, 1955.

F M Leventhal, *Respectable Radical: George Howell and Victorian working-class politics*, Weidenfeld & Nicolson, 1971.

R H Tawney (pref.), *The Life and Struggles of William Lovett*, Macgibbon & Kee, 1967.

K Hughes, *The Short Life and Long Times of Mrs Beeton*, Fourth Estate, 2005.

H Spencer, *Railway Morals and Railway Policy* (reprinted from the Edinburgh Review), 1855.

A Vaughan, *Railways, Politics and Money*, John Murray, 1997.

A A Jackson, *London's Termini*, David & Charles, 1986.

M Casson, *The World's First Railway System: enterprise, competition, and regulation in Victorian Britain*, Oxford University Press, 2009.

Christian Woolmar, *Fire and Steam: a new history of the railways in Britain*, Atlantic, 2007.

Robert Beaumont, *The Railway King: a biography of George Hudson*, Review, 2002.

Ralph Waldo Emerson, *The Early Lectures of Ralph Waldo Emerson*, Vol. 2, Harvard University Press, 1964.

A O J Cockshut, *Truth to Life: the art of biography in the nineteenth century*, Collins, 1974.

E M Sigsworth (ed.), *In search of Victorian Values: aspects of nineteenth century thought and society*, Manchester University Press, 1988.

L Merrill, *When Romeo was a Woman*, University of Michigan Press,2000.

S Bakewell, *The Way to Live: A Life of Montaigne*, Chatto and Windus, 2010.

V E Frankl, *Man's Search for Meaning*, Rider, 2004, first published in German, 1946.

NOTES AND REFERENCES

MONEY VALUES THEN AND NOW

In the very few places where I have resorted to 'today's equivalent', I indicate, in the relevant note, the formula used. Meaningful value comparisons across a hundred-and-fifty years are immensely complex, and are always open to question, given the range of variables that need to be taken into account. The complexity of the subject is clear from a reading of Exeter University's excellent web page:

www.projects.exeter.ac.uk (and follow the links).

ARCHIVE SOURCES

The main repositories of Smiles correspondence and papers used are:

The West Yorkshire Archive Service, Leeds. Individual documents are listed in the comprehensive online catalogue, www.archives.wygs.org.uk. Smiles papers are listed in series WYL78/ ...

Public Record Office of Northern Ireland, Belfast. Smiles papers are listed in series D34378/A ...

National Library of Scotland, Edinburgh – the John Murray Archive. Smiles letters listed in series 41100-41102.

The National Archives, Kew. Smiles papers and relevant documents listed in original card index under Smiles.

ABBREVIATIONS

Auto	Samuel Smiles, *The Autobiography of Samuel Smiles*, ed. Thomas Mackay, John Murray, 1905.
Aileen	Aileen Smiles, *Samuel Smiles and his Surroundings*, Robert Hale, 1956.
BL	British Library
EC	Eliza Cook
Jack	Jack Hartree, Smiles's son-in-law
Janet	Janet Hartree, Smiles's eldest daughter
JM	John Murray. Samuel Smiles dealt with both John Murray III, 1808-1892, and his son John Murray IV, 1851-1926. Where original correspondence allowed it, I have indicated which John Murray was involved.
JMA	John Murray Archive at National Library of Scotland
JWC	Jane Welsh Carlyle
Kew	The National Archives, Kew
LoE	Samuel Smiles, *Lives of the Engineers*
LoGS	Samuel Smiles, *Life of George Stephenson*
Manchester	Manchester Public Libraries, Archive and Information Service
NRM	National Railway Museum

PRONI   Public Record office off Northern Ireland
SH   Samuel Smiles, *Self-Help*
SS   Samuel Smiles
WYAS   West Yorkshire Archive Service

INTRODUCTION

1 Scott, Byron, Irvine, Austen, Darwin, and Smiles were all published by John Murray of Albemarle Street, London, whose archive is held by the National Library of Scotland.
2 SS to JM, 2 May 1891. JMA.
3 *Auto*, p.229.
4 Friedrich Engels, *The Condition of the Working Class in England, 1844.*
5 Matthew Arnold, *Culture and Anarchy*, first published 1867-1868 as a series of essays in the *Cornhill Magazine,* and as a book in 1869.
6 *Leeds Times,* 3 August 1839.
7 Asa Briggs, Introduction to *Self-Help*, centenary edition (John Murray, 1958).

PROLOGUE

1 Most online spellings of Mrs Smiles's name show 'Ann', probably copied from *Aileen* (*q.v.*) All documents I have seen written by her mother use 'Anne', so I have followed.
2 *Leeds Times,* 3 August 1840.
3 Humphrey Carpenter, *The Seven Lives of John Murray*, ed. Candida Brazil with additional material by James Hamilton, p.195 (John Murray, 2008).

CHAPTER 1

1 Quotes from Samuel Smiles not referenced are from *The Autobiography of Samuel Smiles*, ed. Thomas Mackay (John Murray, 1905).
2 Obituarist in the *London Standard*, 18 April 1904.
3 '... born in 1812'. Charles Dickens was born in the same year (10 February) – it was a good year for writers of huge industry and dedication.
4 *Early Letters of Jane Welsh Carlyle*, q. *Auto*, p.6.
5 Jane Welsh Carlyle to Thomas Carlyle, 18 July 1849. *Carlyle Letters Online.*

CHAPTER 2

1 *The World*, 14 February 1883.
2 ... Minutes of the Committee of the Haddington Public Dispensary, 1819, q. R J Morris, *Transactions of the East Lothian Antiquarian and Field Naturalists' Association*, 22nd vol., 1993, p.97.
3 East Lothian Itinerating Libraries: see W F Grey and H Jamieson, *A Short History of Haddington* (Spa Books, 1986).
4 George Tait, in John Martine, *Reminiscences of The Royal Borough of Haddington* (1883).

CHAPTER 3

1 A Brack, *Journal of the Isle of Man History Society*, vol.2, no.3, July 1980: 'He [Dr Lewins] married a young widow from Leeds and practised in Haddington until she died in 1828.'
2 Letter from Smiles's parents, Haddington, 17 October 1829, possibly a copy transcribed by another, preserving the original spelling. WYAS.
3 In 1826 Professor Andrew Duncan called Edinburgh 'the first medical school in the Empire'. Lisa Rosner, *Medical Education in the Age of Improvement,* p.24 (Edinburgh University Press, 1991).

4 *Regulations to be observed by Candidates previously to their being taken upon trial for obtaining Diplomas from the Royal College of Surgeons of Edinburgh.*

5 When in 1937 a committee organising a plaque in Leeds in memory of Samuel Smiles wrote to the dean of Edinburgh University medical School for confirmation, the Dean replied that 'No trace of a graduate of that name can be found in the records.' WYAS Kilburn Scott archive WYL/KCS8/145.

6 *Regulations, op cit.*

7 The Old Surgeons' Hall. The New Surgeons' Hall in Nicolson Street, designed by William Playfair, was opened in 1832, three years after Smiles's matriculation.

8 *Pamphleteer,* 1814, q. Rosner *op cit.*

9 M. Cosh, *Edinburgh in the Golden Age,* p.812 (John Donald, 2003).

10 Thomas Alcock, *An Essay on the Education and Duties of the general practitioner in Medicine and Surgery,* q. Rosner, *op cit,* p.21.

11 Darwin, who never completed his medical training, nevertheless found himself able to come to his wife's help when, in 1850, he administered chloroform to ease her pain during childbirth. Three years later Queen Victoria was given chloroform in similar circumstances, at the birth of her eighth child, effectively ending the prejudice which had deprived women of this relief.

12 R Gordon, *Great Medical Disasters,* pp.13-15 (Hutchinson, 1983).

13 Helen Dingwall, *A Famous and Flourishing Society: the history of the Royal College of Surgeons of Edinburgh 1505-2005,* p.135 (Edinburgh University Press, 2005).

14 Robert Lewins, *Biographical Memoir of John Fletcher MD* (Edinburgh, 1837).

15 The biggest of all despots ... *Auto,* p.37. Smiles describes graphically how in George Street the mob came to a large house not lit up in celebration. 'They began to smash, when suddenly three beautiful women came forward, on to the balcony, each with a lighted candle in her hand. They saved the house. The mob worships beauty and courage.' (*Auto,* p.37.)

16 *Regulations, op cit.*

17 W F Grey and J H Jamison, *op cit,* p.88.

18 Rosner, p,154, *op cit.*

19 *Ibid,* p.153.

CHAPTER 4

1 Aileen, p.32.

2 Louis Aimé Martin ... Aimé Martin was a strong advocate of the 'power-behind-the-throne' role of women. 'The man carries to the forum the notions which the woman has discussed with him by the domestic hearth. His strength there realises what her gentle insinuations have inspired.' Martin's ideas were promoted in England by Sarah Lewis in *Woman's Mission,* a book much admired by George Eliot among others. This quotation is from the preface to the fourth edition, London, 1839. Smiles would have read Martin's work in French, published 1834.

3 De Gérando, *Self-Education,* translated by the Unitarian Transcendentalist Elizabeth Peabody in 1830.

4 Ralph Waldo Emerson, The American Scholar, a speech delivered in 1837.

5 'We must above all seek elevation of character'. *S-H* p.v.

6 *Tait's Edinburgh Magazine.* For John and Isobel Johnstone's involvement see *Oxford Dictionary of National Biography,* Johnstone, Isobel.

7 *Tait's Edinburgh Magazine,* October 1833.

8 *Ibid.*

9 A newspaper commended for its radical stance ... 'With much satisfaction we observe a number of additions to the Newspaper Press, all on the side of the people. We have the Glasgow Argus, the Leeds Times, and the Devonport Independent, advocating Radical Reform, in the best sense of the term.' *Tait's Edinburgh Magazine,* May 1833.

10   The six aims of the People's Charter were: a vote for every man of 21 years or over, of sound mind and not undergoing punishment for crime; a secret ballot for parliamentary elections; no property qualifications for MPs; payment for Members; equal constituencies by number of electors; annual elections.

11   See Preface to *Self-Help*, p.ix: 'he addressed them [a group of young working men] citing examples of what other men had done, as illustrating what each might, in a greater or less degree, do for himself ... and above all on that honest and upright performance of individual duty, which is the glory of manly character.'

12   Hazelwood School was opened by the Hill family at Edgbaston, near Birmingham, in 1819, to provide an education on liberal principles. It was enthusiastically endorsed by Jeremy Bentham and a London school, Bruce Castle in Tottenham, opened in 1827.

13   'Bowring ...' John Bowring lost his Kilmarnock seat in parliament in 1837, allegedly on religious grounds. 'The defeat of Dr Bowring in Kilmarnock is not to be attributed to political feeling but to religious bigotry. Our straitlaced neighbours cannot reconcile their conscience to return a Unitarian of their own political sentiments; they prefer a Tory ...' *Tait's Edinburgh Magazine*, October 1837.

14   Octavia Hill is best known today as a founding figure, in 1894, of England's National Trust, but all her life she was concerned for the plight of the urban poor, and particularly for their right to open space and beauty near their cramped and over-crowded homes. As an instinctive opponent of the sort of 'progress' espoused by Samuel Smiles, she might have had little in common with him. But as a strong-minded, independent woman intolerant of collective apathy, Hill was also a natural believer in self-help. 'We have made many mistakes with our alms', she wrote, 'eaten out the heart of the independent, bolstered up the drunkard in his indulgence, subsidized his wages, discouraged thrift, assumed that many of the ordinary wants of a working man's family must be met by our wretched and intermittent doles.' Quoted in Robert Whelan, ed., *Octavia Hill: Letters to fellow Workers 1872-1912* (Kyrle Books, 2005).

15   *Life and Struggles of William Lovett*, 1876, p.143 (new edition, Macgibbon and Kee, 1967).

CHAPTER 5

1   *Directory and Topography of the Borough of Leeds* ..., William White, 1842.

2   Maurice Beresford, *East End, West End: the face of Leeds during urbanisation*, p.392, Thoresby Society, vols LX and LXI, 1985-1986.

3   White, *op cit*.

4   *Leeds Intelligencer*, 5 January 1839.

5   *Leeds Intelligencer*, 1 December 1838.

6   *Leeds Mercury*, 29 December 1838.

7   *Leeds Times*, 29 December 1838.

8   *Leeds Times*, 27 January 1838.

9   Every editor loved the People ... all quotations in this paragraph are from the Leeds papers' new year messages on 5 January 1839.

10   *Northern Star*, 22 December 1838.

11   *Leeds Intelligencer*, 22 December 1838.

12   At one time the voice of the left ... 'left' and 'right', applied to politics, were not in use until much later. The *Oxford English Dictionary* cites J Bodley, France, in 1898: 'the Socialists, who now compose the Radical left wing'. Jacobins and Girondins sat left and right of the Chair in the Assembly in Revolutionary France.

13   Edward Baines, *The Life of Edward Baines* (Longmans Brown, Green, and Longmans 1851).

14   In its new year address the *Leeds Mercury* announced ... '[the paper] now contains five times as much matter as when it came into the hands of Mr Baines in 1801.' In *Life of*

Edward Baines the word count for a copy of the *Mercury* in 1801 is given as 21,376, increased by 1848 to 180,000.

15 *The Annals of Yorkshire – Leeds, from the Earliest Times to the Present Time* (John Hall, 1860).

16 During a great storm at Sidmouth in 1824 Mrs Partington tried to push back the ocean with her mop. *Brewer's Dictionary of Phrase and Fable*, 15th edition, Cassell, 1995.

17 Robert Nicoll, q. in *Annals of Yorkshire, op cit.*

18 All quotations from the *Leeds Times* in the preceding paragraph are from the issue of 5 January 1839.

CHAPTER 6

1   *Northern Star*, 19 January 1839.

2   O'Connor's amendment declared: 'That we consider all restriction of foreign grain is unjust in principle and injurious in its effects, nevertheless we are of opinion that no salutary alteration can be made in the present system until those for whose benefit the change is contemplated, shall have a voice in the choice of those representatives to whom shall be entrusted the power of preventing so great an evil as the present Corn laws.' (*Ibid.*)

3   *Auto*, p.88.

4   *Northern Star*, 19 January 1839.

5   *Leeds Times*, 19 January 1839.

6   *Leeds Times*, 26 January 1839.

7   *Ibid.*

8   *Ibid.*

9   *Leeds Times*, 25 May 1839.

10 *Leeds Times*, 16 November 1839.

11 *Leeds Times* 7 December 1839.

12 *Leeds Times*, 3 August 1839.

13 *Leeds Times*, 10 August 1839.

14 *Leeds Mercury*, 17 August 1839.

15 *Leeds Times*, 2 February 1839.

16 *Leeds Mercury*, 24 August 1839.

17 *Leeds Times*, 7 September 1839.

18 William Lovett, *op cit.*

19 *Leeds Times*, 26 January 1839.

CHAPTER 7

1   *Leeds Times*, 21 December, 1839.

2   *Leeds Times*, 4 January 1840.

3   *Ibid.*

4   *Leeds Times*, 9 October 1841.

5   *Leeds Times*, 8 August 1840.

6   *The Times*, 5 May 1840.

7   *Leeds Times*, 1 February 1840.

8   *Auto*, p.92.

9   *Leeds Mercury*, 5 December 1840.

10 *Leeds Times*, 19 December 1840.

11 *Leeds Times*, 12 December 1840.

12 *Leeds Times*, 26 December 1840.

13 *Leeds Times*, 23 January 1841.

14 Fifty years later Smiles remembered ... see *Auto*, p.95.

15 *Leeds Times*, 23 January 1841.

16 *Leeds Times*, 30 January 1841.

17 *Auto*, p.96.

18 *Ibid*, p.110.

19 B L Cobden papers, ADD MS 43667, f57, SS to R Cobden, 20 September 1841.

20 *Leeds Times*, 23 October 1841.

21 *Ibid*.

22 *Auto*, p.119.

23 '... mere operatives ...' Joshua Hobson, editor of the *Northern Star*, led a deputation in January 1842 to lobby Peel on behalf of the Ten Hours Bill. Hobson and his group used the report of the Leeds Enumeration Committee to support their case, then claimed that Peel had been so moved by the evidence that he agreed to give serious consideration to the deputation's demands. But Peel, in presenting proposals for Corn Law revision in February, claimed that he had been deceived by Hobson's figures. William Beckett, one of Leeds's two Liberal MPs, did speak to the Peel motion on the Corn Laws, and remarked that 'a strict examination of the condition of the manufacturing interests would prove that distress was fearfully on the increase.' See reports in *The Times*, 20 January and 3 February 1842.

24 *Leeds Times*, 5 February 1842.

25 Though the Overseers final audit seemed to prove that things were even worse than suggested, the effect of the variations was to diminish the credibility of the Operatives Enumeration Committee. See *Leeds Times*, 12 March 1842.

26 *Northern Star*, 2 July 1842.

27 *Northern Star*, 20 August 1842.

28 *Ibid*.

29 *Leeds Times*, 13 August 1842.

CHAPTER 8

1   Aileen, p.6.

2   Correspondence between Sarah Anne, her mother, and Miss Martineau, dated 1838-39, in Smiles archive, WYAS,WYL78/A/III/2&ff.

3   WYAS, undated WYL78/A/III/16.

4   'I was introduced to good society ...' *Auto*, p.126.

5   *London Gazette*, 20 December 1842.

6   *Auto*, p.129.

7   A correspondent in the *Yorkshire Post* in December 1937 wrote: 'When Dr Smiles gave up his practice in 1845 it was carried on by my uncle, Dr William Scott and he afterwards had a partner, Dr Pierson, who also lived in Springfield House [Smiles's house] ... Dr Pierson's practice was purchased by Dr S Moore of Domestic Street who started practice in 1886 ... his son Dr John E Moore is carrying on very near the origin [sic] house where Dr Smiles lived.' Kilburn Scott file, WYAS.

8   *Auto*, p.303.

9   Alice Mann, who carried on the business after her father's death, had strong radical connections, and was associated with Joshua Hobson, editor of the *Northern Star*. See John Harrison, *Robert Owen and the Owenites*, p.190 (Routledge Revivals).

10 *Leeds Times*, 12 November 1842.

11 *Leeds Times*, 9 December 1843.

12 Fragment of an account by SS, undated WYAS 78A/III/16.

13 *Leeds Times*, 6 January, 1844.

14 *Auto*, p.129.

15 '... the now combined Mechanics' Institution and Literary Society ...' The two bodies amalgamated in 1842.

CHAPTER 9

1 *Leeds Times*, 12 October 1844.
2 *Leeds Times*, 29 March 1845.
3 *Leeds Times*, 5 October 1839.
4 *Leeds Times*, 29 March 1845.
5 *Auto*, p.134.
6 Trygve Tholfsen, *Working Class Radicalism in mid-Victorian England* (Croom Helm, 1976).
7 *Leeds Times*, 2 February 1839.
8 *Auto*, p.134.
9 *Leeds Times*, 25 May 1839.
10 The impact on an author of family life, exemplified by 'the pram in the hall', was identified by Cyril Connolly in his book, *Enemies of Promise*, 1938.

CHAPTER 10

1 *Auto*, p.139.
2 Report in *Leeds Times*, 31 May 1845.
3 Kew, Report of Directors of Leeds and Thirsk Railway Company.
4 George Grainger FRSE, Scottish engineer, 1793-1852, great-grandfather of composer Percy Grainger. He was killed in an accident on the line in 1852, shortly after it opened.
5 Kew, Report of Directors of the Leeds and Thirsk Railway Company.
6 wwwGracesGuide.co.uk
7 Henry Mayhew, *London Labour and the London Poor*, ed. Victor Neuberg, pp.424-425 (Penguin Classics, 1985).
8 See *Leeds Times*, 4 July 1846.
9 *Leeds Times*, 25 August 1846.
10 *Leeds Times*, 5 September 1846.
11 *Auto*, p.153.
12 'Generally you will find the successful literary man a person of industry ...' In *Character* (1871) Smiles cited a number of examples, though they could hardly have been described as contemporaries – Chaucer, a comptroller of petty customs; Bacon, a lawyer; Addison, Secretary of State ... The obvious example from his own time was, of course, Anthony Trollope, who combined novel production on an industrial scale with his work as a Post Office Surveyor.
13 'Sam Goldwyn's remark ...' Goldwyn, on being told by a writer that his movie script had a message, is said to have replied: 'Pictures are for entertainment, messages should be delivered by Western Union.'
14 The Odd Fellows Society. Figures quoted are from the speech delivered by Alexander Sherriff, Chairman of the Leeds meeting, on 21 September 1846. The *Quarterly Magazine of the Society of Odd Fellows*, published in Manchester, gives, in its April 1846 number, an account of the origins of the movement, probably in the guilds of the mid-eighteenth century, part of 'the mania for Free-Masonry' – resuscitated in its current form at the beginning of the nineteenth century. The same magazine claims, in its January 1847 issue, the number of members worldwide as 257,905.
15 *Leeds Times*, 26 December 1846.
16 Andrew King, blog, 'Greenwich English Prof', 20 May 2013 (www.gre.ac.uk).
17 Mary Howitt, *Autobiography*, edited by her daughter, Margaret Howitt, 1889.
18 'If not necessarily a commercial success ...' *Howitt's Journal* lasted for only eighteen months, from January 1847 to mid-1848, with William and Mary Howitt as joint editors.
19 The *People's Journal* published 'A Scheme of Free Libraries' by Dr Samuel Smiles (vol.1, p.119).
20 Lord Campbell's Obscene Publications Act. In fact the 1857 Act struggled to reach the

statute book. In Paris the same year Gustave Flaubert was acquitted on charges of obscenity in the *Madame Bovary* trial. But thirty years later in England, with the rising economic tide had come the rising tide of national self-congratulation, and the rise of morality as a patriotic imperative. Attacking Zola in the House of Commons in 1888, Mr Samuel Smith, Member for Flintshire, asked: 'Were we to wait until the moral fibre of the English race was eaten out, as that of the French was almost ... Such garbage was simply the death of a nation. Were they to wait till this deadly poison spread itself over the soil and killed the life of this great and noble people.' *Parliamentary Debates*, 3rd series, vol.cccxv, 8 May 1888.

21 'Smiles's mini-biography ...' See *Howitt's Journal*, vol.1, February 1847.
22 '... inscribe our local curé in place of Napoleon ...' Smiles later wrote of Napoleon in *Self-Help*: 'Napoleon's intense selfishness was his ruin ... his life taught the lesson that power, however energetically wielded, without beneficence, is fatal to its possessor and to its subjects; and that knowledge or knowingness without goodness, is but the incarnate principle of evil' (p.229).

CHAPTER 11

1 see Lisa Merrill, *When Romeo was a Woman: Charlotte Cushman and her Circle of Female Spectators* (University of Michigan Press, November 2000).
2 Aileen p.68.
3 '... a woman's declaration of independence ...' Alex Tyrell, *The Journal of British Studies*, vol.39, no.2, April 2000: 'Samuel Smiles and the Woman Question in early Victorian Britain'. This essay was my main source for an understanding of Smiles's attitude to women at the time.
4 EC to SS, 14 October 1848. WYAS WYL78/A/IX/40.
5 EC to SS, 13 November 1848. WYAS WYL78/A/IX/41.
6 'Over the life of *Eliza Cook's Journal* ...' The scholarly work of Tim Travers has identified many of Smiles's contributions. See *Victorian Periodicals Newsletter*, no.20, June 1973, pp.41-45: 'The Problem of Identification of Articles: Samuel Smiles and Eliza Cook's Journal 1849-54'.
7 *Auto*, p.165.
8 Adrian Jarvis: *Samuel Smiles and the Construction of Victorian Values* (Sutton Publishing, 1997).
9 *Auto*, p.134.
10 *Auto*, p.160.
11 *Eliza Cook's Journal*, vol.1, no.7, 16 June 1849.
12 *Ibid*, 19 May 1849.
13 *Auto*, p.166.
14 'Open letter from Dr Smiles of Leeds to Edward Baines Esq', February 1852, Manchester M136/3/9/247.
15 *Ibid*, p.2.
16 *Ibid*.
17 SS to Robert Smiles, 10 April 1850. Manchester M136/2/3/3048.
18 SS to Robert Smiles, 17 April 1850. Manchester M136/2/3/3051.
19 SS to Robert Smiles, 16 April 1850. Manchester M136/2/3/3050.
20 SS to Robert Smiles, 29 March 1851. Manchester M136/2/3/070.
21 SS to Robert Smiles, 29 December 1849. Manchester M136/3/9/247.
22 *S-H*, p.16.
23 Report in *Leeds Times*, 11 June 1853.
24 '*Eliza Cook's Journal* was a success ...' Circulation quoted in *Oxford Dictionary of National Biography*, from 'Altick' (R D Altick, *The English Common Reader*, 1957, p.394).

25 SS to Robert Smiles, 11 May 1850. Manchester M136/2/3/3055.
26 *Auto*, p.165.

CHAPTER 12

1   *Leeds Times*, 10 September 1842.
2   *Auto*, p.177.
3   *Auto*, p.183.
4   *Auto*, p.186.
5   *Auto*, p.163.
6   *Auto*, p.186.
7   Robert Stephenson to SS, 9 October 1854. NRM.
8   *Auto*, p.192.
9   q. Aileen, p.80.
10 Gerald Massey to SS U/D 1854? WYAS WYL78/A/IX/105.
11 Kew, Minutes of AGM, South Eastern Railway, 9 March 1855.
12 Robert Stephenson to SS, 29 November 1854. NRM.
13 George Parker Bidder (1806-1878), who had worked with the Stephensons on the London
    and Birmingham Railway, and whose prodigious mathematical skill made him a prized
    witness when submitting railway proposals to Parliamentary commissions.
14 Board minutes of South Eastern Railway, 9 November 1854. Kew.
15 'A suburban bank manager's salary ... about £90 per annum.' *Tempted London*, 1889
    (www. victorianlondon.org).
16 Robert Stephenson to SS, 4 October 1855. NRM.
17 Herbert Spencer, 'Railway Morals and Railway Policy', 1855, reprinted from the *Edinburgh
    Review*.
18 *Auto*, p.196.
19 *Auto*, p.210.
20 Robert Stephenson to SS, 4 October 1855. NRM.
21 *The Times*, 19 March 1855.
22 *Auto*, p.197.
23 'The Smiles home in Glenmohr Terrace ...' In Charles Booth's *Survey of life and labour in
    London* (1886-1903), Glenmohr Terrace was marked red, classified as 'middle-class
    well-to-do' (quotation courtesy of Charles Booth Online Archive, London School of Eco-
    nomics).
24 SS to Mrs Holmes, 5 March 1855. WYAS WYL78/A/III/8.
25 *S-H*, pp.264-266.

CHAPTER 13

1   '... a live-in cook and housemaid (they'd had both in Leeds) ...' The 1851 census shows
    the Smiles family at 9 Blenheim Square Leeds (without the head of the house, who must
    have been away on business on census day), together with Hannah Halliley, cook, and
    Sarah Lydia Emmitt, housemaid.
2   *Duty*, pp.64-65.
3   David Ross, *George and Robert Stephenson: A Passion for Success*, p.62 (The History Press, 2010).
4   'The Liverpool and Manchester Railway, going further, faster ...' It was on the famous
    Rainhill trials that Stephenson's immortal 'Rocket' showed its paces, though in fact, like
    most of George Stephenson's creations, it was the fruit of several people's work. See
    Jarvis, *op cit* and *George Stephenson* (Shire Publications, 2006).
5   *LoGS*, p.82.
6   *LoGS*, p.147.
7   *LoGS* p.411.

8 *LoGS* p.459.
9 SS to JM, 10 December 1856. NLS/JMA.
10 *Ibid.*
11 SS to JM, 30 March 1857. NLS/JMA.
12 John Lucas, fashionable London portrait painter; his subjects included the Duke of Wellington and the Prince Consort.
13 SS to JM, 4 April 1857. NLS/JMA.
14 Spencer, *op cit*, p.19.
15 'Over the years Smiles made many revisions ...' A thorough analysis of changes to the text in successive editions of the *Life* has been made by Adrian Jarvis in *Samuel Smiles ... op cit.*
16 'George Eliot wrote to a friend ...' 26 July 1857, *Letters of George Eliot*, vol.12, p.349. Eliot's *Adam Bede*, another book born in that *annus mirabilis* for English publishing, 1859, reveals her sympathy for the qualities of self-help: 'such men as he', she writes, 'are reared here and there in every generation of our peasant artisans ... they make their way upward, rarely as geniuses, most commonly as painstaking honest men, with the skill and conscience to do well the tasks that lie before them.' Q. Kathryn Hughes, *George Eliot: the Last Victorian* (Fourth Estate, 1998).

CHAPTER 14

1 SS to JM, 31 August 1857. NLS/JMA.
2 SS to JM, 11 January 1858. NLS/JMA.
3 SS to JM, 28 August 1858. NLS/JMA.
4 M to SS, 3 July 1858. NLS/JMA.
5 SS to JM, 28 May 1858. NLS/JMA.
6 JM to SS, 31 May 1858. NLS/JMA.
7 *Auto*, p.236.
8 '... the *Statement* took little account of the poor families ...' See Linda Neate, *Victorian Babylon* (Yale University Press, 2000), p34: 'In the 1860's the railways ploughed into the heart of London, causing major displacements of mostly labouring populations through enforced demolition ... In preparing the routes for their lines, the railway companies usually planned them to pass through working-class districts, where land and compensation were cheaper.'
9 SS to JM, 28 December 1857. NLS/JMA.
10 The equivalent today of about £80,000,000, if one takes building costs as a guide to property value. A building craftsman's wages recorded for 1860 at £2-6-4 for eleven days, would now perhaps be something over £1000 for the same time, a multiple of about 275. The arbitrator at the time used a crude average of surveyors' calculations to arrive at a figure. 1860 figure from Kew, 2005 (wwwnationalarchives.gov.uk/currency – this website is no longer updated).
11 SS to JM, 25 August 1858. NLS/JMA.
12 SS to JM, 3 July 1858. NLS/JMA.
13 SS to JM, 6 July 1858. NLS/JMA.
14 *Auto*, p.222.
15 'His terms again ...' Murray's selective attitude to his authors is seen in an interesting light by his correspondence with Charles Darwin at the same time. On the subject of *The Origin of Species* he wrote: 'I have no hesitation in swerving from my usual routine and stating at once and even without seeing the manuscript ... I can ascertain to 2/3 of net proceeds of the edition.' JM to Charles Darwin, John Murray letter book, April 1859. NLS/JMA.
16 SS to JM, 18 July 1859. NLS/JMA.

17 *Auto*, p.223.
18 J C Jeaffreson, *A Book of Recollections*, 1894, quoted in David Ross, *op cit*, p.285.
19 SS to JM, 27 October 1859. NLS/JMA.
20 SS to JM, 26 November 1859. NLS/JMA.
21 *Ibid.*
22 SS to JM, 30 November 1859. NLS/JMA.
23 SS to JM IV, 29 March 1891. NLS/JMA.

CHAPTER 15

1   *Leeds Times*, 26 November 1859.
2   *Self-Help*, Introduction.
3   *The Athenaeum*, 23 April 1904.
4   Henry Mayhew, *London Labour and the London Poor*, 4 vols, 1861-1862.
5   SS to JM, 13 January 1860. NLS/JMA.
6   SS to JM, 26 November 1859. NLS/JMA.
7   *Fraser's Magazine*, December 1859.
8   Aileen, p.100.
9   'Mrs Gaskell's North ...' Elizabeth Gaskell (who had contributed to the *People's Journal* at the same time as Smiles), published her novel, *North and South*, dramatising the differences between the industrial north and the conservative south, in 1855.
10 George Potter, b.1832, was Secretary to the Progressive Societies of Carpenters and Joiners, and leader of the Confederation of United Building Trades in the 1859 dispute over a nine-hour day.
11 *LoE*, Preface, p.iv.
12 SS to JM, 8 December 1860. NLS/JMA.
13 SS to JM, 29 August 1860. NLS/JMA.
14 *LoE*, vol.I, p.152.
15 *LoE*, vol.II, p.294.
16 *ibid*, pp.308-310.
17 *ibid*, p.325.
18 *ibid*, p.462.
19 *LoE*, vol.III, p.14.
20 *Leeds Times*, 25 May 1839.
21 *LoE*, vol.II, p.327.
22 *ibid*, p.87.

CHAPTER 16

1   SS to JM, 29 August 1860. NLS/JMA.
2   SS to JM, 7 December 1860. NLS/JMA.
3   SS to JM, 7 December 1860. NLS/JMA.
4   SS to JM, 21 September 1860.
5   *Auto*, p.251.
6   'The three handsome volumes ...' Probably because *Lives of the Engineers* is referred to as a 3-volume work, and the third volume did not appear until 1862, that year is usually given as the date of publication of the whole. The first, and more important two, in fact appeared in 1861 and were reviewed in that year.
7   SS to JM, 25 November 1861. NLS/JMA.
8   *The Times*, 21 November 1861.
9   *The Times*, 24 December 1861. The Times Online © Times Newspapers.
10 'It now became respectable to praise industry ...' Courtney Salvey argues that the publication of Samuel Smiles's biographies 'was a small tipping-point in Victorian culture,

subtly impacting the literati's image of the machine age and its creators.' *Samuel Smiles and the Literati – the image of the Victorian engineer*, Indiana First West University Victorian Studies Association.

11 Sir Stafford Northcote was one of the secretaries of the Great Exhibition of 1851. Between 1841 and 1852 he was a member of Gladstone's political staff, but in 1852 switched sides to join Disraeli's inner circle (see *Oxford Dictionary of National Biography*).

12 *Auto*, p.257.

13 Aileen, p.94.

14 SS to JWC, 13 December 1859, Carlyle Letters online.

15 SS to Janet, 2 May 1860. WYAS WYL78/A/1/4.

16 SS to Janet, 21 March 1860. WYAS WYL78/A/1/3.

17 SS to JM, 20 March 1862. NLS/JMA.

18 *Ibid.*

19 'A judge and Archdeacon would propose him ...' He was never elected. In 1862 he told John Murray that 'The Honourable Justice Byng and Archdeacon Browne have put themselves down as my proposer and seconder for election as a member of the Athenaeum.' SS to JM, 29 December 1862. NLS/JMA. The Club's records show that his nomination was withdrawn in 1874, perhaps because he tired of spending so long on the waiting list (information courtesy of the Athenaeum archive).

20 Smiles account book, in Samuel Smiles archive. WYAS.

21 Aileen, p.95 (in her book Aileen Smiles spells the house name 'Westbank'. In Smiles's correspondence he uses 'West Bank').

22 Aileen, p.96.

23 SS to JM, 10 April 1863. NLS/JMA.

24 Aileen, p.94.

25 SS to JM, 11 August 1885.

26 Document dated 29 September 1865. Kew.

27 Robert Stephenson to SS, 4 October 1855. NRM.

28 SS to JM, 5 July 1892. NLS/JMA.

29 *Auto*, p.251.

30 SS to JM, 11 August 1865. NLS/JMA.

31 *The Times*, 23 January 1886.

32 *Pall Mall Gazette*, 1 February 1886.

33 Account book at WYAS.

34 SS to Janet, 1 November 1881. WYAS WYL78/A/1/128a.

35 Minutes of quarterly meeting of South Eastern Railway, 30 August 1866. Kew.

CHAPTER 17

1 Q. in Norman Toulson, *The Squirrel and the Clock*, p.118 (Henry Melland, 1985).

2 Aileen, p.102.

3 *S-H*, p.5.

4 *S-H* p.12.

5 SS to JM, 16 January 1867. NLS/JMA.

6 '... rubbished the Orange "triumph" ...' In *The History of Ireland* he wrote: 'though "the Boyne" has become a party word of triumph among the protestants of Ireland it seems to us that after all there was very little to boast of at the close of the day's battle. There is very little doubt that had not the Irish been commanded by a coward, the result would have been very different ... The Boyne was neither more nor less than a drawn battle, though to William it had all the advantage of a complete victory.'

7 SS to JM, 15 March 1857. NLS/JMA.

8 *Huguenots*, p.288.

9 Jules Michelet, *Le Peuple*: 'Was one emigration greater than the other? ... there was this great difference between them: France, at the emigration of '89 lost its idlers; at the other its workers.'

10 *Huguenots*, p.447.

11 *Ibid*.

12 The Annual Soirée of the Huddersfield Mechanics' Institution ... report in the *Huddersfield Chronicle*, 2 November 1867.

13 Robert Cooke, 1816-91, John Murray III's cousin, joined the firm in 1837, became a partner and was JM III's right-hand man.

14 *Auto*, p.223.

15 Harper Bros, New York, to JM, 1 August 1894. NLS/JMA.

16 SS to JM, 28 July 1868. NLS/JMA.

17 SS to JM, 8 March 1869. NLS/JMA.

18 Sam S to his brother Willie, 1 July 1867. PRONI D3437/4.

19 *S-H*, p.399.

20 SS to JM, 24 December 1868. NLS/JMA.

21 Aileen, p.104.

22 Aileen, p.107.

23 SS to Janet, 9 October 1868. WYAS WYL78/A/1/31.

24 SS to R Cooke, 15 April 1869. NLS/JMA.

25 SS to JM, 1 April 1869. NLS/JMA.

26 'Nakamura's translation ...' For an understanding of Smiles's attraction for the Japanese I relied heavily on Sarah Metzger-Court's April 1991 article, 'Economic Progress and Social Cohesion: 'Self-Help' and the achieving of a delicate balance in Meiji Japan', *Japan Forum*, vol.3, no.1, April 1991.

27 See Earl H Kinmouth: ' Nakamura Keiū and Samuel Smiles: A Victorian Confucian and a Confucian Victorian', in *The American Historical Review*, vol.85, no.3, June 1980.

28 Smiles's account book. WYAS. West Bank is no longer standing. Detached houses in Blackheath in 2014 were routinely advertised for between £2,000,000 and £3,000,000.

29 *Auto*, p.293.

CHAPTER 18

1 SS to JM, August 1871. NLS/JMA.

2 *Auto*, p.275.

3 *Ibid*.

4 SS to JM, 23 November 1869. NLS/JMA.

5 *Auto*, p.298.

6 SS to JMA. NLS/JMA.

7 SS to R Cooke, 16 October 1871. NLS/JMA.

8 SS to R Cooke, 16 October 1871. NLS/JMA.

9 *Auto*, pp.288-289.

10 SS to W.Lovett, 20 February 1872. BL add ms 78/6/1 f386.

11 *Morning Post*, 25 September 1871.

12 SS account book. WYAS WYL78/A/2/71.

13 *Morning Post*, 23 November 1871.

14 Smiles's account book shows a net contribution from *Boy's Voyage* of £116-12-6 in the period to June 1872 and £127-7-6 in the subsequent twelve months. WYAS.

15 All figures from Smiles's account book. WYAS.

16 Kathryn Hughes, *The Short Life and Long Times of Mrs Beeton,* p.74 (Fourth Estate, 2005).

17 Thomas Carlyle, *Past and Present*, 1843, chapter 11.

18 Burton, *The Anatomy of Melancholy*, Robert Burton, 1621.

19 *Character*, p.92.
20 *Character*, p.97.
21 *Character*, p.62.
22 Aileen, p.114.
23 A number of his drawings and watercolours are in the Smiles archive at PRONI.
24 SS to Sam, 3 July 1873. WYAS WYL78/A/III/19.
25 SS to R Cooke, 28 March 1874. NLS/JMA.
26 Letter q. in Aileen, p.123.
27 SS to JM, 28 July 1874. NLS/JMA.

CHAPTER 19

1   'I have had some thoughts about bringing out a cheaper edition ...' SS to R Cooke, 15 June 1875. NLS/JMA.
2   *Ibid.*
3   SS to R Cooke, 11 June 1875. NLS/JMA.
4   'Characteristics of Biography' is a title Smiles mentioned several times in his correspondence, but the book never appeared. 'Ships and Shipbuilders' and 'Men of Business' were ideas inspired mainly by his visits to Willie's high-flying business circle in Belfast. This material resurfaced as *Men of Invention* in 1884.
5   SS to Jack, 26 September 1875. WYAS WYL78/A/1/59.
6   Sir Gildsworthy Gurney, 1793-1875, had built a steam carriage in 1829 which ran between London and Bath.
7   SS to Jack, 27 October 1875. WYAS WYL78/A/1/64.
8   SS to Jack, 6 November 1875. WYAS WYL78/A/1/66.
9   *Thrift*, p.37.
10 *Thrift*, p.34.
11 *Thrift*, p.42.
12 *Thrift*, p.45.
13 SS to Janet, 4 January 1878. WYAS WYL78/A/1/81.
14 SS to Janet, 13 February 1876. Novels were often subscribed for in parts – 'taken' in the way gentlemen in later years 'took *The Times*'. WYAS WYL78/A/1/67.
15 SS to Janet, 10 March 1876. WYAS WYL78/A/1/68.
16 'On Sunday we were at Mrs Harty's ...' *Ibid.* 'Harrison the Comptist' was probably Frederic Harrison, English historian and positivist philosopher, who was a follower of Auguste Compte. 'Miss Sitwell' was probably Florence Sitwell (1858-1930), devoutly religious, aspiring poet, maiden aunt of Edith, Osbert and Sacheverell Sitwell. She would have been no more than nineteen years old when Smiles encountered her. (I am grateful to Alexandra Sitwell Hayward for help in tracing her forbear's identity.)
17 SS to Jack, 21 December 1876. WYAS WYL78/A/1/72.
18 *Ibid.*
19 SS to Janet, 29 December 1876. WYAS WYL78/A/1/73.
20 G Reid to SS, 3 April 1877. WYAS WYL78/A/V/58.
21 SS to Janet, 4 January 1878. WYAS WYL78/A/1/81.
22 SS to Sarah Anne, 16 April 1877. WYAS WYL78/A/III/10.

CHAPTER 20

1   SS to JM, 4 May 1877. NLS/JMA.
2   SS to JM, 18 May 1887. NLS/JMA.
3   SS to Janet, 17 July 1877. WYAS WYL78/A/1/77.
4   SS to JM, 8 September 1877. NLS/JMA.

5   *Ibid.*

6   SS to Janet, 31 January 1878. WYAS WYL78/A/1/84.

7   SS to JM, 21 August 1878. NLS/JMA.

8   SS to Jack, 6 September 1878. WYAS WYL78/A/1/90.

9   '... later that night Cooke "called on Mr Miles, of Simpkin Marshall ..."' SS to Jack, 9 November 1878. WYAS WYL78/A/1/93. *Reminiscences of Literary London from 1779-1853* said of Simpkin & Marshall: 'Though not distinguished as publishers, this firm carries on the largest business in the book trade of any house in Europe.' Back in 1838 the same 'undistinguished publishers' had produced Smiles's *Physical Education* in London.

10 *Auto*, p.327.

11 James Byng to SS, 12 February 1879. WYAS WYL78/A/X/32.

12 SS to JM, 30 March 1879. NLS/JMA.

13 SS to JM, 13 November 1878. NLS/JMA.

14 'Smiles declined an invitation ...' See BL ADD MS 44108 ff 279-282. Smiles explains to Mrs Bennett (Gladstone's cousin) why he cannot accept the invitation. The Murray Memoir (though he doesn't mention it by name) has taught him a lesson: 'I shrink from undertaking another.'

15 SS to JM, 30 March 1879. NLS/JMA.

16 *Auto*, p.338.

17 *Auto*, p.335.

18 *Auto*, p.343.

19 SS to Menebria, 18 November 1879. WYASWYL78/A/IV/4.

20 Draft letter, SS to Secretary of the French Academy, 15 December 1879. WYAS WYL78/A/IX/7. His nomination was not successful. In 1879 the Montyon Prize was awarded to the American engineer George Henry Corliss, inventor of the Corliss steam engine.

21 G Reid to SS, 14 October 1879. WYAS WYL78/A/II/99.

22 JM to SS, August 1879. NLS/JMA.

23 SS to Italian Chargé d'Affaires, London, 10 January 1880. WYAS WYL78/A/IV/17.

24 SS to Jack, 25 October 1880. WYAS WYL78/A/1/120.

25 SS to Jack, 6 November 1880. WYAS WYL78/A/1/123. The distinction between 'booksellers' and 'publishers' was blurred at this time. In an article on 'Authors and Publishers' in *Murray's Magazine* in 1890, Smiles used 'booksellers' and 'publishers' interchangeably.

26 *Duty*, p.9.

27 *Duty*, p.423.

CHAPTER 21

1   SS to Jack, 25 October 1880. WYAS WYL78/A/1/120.

2   *Industrial Biography*, p.276.

3   SS to Mrs Lington, 2 December 1880. WYAS WYL78/A/IV/2a.

4   *Ibid.*

5   SS to Janet, 11 November 1881. WYAS WYL78/A/1/128.

6   SS to Janet, 13 December 1880. WYASWYL78A/1/125.

7   *Auto*, p.349.

8   SS to Janet, 19 February 1882. WYAS WYL78/A/1/135.

9   *Ibid.*

10 'I will tell them to go to Ouida ...' SS to Janet, 10 January 1882. WYAS WYL78/A/1/134. 'Ouida' was the pen-name of Marie Louise Ramée, hugely popular writer of highly-charged romantic novels.

11 *Men of Invention and Industry.*

12 SS to Janet, 12 July 1882. WYAS WYL78/a/1/141. The reference is to the practice of some evicted Irish tenants, who protested by maiming their landlords' cattle in night raids.
13 SS to Jack, August 1882. WYAS WYL78/A/1/145.
14 SS to Janet, 4 January 1883. WYAS WYL78/A/1/132.
15 SS to Janet, 3 January 1883. WYAS WYL78/A/1/151.
16 SS to Janet, 8 January 1883. WYAS WYL78/A/1/152.
17 SS wrote to JM, 23 January 1888: 'I intended to have finished this work (as stated to Mr John Murray junior) by the end of 1886.' NLS/JMA.
18 SS to Janet, 19 March 1883. WYAS WYL78/A/1/162.
19 *Auto,* p.366.
20 SS to Janet, March 1883. WYAS WYL78/A/1/174.
21 '... to found industries that give employment to large numbers of persons ...' Modern Irish governments evidently agreed, as shown by the success in more recent times of Ireland's Industrial Development Authority, and the emergence of the 'Celtic Tiger'.
22 Sets of Smiles's other books were presented to both of Dublin's Free Libraries by the city's Lord Mayor in October 1884. *Freeman's Journal,* 2 October 1844.
23 SS to R. Cooke, 27 November 1884. NLS/JMA.
24 *Ibid.*
25 SS to JM, 8 August 1885. NLS/JMA. In *Self-Help* Smiles recounted the famous story of the accidental burning by J S Mill's maid of the manuscript of the first volume of Carlyle's *History of the French Revolution* (he did not identify Mill).
26 All these questions are from Smile's 1886 letters to JM. NLS/JMA.
27 'In his youth he made pencil and watercolour sketches ...' Examples are in the Smiles archive at PRONI.
28 SS to Janet, 24 December 1886. WYAS WYL78/A/1/189.
29 SS to JM, 21 February 1887. NLS/JMA.
30 SS to Janet, 28 February 1887. WYAS WYL78/A/1/191.
31 Sarah Anne to Janet, 2 April 1887. WYAS WYAS WYL78/A/III/13.
32 SS to R.Cooke, 11 May1887. NLS/JMA.
33 'All honour to that thoroughly good ...' *Auto,* p.397. In their attitude to 'the People' and the idle rich, the Queen and Smiles were very much on the same side. Elizabeth Longford quotes from one of Victoria's letters in 1867: 'The lower classes are becoming so well-informed – are so intelligent and earn their bread and riches so deservedly that they cannot and ought not to be kept back – to be abused by wretched high born beings, who live only to kill time.' *Victoria,* Elizabeth Longford (Weidenfeld and Nicolson, 1964).

CHAPTER 22

1 'My "wee bookie" is nearly corrected ...' SS to Janet, 28 August 1887. WYAS WYL78/A/1/198.
2 SS to Janet, 29 August 1887. WYAS WYL78/A/1/199.
3 'The new book, now with the title ...' 'The title I fixed on many years ago was "Characteristics of Biography" but have not been satisfied with this title.' SS to JM, 11 May 1887. NLS/JMA.
4 SS to JM. NLS/JMA.
5 *Pall Mall Gazette,* 10 January 1888.
6 *Life and Labour,* p.254.
7 *Life and Labour,* p.255.
8 *Life and Labour,* p.245.
9 *Leeds Times,* 29 March 1845.
10 SS to JM, 23 January 1888. NLS/JMA.
11 SS to JM, 27 January 1888. NLS/JMA.

12 SS to JM, 28 January 1888. NLS/JMA.
13 SS to JM, 6 February 1888. NLS/JMA.
14 SS to Jack, 5 February 1888. WYAS WYL78/A/1/204.
15 SS to JM, 13 March 1888. NLS/JMA.
16 1 June 1888. NLS/JMA.
17 SS to JM, 13 July, 1888. NLS/JMA.
18 *Auto*, p.402.
19 SS to JM, 28 July 1888. NLS/JMA.
20 SS to JM, 31 July 1888. NLS/JMA.
21 'Even when he had given Murray the completed first draft ...' Smiles wrote in his *Auto-biography* (p.408), that 'I was able to hand Mr Murray chapter xxxiv, being the end of the work, at the end of January 1889'. Yet letters in the John Murray archive show that Smiles was still writing to Murray about the book's content up to the end of that year.
22 JM to SS, 21 January 1889. NLS/JMA.
23 SS to JM, 21 April 1889. NLS/JMA.
24 *Jasmin – Barber, Poet, Philanthropist*, p.231.
25 SS to JM, 12 April 1889. NLS/JMA.
26 SS to JM, 20 December 1889. NLS/JMA.
27 JM to SS, 29 July 1890. NLS/JMA.
28 SS to JM, 18 August 1890. NLS/JMA.
29 SS to JM, 5 October 1890. NLS/JMA.
30 SS to JM, 6 November 1890.
31 *Pall Mall Gazette*, 11 March 1891.

CHAPTER 23

1 'Self-Help at Home – an Interview with Dr Smiles', *Pall Mall Gazette*, 4 April 1891.
2 SS to Jack, 8 April 1891. WYAS WYL78/A/1/233.
3 *Self-Help*, Preface to 1869 edition.
4 *Jasmin*, p.230 36.
5 Q. Aileen, p.171.
67 SS to JM, 6 October 1891. NLS/JMA.
7 'Even copyright ...' When John Murray urged Smiles in 1894 to take action to protect himself against an imitation of *Self-Help* called *Leaders of Modern History*, by G Barnett Smith, Smiles politely declined. JM to SS, 7 May 1894. NLS/JMA.
8 SS to Janet, 19 December 1890. WYAS WYL78/A/1/228.
9 SS to his grand-daughter Lily, 3 October 1892. PRONI D3437/A/1/14.
10 SS to Lily, November 1894. PRONI D3437/A/1/22.
11 SS to Lily, 1 May 1894. PRONI D3437/A/1/16.
12 SS to Lily, 30 May 1894. PRONI D3437A/1/17.
13 The quotation is from *The Academy*, February 1894. A complex story lay behind Mr Wedgwood's outburst. Gatty claimed that Godfrey Wedgwood had earlier chosen Smiles to take on the biography which he, Gatty, had started many years before but had been forced to abandon. Wedgwood claimed that Gatty had passed on to Smiles confidential papers without the Wedgwood family's permission. See *The Academy*, 16 February and 25 March 1895. Strangely, back in 1864 Smiles had helped an old friend from the Howitt/Cook days, Elizabeth Meteyard (better known to her readers as 'Silverpen'), to bring her biography of Josiah Wedgwood to publication, by commending her to Gladstone, then Chancellor of the Exchequer. The ubiquitous Anne Bennett (see note 14 to Chapter 20) was the go-between – if Smiles was prepared to endorse Miss Meteyard, she would be bona fide, Bennett told her cousin. 'I am quite persuaded you can depend on what he says,' she advised the great man. Gladstone Papers, BL, ADD. MS 44108 f112.

14 SS to Janet, 22 December 1894. WYAS WYL78/A/1/251.
15 SS to Lily, 18 February 1895. PRONI D3437/A/1/29.
16 SS to Lily, 28 February 1896. PRONI D3437/A/1/34.
17 Letter from representative of the King of Serbia to SS, 5 May 1897. WYAS WYL/ A/IX/118.
18 JM to SS, 9 June 1897. NLS/JMA.
19 JM to SS, 9 June 1897. NLS/JMA.
20 JM to SS, 25 July 1898. NLS/JMA.
21 Hallam Murray to SS, 2 September 1898. WYAS WYL78/A/VII/9.
22 Hallam Murray to William Smiles, 1 July 1902. WYAS WYL78/A/VII/43.
23 JM to Lucy Smiles, 18 April 1904. PRONI D3437/A/1/39.
24 *Daily Telegraph*, 18 April 1904.

AFTERWORD

1 H G C Matthew, *Oxford Dictionary of National Biography* (Oxford University Press, 2004).
2 *Self-Help*, Oxford World's Classics, Oxford University Press, 2002, edited and with an Introduction by Peter Sinnema.
3 *Daily Chronicle*, 18 April 1904.
4 Q. Asa Briggs, *Victorian People* (Odhams, 1954).
5 H G C Matthew later described him ... *op cit*.
6 Robert Tressell, *The Ragged-Trousered Philanthropists*, first published 1914 (reprinted Grafton, 1986).
7 See *The Saturday Review*, 16 and 23 May, 1914.
8 'The Samuel Smiles set – Success story', Martin Page, *Observer Magazine*, 13 September 1970.
9 'The Lost World of Samuel Smiles', *Sunday Times* magazine section, 18 September 1958.
10 Allen McLaurin, 'Re-working Work', in *In Search of Victorian Values*, E M Sigsworth, ed. (Manchester University Press, 1980).

INDEX